Praise from the U.K. for

PASSIONATE

MINDS

"Highly entertaining . . . and holds the most agreeable surprises. . . . A story well worth the retelling, and Bodanis tells it vividly." —*Sunday Times* (London)

"The tale is irresistible." —*Financial Times*

"Bodanis is good at explaining complex science and skillful in weaving together two unconventional, complex, and intellectually reforming lives. . . . David Bodanis has taken up one of the great stories of the period, a potent mix of romance, science, and history. . . . There is never a dull moment." —*Sunday Telegraph*

"Installs Emilie in the front row of the pantheon of Enlightenment natural philosophers." —*The Times* (London)

"This is an absorbing tale based on extensive research, and it takes full advantage of both heroes' propensity for coining quotable witticisms. Bodanis eloquently evokes women's restricted lives during the eighteenth century." —*The Guardian* (U.K.)

PASSIONATE MINDS

Emilie du Châtelet, Voltaire,
and the Great Love Affair of
the Enlightenment

David Bodanis

THREE RIVERS PRESS · NEW YORK

Published in the United States by Three Rivers Press,
an imprint of the Crown Publishing Group,
a division of Random House, Inc., New York.
www.crownpublishing.com

Three Rivers Press and the Tugboat design are registered
trademarks of Random House, Inc.

Originally published in 2006 in Great Britain by Little, Brown,
an imprint of Time Warner Book Group UK, London, and
in hardcover in the United States by Crown Publishers, an
imprint of the Crown Publishing Group, a division of
Random House, Inc., New York.

Crown is a trademark and the Crown colophon is a registered
trademark of Random House, Inc.

Library of Congress Cataloging-in-Publication Data
Bodanis, David.
    Passionate minds : Emilie du Châtelet, Voltaire, and the Great
Love Affair of the Enlightenment / David Bodanis.
        p.   cm.
    Includes bibliographical references.
    1. Voltaire, 1694–1778—Relations with women.   2. Du Châtelet,
Gabrielle Emilie Le Tonnelier de Breteuil, marquise, 1706–1749.
3. Authors, French—18th century—Biography.   4. Scientists—
France—Biography.   5. Mistresses—France—Biography.   I. Title.
    PQ2103.D7B63 2006
    848'.509—dc22   2006008059

ISBN 978-0-307-23721-7

Printed in the United States of America

DESIGN BY BARBARA STURMAN

10 9 8 7 6

First Paperback Edition

For Sophie

A life to imagine

Contents

V. TRAVELS

VI. APART

VII. LUNEVILLE

VIII. FINALE

PASSIONATE MINDS

Preface

Back at the end of the 1990s I was researching a book on Einstein when I came across a footnote about an obscure French woman of the early eighteenth century, Emilie du Châtelet. The note said she'd played a minor role in developing the modern concept of energy, then added that she had acquired a certain notoriety in her time.

I was intrigued, and a few days later ended up at the science library of University College London—not in the modern, well-lit stacks upstairs, but deep in the darker ground-floor recesses, where the stacked journals had enough dust on them to reveal they hadn't been touched for years. What I discovered there—and then in other archives, as I tracked down her letters, as well as contemporary accounts of her life—astounded me. The footnote had understated her significance entirely. This woman had played a crucial role in the development of science—and had also had a wild life.

She and the great writer Voltaire were lovers for nearly a decade, though they certainly took their time settling down, having to delay for frantic gallopings across France, sword fights in front of besieged

German fortresses, a wild affair (hers) with a gallant pirate's son, and a deadly burning of books (his) by the public executioner at the base of the grand stairwell of the Palais de Justice in Paris. There was also rigging the French national lottery to guarantee a multimillion-franc payout, and investing in North African grain futures with the proceeds.

Then, when she and Voltaire finally did commit to each other, things started getting more interesting. They'd decided to create a research institute, in an isolated château they'd rebuilt, that in many respects was a century or more ahead of its time. It was like a berthed laboratory from the future. Visitors from intellectual centers in Italy and Basle and Paris came to scoff, but they stayed, awed by what they saw. There are accounts of Emilie and Voltaire at breakfast, reading from the letters they received—from Bernoulli, and Frederick the Great; earlier there had been correspondence with Bolingbroke and Jonathan Swift—and in their quick teasing at what they heard, they'd come up with fresh ideas, then return to their separate wings of the house and compete to elaborate them.

When they ran out of money, Emilie would sometimes resort to the gambling tables at Versailles—since she was so much quicker than anyone else at mathematics, she could often be counted on to win. Voltaire wrote proudly that "the court ladies, playing cards with her in the company of the queen, were far from suspecting that they were sitting next to Newton's commentator."

Voltaire wasn't much of a scientist, but Emilie was a skilled theoretician. Once, working secretly at night at the château over a single intense summer month, hushing the servants not to spoil the surprise for Voltaire, she came up with insights on the nature of light that set the stage for the future discovery of photography, as well as of infrared radiation. Her later work was even more fundamental, for she played a key role in transforming Newton's thought for the modern era. The research she did on what later became termed the conservation of energy was crucial here, and the "squared" in Einstein's famous equation $E=mc^2$ came, in fact, directly from her work.

In the evening of ordinary days, when she and Voltaire did take a break from their separate research, there were candles everywhere, and

Emilie raced in conversation, eyes sparkling, faster than anyone Voltaire had ever met. He adored her youth and intelligence (she was twenty-seven when they met), and she teased him for that; but she was thankful, deeply, that she'd finally found someone with whom she could let her intelligence pour forth. She'd been raised in a world where women weren't educated to any serious level, and she had been too unsure of herself to make these efforts on her own (even though no one who saw her confidence as an adult would have guessed how self-doubting she'd been).

Each of them transformed the other. Before meeting Emilie, Voltaire had been a respected wit, but little of his earlier output would be considered important today. Yet he loved Emilie beyond measure:

> *. . . why did you only reach me so late?*
> *What happened to my life before?*
> *I'd hunted for love, but found only mirages.*

She led him through Newton's great works, and that became the great shift in Voltaire's career, as he started seriously exploring with her how the clear rational laws that Newton had discovered for outer space could apply to improve human institutions here on Earth as well.

I was excited by these first glimpses I was getting. But after collating my notes just enough to write a handful of pages on this couple for my book $E=mc^2$ I was pulled away to other projects. Only in 2003 was I free to get back full time to their story. The wait was worth it, for by then I realized that there was something even more than a love story here. I'd taught intellectual history at Oxford, and knew that many people had contributed to the giant shift in eighteenth-century attitudes known as the Enlightenment.

But I hadn't realized how much du Châtelet and Voltaire's love affair was at the Enlightenment's very heart. The eighteenth century's leading man of reason had been bested by a woman intellectually superior to him, and it had led to their helping shape this powerful, world-shifting movement.

That was the wider story. To make it come alive meant starting inside the early eighteenth century, which even in France, the most advanced country in Europe, would seem deeply bizarre to us if we were sent there now. Women could be whipped and beaten by their husbands, with no recourse in law; homosexuals were liable to be publicly burned or, as in the case of one terrified homosexual abbé who was rescued at the last minute by Voltaire's intervention, preparations would be made to have their bodies pulled apart by iron hooks before they were sent to those salutary public flames.

The belief in the superiority of the rich over the poor was staggering. In France, if the king had chosen to give you a noble title, you often didn't have to pay basic tax—at all. So long as an aristocrat didn't lose that title of nobility, then his children could usually—and quite legally—be exempted from having to pay those taxes either. Or their children, or *their* children either. There were thousands of wealthy families in France that had paid virtually no tax for centuries. Only the little people did. Working for pay was demeaning, and indeed almost the only way for a noble to lose these tax exemptions was to be seen engaging in this scorned activity of paid work.

It also was taken for granted that the government could probe what individuals believed. Censorship was omnipresent, and if what someone believed was deemed wrong, then the government could punish that person as harshly as it wished. There was no space for private religious beliefs.

Voltaire and du Châtelet weren't the first to react against that. Cracks had already begun opening in the old view: from the evidence European explorers found of how different civilizations chose to live; from exhaustion after the continent's religious wars; from the extraordinary corruption of courtly life; from new ideas of the scientific revolution. But du Châtelet and Voltaire went further than most, partly from their sheer intelligence, but also because their unconventional life disproved the standard views. How could anyone believe that women really should have no true rights, or be kept out of education, when du Châtelet's strong, independent actions undercut that bias every day?

Most of the thinkers who began seeing the flaws in the old regime weren't organized at first. They were too isolated to build up any power. That's where the cascade of letters and texts that poured out from Emilie and Voltaire's château was so important. They galvanized such then unknown young men as Helvétius, d'Alembert, and Diderot, whose writings and edited volumes spread Enlightenment ideas even more widely.

It was pretty clear that I was going to have to write a full book: a biography not just of du Châtelet, but of Voltaire wherever he over-lapped with her, and their links with wider trends as well. Although I'd concentrate on France, because of its place at the center of the civilized world, I realized I couldn't help at least touching on how these ideas entered deep into the roots of the American Revolution and Constitu-tion. It's especially poignant today, for these Enlightenment ideas are at the heart of what is hated by groups such as al-Qaeda: the belief that diverse religions should be equally respected; that women can be treated fairly; that church and state can be separated; that old beliefs are not the sole path to truth.

The research was a delight. Du Châtelet had been an inveterate letter writer, sometimes sending four or five messages a day, and Vol-taire wrote constantly too, so what I found about key events was often as dense as an e-mail trail today. Thousands of those letters have sur-vived, as have du Châtelet's own half-dozen books and unprinted man-uscripts (including beautiful, private autobiographical reflections). There also are letters from houseguests and neighbors and purchasing agents and scientists, as well as a vast thicket of police reports, comple-mented by a small layering of servants' memoirs.

The detail was so great that when, for example, I describe Voltaire smiling after being asked a question by a particular police spy in May 1717, his smiling is not a random guess, but appears in a report the spy wrote that very evening. If du Châtelet looks out of a window, it's something mentioned in letters, or impossible to avoid by the layout of the room she's in—through the kindness of the present owners of the château where she and Voltaire lived, I was able to track their daily pat-terns, and spend time banging on walls, as well as examining door hinges and stairwell foundations and layers of wall paint, to work out what their living space had been like at the time.

Whenever the story seemed to slow, my characters would help me. Since Voltaire and Emilie often got restless after a few months at the château—or the government would draw up arrest warrants again—their shared decade wasn't just one of quiet reading and conversation. There were border escapes and Versailles card cheats; Paris throngs, and torn passion with the man who inspired the heartlessly sexy aristocrat Valmont in *Les Liaisons Dangereuses* (". . . and if you are still interested," du Châtelet wrote him one delicate time, "oh *felix culpa*"). There's a carriage overturning in deep snowdrifts at night, even an expedition through the frozen wastes of northern Lapland, in search of the truth about God's plans for the universe in the cold of Earth's Arctic latitudes.

There was so much material that the eavesdropping almost got too vivid. I found du Châtelet's account of how she would binge-eat when she was depressed, then make herself quickly stop before any of her friends could tell she'd gained weight; there's Voltaire mulling over the sexual exhaustion of his "little machine," and then reporting with satisfaction when it was back in order.

One of the most painful parts in my writing came when I reached the moment where the idyll started crashing apart. It was like watching friends you've loved destroying themselves in a divorce. Voltaire and Emilie had always had sudden quarrels, but those were usually patched up by an afternoon in the bedroom and then, if they were at the château and the weather was good, a picnic nearby, for which they'd bring wine, food, and—to new visitors' puzzlement—an extra crate with books, writing paper, quills, and ink. But in time these resolutions came further and further apart.

Voltaire fell out of love first. Emilie knew she should still be able to have a satisfying life, and at one point wrote how ridiculous it was to think that an intelligent woman really needed a man to be happy. Yet she did need that warmth, and the main text shows the resultant catastrophe that led to her sudden death in her early forties.

Voltaire was devastated ("I have lost the greatest part of myself"), and if there's a bitterness, an angry bite to his satires after that, it's largely due to this awful injustice at the end. It's especially strong in

Candide, the satirical philosophical story he wrote a decade later, built on themes the two of them had spent innumerable hours arguing over.

WHY isn't the story better known? Almost immediately after Emilie's death, sharp-tongued gossips began to disparage what she'd done. Since her main work was so technical, the women who ran Paris's salons had had no way of understanding its importance. Then, when her insights did enter the scientific mainstream, the idea that a woman had created these thoughts was considered so odd that the male researchers who used her ideas came to forget who had originated them. Voltaire did what he could, but even before his own death memory of her was being lost. By the end of the eighteenth century Immanuel Kant was writing that to imagine Madame du Châtelet a great thinker was as preposterous as imagining a woman to possess a beard; by the Victorian era of the nineteenth century, all but the briefest references to her name were gone.

Now is a good time to bring her back. A number of eighteenth-century women have been written about recently, but usually just because they had affairs with notable men or married into wealthy or important families. Du Châtelet's achievement is on an entirely different level.

Recent historical styles help. For a long time the chief Enlightenment thinkers were treated as a unified group, nobly striving for the betterment of all mankind, either as divinely inspired sages or as representatives of an inevitably rising new class. Much of that was a fantasy of French historians, projecting onto the past one side of the harsh, ongoing nineteenth-century battles left over from the French Revolution.

Conservative thinkers reacted against that, with their views reaching a head as the communist and fascist regimes of the early and mid-twentieth century showed the ways that insistent, misguided ideas could produce great evil. A gentler critique came from the American academic Carl Becker, who concentrated on the way many Enlightenment thinkers seemed just to be transposing the religious ideals they'd been brought up with, even in their recommendations about ostensibly secular policies. As Simone Weil put it in a different context, it was as if they believed one could get to heaven simply by marching straight ahead.

Yet that naiveté also was an exaggeration. One of the most important correctives in the immediate postwar years came from Peter Gay, then a young German refugee, working at Columbia University in New York. Among other things he pointed out the absurdity of holding that Voltaire ever believed in the infinite malleability of mankind, given that Voltaire put individuals driven by illogical emotion at the center of so much of his work.

About two decades later, Robert Darnton, whose father and brother had been notable *New York Times* reporters—and who briefly tried that career himself—began looking at the practicalities of what it really meant to be a writer or publisher in eighteenth-century France. He hunted in old archives and police transcripts—think of an on-the-scene tabloid photographer, but with a Ph.D.—till he brought back to life the travails of exhausted pamphleteers, under-the-counter booksellers, police spies, and everyone else who created the actual networks of communication used in France then.

It was an ingenious way of extending work of the French Annales school, which used a mix of economics, statistical research, and cognitive anthropology to open up a dense history from below, where cheap, massively popular thrillers of political pornography were more important than grand treatises of political theory. A later generation of historians has corrected some of Darnton's exuberance, yet continues his approach of looking at every aspect of the Enlightenment through fresh lenses, finally getting away from the left-wing/right-wing categories that had oversimplified much earlier work.

Du Châtelet's role as anything more than a sexy mistress took a long time to be accepted, and it was only the work of the immensely conscientious Princeton scholar Ira O. Wade that showed how important and creative she'd been. Wade was publishing this as far back as the 1940s, but although a diligent man, he seems to have trained at the Immanuel Kant school of expository prose: he was a terrible writer.

Only with a fresh generation of feminist scholars, especially from the 1970s on, did more serious attention go to her.

There had, I found out, been a few popular biographies even before this—most notably Nancy Mitford's 1957 biography of Voltaire that included this period in his life. But along with lacking many of the most important letters, Mitford knew little about science. Since du Châtelet's life was focused on science, the result was a cutout character who had dashing adventures, but for no discernible reason—like writing the life of Winston Churchill but leaving out the politics.

Voltaire was luckier in his biographers, not least because his letters have always been easily accessible—he lived long enough to ensure that—and because his writings are so catchy. But his biographers also often downplayed the role of science in shaping his life, which inevitably meant downplaying du Châtelet as well.

It's a pleasure to change that finally, and do justice to our characters by bringing back the science that had been so important to them both. But I also realized that it was important I didn't overemphasize that and produce merely another one-sided view. Instead I've concentrated on their love and built a narrative around that. It's the most vivid way I know to illustrate the subtle, often barely seen cultural shifts of the early Enlightenment: a way of making two long-gone individuals come back to life, in all their stumbling excitement and fears.

Author's Note

Throughout the book I call du Châtelet by her first name, and Voltaire by his last—which seems unfair, except that this is often how the two referred to each other. The name *du Châtelet* wasn't what our heroine was born with, nor what she chose, and when it came to teasing her male friends, she'd often write that they were one of her Emiliens. *Voltaire,* by contrast, was a name that our hero chose, and by which he did like to be referred to.

Translations presented more of a difficulty. Voltaire reads very easily in French, but literal translations—especially of his poetry—make him sound too mannered. To avoid that, although the prose translations are fairly neutral, the poetry translations are very liberal, at times almost paraphrases. This is actually the approach Emilie and Voltaire took when they did translations themselves: freely dropping and adding words to make writers come out as they felt they should. Some of the translations are my own, or by other recent authors; others are by contemporaries of our protagonists, to even better capture the style of their time.

. . . You are beautiful
*   so half the human race will be your enemy*
You are brilliant
*   and you will be feared*
You are trusting
*   and you will be betrayed . . .*

—VOLTAIRE, "Epistle on Calumny," 1733,
    soon after meeting Emilie (everything he
    predicted came true)

Prologue

Cirey, France, late June 1749

Alone, after dinner. Through the long window leading to her terrace the low hills of eastern France were barely visible in the dusk. She'd loved this house, her home, but after a decade spent with François, the man she'd lived for above all others, their life together had begun to shatter.

In his place she'd thought she'd found a better man, younger and more handsome, but then he too had turned cool to her. She'd tried to avoid admitting it at first ("illusion is not something you can have if it is not in your nature. However, you can avoid looking behind the scenes"), but his coldness never ended: she was experienced with men, and knew when passion was over.

A turn from the window: it was time to get back to work. The servants had lit the numerous candles on her table, and her manuscript was where she'd left it. She sat on the white taffeta chair. It was comforting to be back here after Paris, with the panels she'd commissioned from Watteau's workshop on the wall around her, her dog's basket beside her bedroom, her library through the doorway beyond.

In his own wing of the château, François was at his writing table too, the blank manuscript sheets for the play he was working on stacked beside him. If he was lucky, the play would bring him back into the king's favor and make up for the catastrophe during his last visit to Paris; there were important governmental reforms to work on as well.

He also had a mistress waiting in Paris, who was sending enticingly sultry letters, but he was getting tired of her. And how could she compare with Emilie, his one great love, the woman he'd shared so many years with? They weren't lovers anymore, but they had a bond that was deeper than in their years of first passion so long ago.

They would never abandon each other.

Back in her room, facing the long window and the river, Emilie was ready to start her night's work. Her hair was still thick, dense with dark curls, but she was graying in front. She had her diamonds on, and now reached for her quill. It was very quiet at the château. The moonlight that streamed past her angled onto the lace pillows at the head of her bed. The mathematics was getting harder. She was in her forties, nearing the final stages of pregnancy, and convinced that she was unlikely to survive the labor that would soon come. Some of her friends had tried to chide her out of that worry, but François knew her better than anyone else. He understood that she wasn't angry, just disappointed that she would have to leave before she was ready.

What could make a life worthwhile once love has faded? The great Isaac Newton had created modern science, yet his work had been incomplete at his death. She knew how to bring out Newton's most important, hidden truths about how gravitation worked and what those detailed workings might reveal about God's intentions for us. She'd also begun to glimpse her own powerful insights about the way energy that seemed to be used up in one part of the universe could instantly appear in another part, to keep the overall balance unchanged. She'd worked on her book bringing those all together for years, and was close to the end now. Maybe she would have enough time to finish it. If she succeeded, its memory could last for centuries.

She lifted the quill, then dipped it in the open ink pot.

I

BEFORE

1

Emilie

Gabrielle Emilie Le Tonnelier de Breteuil, just ten years old, sitting at the grown-ups' dinner table, her wavy hair pinned tight in yet another effort to keep it in place, was straining to follow the words of the visitor her father had brought to their Paris mansion this Thursday night. His name was Bernard le Bovier de Fontenelle, and she'd heard he was a famous scientist. He was talking about the distant stars.

He was explaining that they are huge suns like our own, with inhabited planets around them. That shouldn't terrify her, he went on, for it means we no longer have to feel oppressed, pinned down on our one small planet. Instead, we should gaze outward and breathe freely. "Nothing is so beautiful to visualize as this prodigious number of [solar systems], each with a sun at its center making planets rotate around it."

Emilie listened, rapt. It was dark outside, and the light from more than a dozen candles filled the room; the servants worked quietly amidst the glasses and plates and silver serving trays. This was one of the first times she had been allowed to stay up so late. Even better, Fontenelle was scarcely paying attention to anyone else.

Emilie's elderly father, Louis-Nicolas, looked on thoughtfully. He had arranged this evening, for he recognized that his daughter was different from other children, badgering him with constant questions about history and the court and the stars and religion. But he also knew that Emilie's excitement at learning didn't find favor with everyone. Her mother, Gabrielle-Anne, was also at the table—and she was distinctly not amused.

Gabrielle-Anne was one of those once-beautiful women who forever remain unhappy in life, however wealthy they are. "I don't think that anyone ever saw her smile," a regular visitor remarked, "except in a weary, condescending way." She'd been brought up in a convent, where the most important knowledge was how to maintain your social position, and the most intellectually complex instruction had been needlepoint. For years she'd tried to instill in Emilie the only kind of advice she felt a girl needed. The rules were legion:

"Don't ever blow your nose on your napkin—you might think I don't have to tell you, but the Montesquieu brothers blow theirs on the tablecloths, and it's disgusting. Break your bread rather than cut it (and break the bottom of your soft-boiled eggs when you're done so that the servants won't send them rolling off the plate onto you). . . . Never, ever comb your hair in church. You must be careful with the word *monseigneur,* it is pronounced differently for a prince of the Church and for a prince of the blood. And when a priest's in the room, always give him the chair nearest the fire and serve him first at meals, even if he's at the bottom of the table."

The mother had even tried sending Emilie to formal infant balls, where children arrived in miniature carriages and were supposed to remain for hours, showing off their bouquets, remarking on the goblets and furnishings and each other's clothes. But Emilie had been bored and showed it.

Making it even worse at the Breteuil table this Thursday night was Emilie's fourteen-year-old cousin Renée-Caroline. She was cross, for she wasn't used to being ignored. In the past few months, since she'd moved into the Breteuil home, she'd been the favored girl. She was everything a mother could hope for: compliant, pretty, and always wearing the right clothes.

For hours on end she would happily gossip with Gabrielle-Anne, talking about fashion and etiquette, and the quite embarrassing weakness of the father's family, which had been ennobled for scarcely two centuries—a sad contrast to Gabrielle-Anne and Renée-Caroline's notably more distinguished, if not quite so wealthy, family. ("When we spoke about such nobles of the second rank," Renée-Caroline recounted, "we were careful to look sideways to be sure our words didn't offend them—as one would if speaking about hunchbacks or redheads.") The mother gave this newcomer all the approval she withheld from her daughter.

Emilie had desperately wanted to join them, but she could never quite say or do the right thing. If she did try, she was more likely to blurt out some complex question in philosophy or theology. She would have been better off asking about fashion. "She was so confused and pedantic," Renée-Caroline remembered. "She wanted us to think she understood everything." Her mother and cousin just sighed.

Renée-Caroline had even convinced Gabrielle-Anne to kick Emilie out of the attractive upstairs bedroom that overlooked the Tuileries, letting herself move there instead. Emilie was relegated to small ground-floor rooms, looking out on a wall. "I don't believe there's anyone on earth who can feel despised without becoming despondent," Emilie wrote later. "Public scorn is a worse torture than the law can inflict, because it doesn't go away."

Now, though, at the dinner table, in her father's encouraging presence, and with the dinner guest focusing on her, she was able to escape into the wondrous world of science. Fontenelle told the ten-year-old Emilie about the thick band of white in the night sky called the Milky Way, and explained that this too was but a seeding of worlds, in far greater number than we could imagine. Experienced visitors from those distant stars might call out to new passengers as they entered our solar system, "You will soon discover a planet which has a great ring around it"—and so Saturn would be a floating navigation beacon for them to use.

Emilie was entranced with what might lie out there in space. According to Fontenelle, it seemed impossible that anyone on Earth could possibly weigh distant Saturn, or determine the temperature there. But what might be discovered in the future if you really used your mind?

Her father was unusual. Most European thinkers of the time were convinced that human adults were actually two different species, with males having been created with superior intellects to match their superior strength. But Louis-Nicolas knew how bright his daughter was, so quick in her thoughts, and he didn't see why he shouldn't help her.

Even when Emilie had been younger, and often clumsy as a little girl, he'd encouraged her in physical activities such as supervised horse riding and fencing. Now he began to bring tutors to the house for her. As the years went on, she translated Virgil and learned to read Tasso in the original Italian; she had the pleasure of memorizing long stretches of Lucretius and Horace as well. "Men can choose lots of ways to achieve glory," Emilie wrote, looking back, ". . . but women can not. Yet when someone is born with a soul that wants more, at least solitary study is there to console them."

Gabrielle-Anne was horrified at her daughter's progress and fought her husband at every step, at one point even trying to get Emilie sent away to a locked convent. That would have been a catastrophe for Emilie. Even the most distinguished girls' school, located outside Paris, had no significant studies, and allowed only a single thirty-minute visit with parents every three months. Punishment at elite convent schools included sending young girls, repeatedly and alone, to pray in stifling dark burial vaults. (One of Louis XV's daughters suffered such fits of terror from being forced to do this that she never recovered.) Fortunately for Emilie, her father managed to hold out against the convent.

But even though she got to study, she was still lonely—and could scarcely leave the house. If she went to the front of their mansion, when the staff went in and out on errands, at best she could see the open Paris streets beyond, and the king's private Louvre palace in the distance. It wasn't becoming for a female to explore on her own, and it was also too dangerous—not just at night, when, as her two older brothers had taught her, knife-wielding killers and the ghosts of the dead and carriers of plague roamed, but even during the day, when mutilated beggars would defecate under the yew trees in the Tuileries beside the old clay quarries there, and huge wooden carriages would jounce past while groups of restless policemen with thick cudgels watched the crowds. She was constrained to stay in.

As time passed, she realized that her protective father wouldn't be there forever. She had exactly two alternatives in life: either she could marry into a family that would keep her well or she really could be sent to a convent. Only this time it would be not just for a few years of education but to stay for the rest of her life, amid women who'd been disfigured by smallpox, or who'd been considering marrying beneath them, or—perhaps the majority—whose parents were simply unwilling to waste the funds to send a daughter out into any suitable family at all. It was not a biological clock but a financial one that now began to tick.

To make it harder, her father's income had gone down. For many years he had been chief of etiquette at Versailles and had earned a great deal by negotiating with foreign dignitaries to give them access to the king. After Louis XIV died, however, in 1715, that had stopped. Emilie's dowry—crucial to help pull in a spouse—was only medium-sized.

Luckily, though, when Emilie was fifteen—in 1721—something began to happen that tormented Renée-Caroline, still a regular visitor, more than ever. Emilie had been lanky and awkward as a child ("my cousin was three or four years younger than me," Renée-Caroline wrote, "but she was at least five or six inches taller"). Now, though, Emilie filled out. Her face took on an attractive oval shape, her hazel eyes widened, and she became, if not the perfect beauty that her mother had been, then a tall young woman who was very fit and very confident.

This could be her escape route. At age sixteen she was sent to live at court, to see what man she could attract with her mix of beauty and money—and with luck she wouldn't say too much to put him off. The purpose, as every woman understood, was to get a man who, in the later immortal words of Dorothy Parker, should be wealthy, loyal, and dumb.

But although Emilie didn't want the convent, she still was choosy. She was realistic enough to know that she wasn't going to find a man who would stimulate her creativity. But she also didn't want the standard life of a wealthy married woman, and needed someone who would at least give her the space to keep on studying.

It didn't help that since the recent death of Louis XIV the court had been run by a regent, who encouraged a sensual indulgence in his own life and among his courtiers that the old king hadn't allowed for decades. Since the most ridiculous of the fops, officers, and gamblers at Court wouldn't leave her alone, Emilie had to come up with a plan to show she was serious. As one account has it, she simply challenged the chief of the royal household guard, Jacques de Brun, to a sword fight.

De Brun was an experienced soldier and might have thought this was madness, barely worth lifting a weapon, but Emilie knew what she was doing. They wouldn't use their swords to try to kill, but the spectacle of her having to take off her formal dress and squaring up against this professional soldier would bring as many of the nobles as could manage to circle around and watch.

The years of fencing lessons Emilie's father had given her now paid off. One soldier who knew her well—and had himself killed a man in a duel—wrote, "She . . . wields a sword like a hussar, and becomes so ferocious when [a man] vexes her that she would not hesitate to run him through." She didn't defeat de Brun, but he didn't defeat her either. They each put down their swords, panting.

To her mother this was the worst possible thing she could have done. "My youngest . . . frightens away the suitors. . . . We may be forced to send her to a convent [after all], but no abbess would accept her." There was still no sign of the ideal suitor at Versailles, but Emilie could now go back to her studies, at least for a while.

It was harder than at home, because she'd gone beyond what her Paris tutors could teach her and there was no one at Versailles she could share her interests with, especially in philosophy and science. She began to study and read on her own. What she learned went roughly like this:

In medieval times, several hundred years earlier, there had been virtually no science. The universe was felt to be very simple. There was God on high, and kings and the Pope and cardinals below Him, and the chain of authority continued on, down through bishops, and knights, and monks, all the way to the humblest peasant. Everyone was in his place.

Nothing new was to be discovered. Even the heavens above were unchanging. Earth was at the center of a small universe, and the sun and planets orbited around us not very far away, possibly closer than the moon. At the outer extremity there were tiny flecks of light—the stars—which were affixed to a crystalline shell that slowly rotated overhead through the seasons. No one could question this, for not only was it obvious to direct sight, but the king and the Church derived their authority from the very nature of this unchanging universe. God ruled from a celestial throne, just as our superiors ruled us from their earthly thrones. Questioning the truths of astronomy would be the same as questioning the authority of kings and religious leaders here on Earth. It was a strict theocracy in which Emilie's distant ancestors lived.

For centuries on end that vision barely changed. But then—again, according to the standard texts she would have read—a few astronomers such as Copernicus and Kepler began to question the science that underpinned those views. They found that the data that had been unquestioned since ancient times were not as true as believed. The sun did not orbit daily around the Earth. The heavens were not changeless after all.

Most impressive of all, these new findings were not just guesses; vague notions that depended on intuition to prove true. There were ways to demonstrate that they were accurate, and to chart the new rules in detail.

Emilie was desperate to learn more—this was what she yearned for—but although she would no doubt drag Louis-Nicolas into nodding agreement when she shared some of these new ideas with him on visits, she couldn't get him to give her extra funds to buy more books. His lowered income didn't allow it.

There was one alternative. Emilie was bright enough at mathematics to teach herself analytic geometry. Shouldn't she be able to count the cards at the gaming tables quickly enough to give her a chance to win in gambling? (Gambling was popular, and well-bred young women were often exposed to it enough to pick up the rudiments.) If she did develop that skill, then with the money she might gain . . .

"My daughter is mad," Louis-Nicolas soon wrote. "Last week she won more than two thousand gold louis at the card tables, and . . . spent . . . half on new books." Louis-Nicolas hadn't pressured her as much as her mother, but where would this end? "I argued with her in vain, yet she would not understand that no great lord will marry a woman who is seen reading every day."

Finally, though, late in 1724, at age seventeen, Emilie realized she had to give in. A few girls managed to still be on the marriage market into their early twenties, but that was rare. (In fact, there had been a small number of women who'd managed to create semi-independent lives, but they were scarcely remembered.) Most women had been signed away in marriage at much younger ages. Girls could be legally married at twelve, and engaged—with no chance of recourse—at age seven.

With some help from her friends, and advice from her father, the teenage Emilie ended up paying special attention to a heavyset, polite man in his thirties, named Florent-Claude, who was the marquis of Châtelet-Lomont. He was a musketeer, his grandfather had been one of the Sun King's senior generals, and although the family estates were divided with his younger brothers, he still had enough inherited money—and would be helped by Louis-Nicolas's dowry gift—to give this young woman a decent life.

There was more. As a du Châtelet, he had a high enough ranking in the nobility that he would be able to call in the help of other powerful families if in the future there were legal attacks against him, his wife, or their income. That was important, for legal courts were so weak at the time, and judges so easily swayed by bribes or political influence, that without such personal connections it was quite possible for a family's inheritance to be gravely diminished. It made sense for Florent-Claude too, since Breteuil had his own useful links at court, aside from the wealth he would transfer in his dowry, and also the power of his wife's family name.

Contracts were now exchanged between the two families, and once the financial details were worked out, Florent-Claude officially proposed. He had been careful about the details but was not as solely mercenary as many others were. (One aristocrat, for example, had signed a marriage contract with the twelve-year-old daughter of a wealthy man and then left his new wife in a convent—she'd been sent back there after the wedding night—where she learned how to read and to sing while he proceeded to spend the dowry on his gambling debts.) Florent-Claude knew that although he and his wife would live quite separate lives, as was the custom, it would also help if they came to like each other.

The marriage was on, and now everything was changing fast. Gabrielle-Anne was in her element: finally her daughter was seeing some sense. There was no time for reading, of course, for instead there were hair styles to consider, and invitations to arrange, and legions of dressmakers to supervise. There was a rush of other activity at Versailles, of course—including a police hunt for someone who'd attacked a nobleman—but that could be ignored. Emilie was primped and styled and made over. Her mother had accumulated cloth for this occasion in a big wooden wedding chest; now there would be a silk veil-like fabric, to be held over Emilie's head at the ceremony (and which everyone knew would also be used in baptizing her first child); the tight bodice to have commissioned; new very high-heeled shoes (so uncomfortable to walk in that they would always have to be exchanged for slippers inside the house); specialists to prepare the rinses of mercury, bismuth, white lead, and rice flour to be rubbed on her face.

And then in June 1725 she was married. Florent-Claude wasn't callous, and understood that it would take his young bride a while to get used to her new life. He was willing to let her visit her brothers, whom she was close to, for a while; she could even continue to ride horses, so long as it was under proper supervision. But in September her formal duties began, for they were going to make a ceremonial entrance to the

town of Semur in Burgundy, a several-day carriage ride southeast from
Paris. He was governor of the castle, ruling over Semur, and this would
be their formal home.

Emilie tried to pack some books, but there wasn't space for many.
At noon on September 29 the town began to assemble, pressing up
against the stone ramparts: the minor nobles in one area, the priests
and monks in another, magistrates and guild artisans and ordinary
people packed in their sections as well. The townsmen waited in the
heat, and then at 4 P.M. there were the first drums announcing that the
town's new masters were in sight. The bells of the three grand churches
sounded, and nobles with swords were soon riding alongside. Everyone wanted to see the new marquise, not least Florent-Claude's four
sisters, who hoped they would soon have someone to give them the
latest gossip about Versailles, and clothes, and fashionable decoration.

The cobblestone and packed-dirt streets in Semur were crowded,
and for almost two more hours Emilie had to stay inside the hot carriage beside Florent-Claude. Guards with pikes and arquebuses marched
behind, and finally they reached the stone château's central court. Even
more dignitaries were waiting there, as well as clusters of everyone who
wanted to be thought a dignitary. Her husband was proud. Emilie got
out of the carriage. Paris and all she'd learned there were impossibly far
away. She was eighteen years old, and surrounded by crowds again, but
she was still alone.

2

François

François-Marie Arouet, still just a minor poet and social butterfly (yet the man who would transform himself to become the great writer Voltaire): young M. Arouet, age twenty-three, partial to wearing black trousers and a white lace shirt, thin and with brilliant eyes, was standing, this Whitsunday morning, amid a group of burly police officers, just outside the Bastille prison in central Paris. He was joking with them, seemingly without a care in the world, explaining that he was happy to see these looming masonry towers of the Bastille, for he had once visited friends there.

But it didn't change the fact that he was under arrest.

When he'd been staying in a Paris inn, a young fellow guest from the provinces had recognized the notorious young poet and asked, awestruck, if it was really true that the latest mocking verses that were going around Paris were his. The verses attacked the sexual escapades of the liberal regent, Philippe d'Orléans, who'd grabbed power after the recent death of the grand Louis XIV.

The lines had, in fact, been written by someone else, but Arouet loved to be the center of attention. He smiled and asked if the rural visitor—whose name was Beauregard—thought the verses were any good. Beauregard said yes, but added that now he had met Arouet, he could see that the poet was too young to have written something so accomplished, and they must have been written by someone else. Arouet quickly replied that no, Beauregard was quite wrong. In fact, he said, he'd secretly written a lot of verses like that.

Beauregard was impressed, and so was the superintendent of police when he saw the report of this one day later—for Beauregard was a police spy, whence young Arouet's position at the Bastille's gates, surrounded by these sturdy police officers.

From our era it might seem excessive to be arrested just for writing poems about a ruler's personal life. But in 1717 France, even seventy years before the Revolution, the royal family and its hangers-on were nervous individuals, with a great deal to be nervous about. Back in the previous century, when Louis XIII had taken the throne, a possible usurper was shot to death inside the royal palace as part of an effort to stop an assassination plot against the king. When that king's successor, Louis XIV, had been a child there had been repeated attempts, by massed armies of nobles who didn't accept the Crown's authority, to snatch the young king from the Paris palaces where his terrified mother kept him partly hidden. On several occasions they'd had to escape in secret to avoid these assassins. The new court that had been built at Versailles was a mark of weakness, stemming from those fearful days: the isolated palace there was more easily defensible against assassins, and several hours' ride from mass assaults in Paris.

For a while the successes in the middle years of Louis XIV's long reign had largely concealed that weakness. In the late 1600s France had dominated the Western world: it had the greatest army, the greatest economy, the greatest architects and engineers and thinkers. But from the latter years of the 1600s, in a decay accelerated by the old Louis's vicious attack on all French Protestants, forcing his country's greatest entrepreneurs to leave, the country's apparent success masked a steady decline. Wars were lost, and the frontiers drew closer: the theater and poetry became stilted. And these failures meant that at the end of Louis XIV's reign there were increasing doubts about the near-magical authority that the Crown had insisted came from God.

Most recently, since Louis XIV's death in 1715, the kingdom had officially been ruled by Louis XV, who was then, however, a mere five-year-old boy. This meant that the powerful army and all the nobles—with their wealth and centuries of pride—were supposed to obey that youngster's divinely authorized will. But since he spoke in a child's voice and had to be kept on reins to keep from running in random directions when he was brought outside, and he also understood nothing of the government he was supposed to run, all practical power was devolved to the regent, Orléans, who, however, was opposed by several powerful factions among the higher aristocracy in holding this patronage-rich position.

That's why the government was so touchy about writings that undercut public support. It didn't help that the popular poem Arouet took credit for was one claiming that the licentious Orléans was having sexual relations with his own daughter—an insult made worse by the fact that it quite likely was true.

Since there were no truly independent law courts in France, Arouet could be kept imprisoned for years. (A little later, for example, when a commoner named Desforges wrote two lines of poetry mocking the king, Desforges was dragged to the fortress of Mont St. Michel, thrown into a constricted iron cage, and kept there for three years.)

None of that was as important to Arouet as keeping up appearances, though, whence the easy banter with the arresting officers, and possibly the mention of his highly sensual girlfriend, an aspiring young actress named Suzanne de Livry, who was earnest and loyal as only a fresh-faced country girl eager to escape from the small village where Arouet had met her can be.

An even greater satisfaction would be to get back at the more senior officer who'd led the arrest, a Monsieur Ysabeau, who had made the unfortunate mistake of trying to bully Arouet when he led the police storming into the inn. As generations of government officials, literary opponents, aristocrats, crown princes, and scientists across Europe would come to learn, such bullying was not a wise course of action to commence.

Arouet was quick-witted, terrifyingly so, and now, at the first interrogations after the arrest, he spitefully told Ysabeau that he'd left the poem on the table in his inn room. Ysabeau replied that there were no papers there. He pressed Arouet again about where they were, till Arouet finally admitted, angry at having to give in, that perhaps he'd thrown them into the toilet.

Upon which news the good bureaucrat Ysabeau quickly returned to the inn, on the not especially salubrious Rue de la Calandre, and found the neighborhood official—the *vidangeuse*, always a woman— who was responsible for emptying the drains. (There was no reliable sewage system in 1710s Paris, and waste built up in underground pipes and chambers.) The local *vidangeuse* opened the top of the drain, lowered a candle on a string, perched over the edge, and after as much of a look as she could bear told Ysabeau that there were no papers floating on the thin layer of water that covered the more solid "*matière grossière.*"

By now it was Friday the twenty-first. Ysabeau told his superior that he was satisfied, and asked if it was truly necessary to investigate further. But the order for Arouet's arrest hadn't been a mere lower court matter: it had come from the pen of the Regent himself. The superior told Ysabeau that he must do his duty.

Back at the Rue de la Calandre soon after, or rather in good part *under* the Rue de la Calandre, officer Ysabeau and *madame la vidangeuse* got to work. The neighbors were beside themselves because of the odor being stirred up—they'd begged for the drain to be closed after the first inspection—but soon there was worse. The drains were built of old brick and mortar. As Ysabeau and the *vidangeuse* pushed in, they brought too much pressure to bear. There was a spurting, perhaps an ominous cracking, and then suddenly, in the cellars beneath the inn where beer and wine were stored, there was an almighty explosion as the old pipes burst, and there appeared, in quick succession, officer Ysabeau, the *vidangeuse,* a great amount of water, and an even greater amount of the *matière grossière* that had accumulated from now-imprisoned poets, visiting informers, and the numerous other guests at the inn.

The beer and wine were ruined (the owner won compensation from the city administration), but in all the torrent, no subversive poems, intact or torn up, were to be found. They'd never been there, as Ysabeau now realized. "It appears," Ysabeau wrote with immense self-control to the police superintendent, that "M. Arouet, with his active imagination, only pretended to have thrown away [the documents] . . . to create unnecessary work."

Across Paris, inside the Bastille, the source of this mischief, young François-Marie Arouet, seemed to be settling in easily. He knew that accounts of Ysabeau's misadventures would add to his own reputation for being able to turn harassment to advantage. He also let his friends know that he would soon be dining at the table of the Bastille's governor, and that he'd received volumes of Homer (in Greek, but with facing Latin translations). He prepared a neatly scripted list of further items for the fortress governor to supply: linen handkerchiefs, a nightcap, two cravats, even a bottle of essence of cloves (to keep his teeth clean). During the day François could visit the billiards room in the wealthier part of the Bastille, or wander and chat with aristocrats in other cells. Only at night was he locked in his cell.

But Arouet's acceptance was just an act. In a poem written much later he described what it really felt like to be locked away as a young man. The cell was deathly silent when the thick bolts of the door were slammed closed: it made the inmate feel separated from the whole universe, like a corpse being wheeled in silence to a cemetery. Arouet had a horror of imprisonment. There were rats and fleas; his cell's walls were at times alive with cockroaches from the cesspools; in neighboring cells there were inmates who had, simply, gone mad. Arouet's cleverness had thrown him into a dead end.

That meant he had to change.

In all of world literature, the play that had most attracted young Arouet was Sophocles' *Oedipus,* with its hard-to-resist motif of a son murdering his father. For Arouet's own father had constantly disparaged him, calling him lazy and "cursed by God." When as a teenager

Arouet had refused to go through the charade of law school that his father had tried forcing him into, he'd been threatened with exile to a miserable, malaria-ridden life on the plantations in the French West Indies. It didn't help that Arouet was probably illegitimate, and that his father had furiously taxed him with this fault as well.

For five years Arouet had been working on and off on a play that was a retelling of Sophocles' tale. There's an advantage in an author not finishing a work, especially a young author who hates limits. Until the work is done, who can possibly know what your limits are? But of course, in all that delaying, you still haven't achieved anything important.

Now Arouet resolved to finish off his play, and he also began detailed plans for another serious work. He would write his way out of the miserable position his vanity had led him to fall into. As would happen many times in his long life to come, he needed to reach that rock bottom before finding the energy—to refute his father's negative judgments?—that would pull him out.

Orléans hadn't been able to write the order for imprisonment on his own. It had to be couched as if it was the will of the now seven-year-old Louis XV. This, clearly, was inane. Arouet thought back to a period when France had been transformed for the better: to the reign of Henri IV, the king who'd declared that Protestants should be treated fairly, thus leading to a century of relative prosperity for France. Arouet wouldn't be able to get ink and paper within the Bastille, but he began a long history in verse anyway, using a pencil stub to scrawl text in the margins of the books that were passed around the prison, then, more carefully, memorizing hundreds of lines of what he composed (for he couldn't trust that he would be allowed to take with him any notebook in which he wrote them down).

He also prepared a deeper change. His father had no respect for him, he knew that. He would now retaliate in kind. He was making a life of his own, and probably wasn't even truly descended from Arouet after all. Molière's original name had been Poquelin. François resolved that when he got out of prison, he would change his name as well. One theory is that he chose an anagram of "Arouet le jeune," for in the style of the time the letters *v* and *u* were often substituted, as were *j* and *i*.

("Arouet le jeune" then become abbreviated as "Arovet l i.") Another theory is that he took a name from a book of pseudonyms available in the prison. Whatever his reasoning, henceforth he would be his own man: the grand

Voltaire

Orléans did in fact let him out, after just eleven months, in April 1718, feeling that enough of an example had been made. Voltaire was supposed to stay away from Paris, but gradually he was allowed back in the city to finish his texts and supervise rehearsals: first for just one day, then for a month, and finally for as long as he wanted.

There were some changes, not least that the fair Suzanne ("who would not sin [for] . . . those alabaster breasts; those lovely eyes") had dumped him for a young man named Génonville, whose merits, aside from not being a convict, included being rich and very easygoing. Voltaire could attest to that, as before his imprisonment Génonville had been a good friend of his as well. But Voltaire's contacts at the official theater, the Comédie Française, were still in place, and once he finished the final editing he was able, on November 18, 1718, to get his *Oedipus* performed after all.

The play was the success of the decade, receiving wave after wave of ovation. Some verses came just from his recent experience:

> *What we are feeling, our Kings cannot know,*
> *They lash at the innocent, with random blows.*

But other lines went further:

> *Yes we can have faith,*
>   *but only in ourselves.*
> *Yes we can look forward,*
>   *but with our vision alone:*
>
> *Not with false guides,*
>   *Nor with false gods.*

It expressed with efficiency the views of the aristocrats and upper professional classes in the audience, who were united in finding most of the Church's guidance laughable. The Reformation had been beaten back so completely in France that this Church had become astoundingly corrupt. Rich youngsters could be created bishops simply because their families bought the position for them. The youngsters so elevated rarely had a religious conviction to match their holy ascendance, and instead used their position almost entirely to accumulate mistresses and wealth.

The audience had further reasons for mistrusting the official attitude about how to live. The top lawyers and physicians among them, for example, recognized that aristocrats were at the pinnacle of society, and they hated the fact that they were looked down upon for failing to have clawed their way up there. The snub was made worse because of the law regulating how an aristocrat could lose his title. Lack of education, lunacy, or profound alcoholism would have no effect at all. But if an aristocrat engaged in the indignity of actually working for a living, then he could be dropped from the nobility (and his family would lose their exemption from tax). As a result, the lawyers and not-yet-ennobled administrators loved dialogue suggesting that professional diligence was the superior guide to follow.

The aristocrats in the audience, for their part, invariably hated the rising professionals. There were ever more of these narrow creatures, who showed a distressing skill at acquiring wealth in business and law, despite the tax disadvantages they suffered from actually working. But the play mocked the administrative positions that many of the rising professionals had purchased for their families as well.

Voltaire was careful never to go too far. The graceful verses in his *Oedipus* play didn't say which particular bishops or pompous officials were unworthy. He wasn't going to chance imprisonment again; the regent was mentioned not at all. All Voltaire was really doing was giving his audience an outlet for their general discontents. Nobody, of course, took it as undercutting the whole system of kings and regents and court appointees, for no one in the audience felt they were living seventy years before the French Revolution. On the contrary, they were part of a world that had existed stably for untold centuries, where there was a royal elite on top of society, peasants at the bottom, and a strict class system safely holding all the parts in between together. To move to better positions within that system might be desirable, and to be reminded of how so many individuals blocked you was satisfying as well. But there was no thought of putting the system as a whole in question.

The play went on to run for more consecutive performances than any other of the time. The British ambassador attended and reported to London that Voltaire was "ye best poet maybe ever was in France." As news of the play's success continued, George I sent this foreign marvel a gold watch and medal. A distinguished prince wrote an ode in Voltaire's honor, exalting him above Pierre Corneille, the great dramatist of the previous century, and inviting the young poet to dine. Voltaire even got his father to attend one performance, and—perhaps despite himself—the old man was seen applauding madly.

Even Orléans relented, bestowing on the new "Voltaire" the closest he could get to an apology: yet another gold watch and, better yet, a substantial annual subsidy. (Though when Orléans personally told him of the annuity, Voltaire replied that although he thanked the regent for helping to pay for his food, in the future he would prefer to take care of his lodgings himself.)

Paris was far more welcoming than before. When he met Suzanne de Livry again she quickly explained that she hadn't really been interested in Génonville—these silly oversights will happen—and as Voltaire would have heard, or at least she would now tell him, she had already dumped that really quite unimpressive young man. It was to Voltaire that she had been attracted all along. Voltaire believed her, sort of, or at least appreciated how she then carried out her apologies. He commissioned a leading artist to paint his portrait for her, which she liked, but when he also accepted her suggestion to cast her as Jocasta (Oedipus' mother) in a planned revival of his great play, she liked that even more.

Unfortunately, Suzanne's skills didn't extend to the theater boards, and when she laboriously declaimed the lines of the queen of Thebes in her strong rural accent the crowd hooted and booed. For a while

Voltaire defended her, and they continued spending time together. But there was also an up-and-coming actress at the Comédie Française, Adrienne Lecouvreur, who had a breezy, natural manner of speaking unknown before. Actresses were usually considered little more than conveniently displayed prostitutes ("it was routine to offer a performance in bed, after a performance in the theater"). That made this new woman's obvious intelligence especially startling. Audiences were enchanted, and to Suzanne's distress, and Lecouvreur's contentment, Voltaire became close with her as well.

Everything was going right. Voltaire made connections at court and at one point was sent by the French prime minister on secretive missions to the German states and to Brussels—somewhat between espionage and diplomacy—where he satisfied the minister, and certainly satisfied himself, playing tennis daily, riding horses, visiting most intriguing brothels, and all in all reporting that he "felt so well that he was astonished."

Back in France he spent weeks on end in the country homes of his new aristocrat friends, spinning out rhymes for his hosts, pleasing them with conversation about music and social intrigue and the arts, putting down anyone who talked too much about finances or politics or real science. Instead, in Rouen he made friends with the marquis de Bernières, made love with the marquis's wife, and when he couldn't be with her in person maintained a correspondence that all three appreciated.

Voltaire remained as wickedly quick as ever. If conversation turned to sibling rivalries, he might point out that indeed it was true that brothers argued—which was why the sovereigns of Europe were called brothers to each other. If they were discussing a poet who was writing an ode to posterity, he could remark that, knowing this poet, he doubted whether the gift would reach its destination.

His long poem on Henri IV was finished, or at least an early version was. Since it lauded that king, who'd encouraged religious minorities, by implication it was critical of Louis XIV, who'd believed in persecuting non-Catholics. (If a suspected Protestant tried not to swallow a wafer being stuffed in his mouth at communion, the penalty—

which king and Church supported—could be to be dragged out of the church and burned alive.) Voltaire arranged for copies to be printed abroad and smuggled past the guards at the gates of Paris, stowed neatly inside the furniture-laden carriages of a wealthy friend; daring readers left it on their tables for visitors to see.

But that was about the extent of his rebellion. Voltaire was aware that the Protestant thinker Pierre Bayle had written deep critiques of the whole French establishment's selfishness and waste, but he was not going to jeopardize his new life by elaborating on that, let alone use his charm to galvanize any unified opposition to the established powers in the land.

The years were passing since he'd been in the Bastille. As his mid-twenties turned into his late twenties and he moved about France ("I spend my days traveling from château to château"), Voltaire especially began spending time with his closest friend, the duc de Sully, who luckily was a bachelor, with an estate on the Loire that was huge, wooded, and inviting. Many distinguished women visited, as well as a number of selected locals. In quiet sections of the forest, Voltaire noted, the bark on the trees was getting ever more carved with intertwined names gouged by the various couples who'd enjoyed time there. There were evenings spent gossiping under the stars, drunkenly trying to make sense of astronomy, though since the visitors used opera glasses rather than telescopes, the locations of the planets were regularly muddled.

Was it enough? To stern lawyers such as Voltaire's father it was the waste of a life. But Voltaire was determined to be accepted among this easy, aristocratic crowd. He knew that his father had never been able to afford a noble title and had constantly suffered insults to his dignity from old-money families who had been ennobled for so long that all doors in top society were open for them. Voltaire once wrote that "in this world one is reduced to being either hammer or anvil." He was not going to be an anvil anymore.

This aimless, lilting life might have gone on forever, but one evening in January 1725, when Voltaire had just turned thirty-one and was at the opera with his friends around him, an arrogant aristocrat whom he'd known vaguely from Sully's circles came up to join them. This was

Auguste de Rohan-Chabot, who was always slower than Voltaire in conversation and must have recognized how much he was shown up at those long picnics or dinners at Sully's estate. Now de Rohan called out words to the effect of Ah, there you are, M. Voltaire, or Arouet, or whatever it is you call yourself. It was a slur, a reminder of Voltaire's origins, but trying to win a match of wits with Voltaire was not an intelligent gambit. Voltaire easily replied: Yes, I am the first to honor my name, but what have you done to honor yours? Then he turned away; the fool had been seen off.

A few days later Voltaire was at the Comédie Française, with Adrienne Lecouvreur—now the most sought-after actress of the time—sitting close to him. The theater was plush but had been built around a long open space, and there were stretches of darkness between the clusters of candles. De Rohan might have been stalking him, for he appeared again. (De Rohan had also had an ancestor who'd been humiliated in love by a lowly playwright—Racine—so seeing Voltaire with Lecouvreur probably made him more upset.) I repeat what I said to you before, de Rohan was said to have muttered. Voltaire looked back at him, unfazed, and responded calmly: I've already told you my reply.

At that de Rohan reached for his cane, to hit Voltaire for his impudence, but Voltaire tried to grab for a weapon as well. There were shrieks, and Lecouvreur conveniently fainted before anything more could happen. De Rohan stormed away.

Everyone talked about it, not least Voltaire, who yet another few days later was dining at Sully's townhouse, on the Rue St. Antoine, when there was a knock on the big gated door. It was cold outside on this winter midday, and one of Sully's servants carried the message in: there was a gentleman outside to see Mr. Voltaire.

Voltaire went out and had only a moment to recognize de Rohan's carriage before a group of de Rohan's bodyguards jumped him. They smashed him with cudgels and kept on beating him, breathing hard, as he went down. De Rohan watched, delighted, from inside his carriage, "supervising the workers," as he later described it. Finally he called them off: it was enough to leave this rascal bleeding and splayed in the dirt.

Somehow Voltaire managed to crawl back to the gates and drag himself into Sully's home. But instead of sympathy or even outrage, he found a great cold distance. Sully and his friends had nothing to say. They certainly wouldn't go to the police with him to back up his complaint. A wordsmith had overstepped certain bounds and now had simply been put in his place.

Voltaire was dumbfounded. How could his friends do this to him? He managed to clean himself up a bit, and set out to reach his other aristocratic friends in Paris. But they too now all withdrew. Jolly rhymes were one thing—that's what clever commoners were brought to great country houses for. But no one was going to turn against a fellow aristocrat who had been in danger of being humbled.

Everything he'd assumed true was falling apart. After one final try at Versailles he gave up on his wealthy friends. Voltaire would take revenge on his own. The sentence for murder was death, but he didn't care.

For several weeks he dropped out of sight, but then reports appeared that Voltaire had begun to take fencing lessons. This was getting too serious. De Rohan's uncle was a cardinal. He had a word with the now fourteen-year-old king, there was a police hunt, and on the night of April 17 Voltaire was arrested.

Voltaire tried a final time, writing with his coldest irony to the secretary of state, Jean-Frédéric Phélypeaux, comte de Maurepas:

> *My lord, I submit very humbly that I have been attacked by the Chevalier de Rohan, helped by six cut-throats, behind whom he had courageously stationed himself. Since then I have sought to restore, not my honor, but his. . . . I am, my lord, your very humble and very obedient servant, Voltaire.*

But Phélypeaux had nothing in common with Voltaire. He had been granted high office as a boy, and the world of inherited privilege—de Rohan's world—was all that he knew. There was a lesson to be taught. When the guards arrested Voltaire, there was only one place for him. Seven years before, Voltaire had been freed from the one confinement he hated more than any other. In all the time since he had trusted the new world of connections he'd built up. Yet where were any of them now?

In April 1725 he was thrown into the Bastille again, but that wasn't enough: he was still a danger from the attention he was getting, plus the likelihood he would try to attack de Rohan again if he was let out. After just two weeks he was escorted to the port of Calais. There were ships there to England, or the forests of America, or the deserts of the Sahara. It didn't matter which he got on, but he was being expelled from France.

3

Young Woman

Emilie's confidence had been knocked out of her by her marriage. Her husband, Florent-Claude, was kind enough, and never criticized her for spending so much time reading—if anything, he seemed proud to have such an intelligent wife. But he was busy supervising his military garrisons and largely left his young bride behind with his sisters, to deal with the two children—a boy and a girl—they'd quickly had.

Even child rearing wasn't something she could take much pride in, for parents of her class were strongly discouraged from spending much time with their children when very young. There were wet nurses and nannies to handle these "primitive" tasks.

She needed to open the door to science again. But how could she? Her father, whom she loved so much, had died recently, and although there was one kindly educated man in a town near Semur who lent her some out-of-date geometry texts, that wasn't what she needed.

It would have been easier for a man. Emilie knew that the great English thinker John Locke two generations before had found a patron in a wealthy aristocrat, and was led through him to interesting

intellectual circles in London. The even greater researcher Isaac Newton had been sheltered and encouraged at Cambridge University. Yet
no woman in France—or England—was allowed to register at a university, let alone at the grand Académie des Sciences in Paris. She was
an outsider, a young isolated parent, and no one from those august institutions would know anything about her, however eager she was for
intellectual companionship.

Florent-Claude realized that something was wrong, and was happy
to set her up at a grand apartment in Paris. It made life easier for him,
for although he would be away almost all the time—on military duties,
let alone his various romantic affairs—it was convenient to have a base
in Paris to return to. He respected Emilie, even if he didn't understand
her, and had no reason to want her to be unhappy.

But Paris wasn't much better at first. Without her adored father
around, she couldn't enjoy the consolation of sharing her feelings with
this one man who'd understood her. Her mother was even colder now
that the flurry of activity from the wedding was long over and the family had broken up; her older brothers were still sweet enough when she
saw them, but busy with their own careers. Even if foreign research
groups might be more welcoming than the Académie des Sciences,
rules of etiquette meant that, as a woman, she could never travel on her
own to visit them.

The first step to getting out of her isolation would be to have female friends here in Paris. But after her experience with her cousin
Renée-Caroline, she still didn't trust that the wealthiest women in the
capital would like her; too many of the ones she did meet were only interested in gossipy details about each other. Although she went through
the motions of teas and lunches and even some outings to the theater,
she was stepping back and analyzing these people she was supposed to
spend her life amidst. Why were they so uniformly unkind? "If I were
king," she mulled in a later writing, ". . . women would be able to take
part in all human rights, especially ones involving our reason. It's because of their lack of education [that] they seem born to deceive."

The level of knowledge was stunningly low. It hadn't been atypical
for Emilie's mother to be so poorly educated at the convent where

she'd spent her years before marriage. The great majority of French women couldn't sign their name in marriage registers, let alone read anything complex. (Decades later, even Olympe de Gouges, author of the stirring "Declaration of the Rights of Women," had to dictate her text because she'd never been taught to write.) Louis XV's daughters remained illiterate, even after several years in convents. An archbishop of a previous generation, who had promisingly written that "nothing is more neglected than the education of girls," went on to explain that it was of course a limited education he had in mind, which should concentrate on managing servants.

In the few schools that were available for women, all science, philosophy, and literature were taboo. A small amount of history was sometimes allowed, but only, as one contemporary put it, "in order not to confuse a Roman emperor with an Emperor of China . . . all this must be accomplished without rules or methods, and only so that girls might be no more ignorant than ordinary people." That was how almost all the women that Emilie was supposed to spend her time with had been educated. (Again, the handful of exceptions—women who were self-educated and had broken through those barriers—were extremely rare, and scarcely known to her then; most of the salons she had access to were more concerned with gossip than anything else.)

It was a desperate time: without good friends, with two small children, and with that door of science seemingly locked forever.

"I felt," she wrote, looking back, "as if I was swimming in an endless sea of uncertainty. In the morning I'd undo whatever I'd decided the day before." She would eat too much ("I gave in too often to my big appetite"), but then immediately go on diets before anyone could see that she'd gained weight. At one point, she even nervously tried an affair with what seemed a pleasant young noble, Guébriant, but it ended quickly. She wanted love, or at least a partner to go forward with in thought. Guébriant was both insincere and entirely vacuous.

She had too much dignity to entirely give up, though. John Locke's writings managed to give her some consolation, for his works spoke to her isolation, showing what a solitary explorer could find.

Locke believed that our mind was a mere blank slate when we

were born, a tabula rasa (a "scraped tablet"). This was revolutionary. If the mind was blank, then it became very important to see who had the power to write on that slate. The writing might be pronouncements from the pulpit of an established church; it might be rules teaching us to defer to the royal family. But if something is wrong with how we think, then the fault is not with any preformed ideas we are born with. Rather, it's the institutions leading us to those misleading or dangerous beliefs that will have to change.

Locke's view made sense to Emilie, explaining how women in modern France were taught to simper or become lost in snide gossip. The "blank slate" they'd been born with had been filled in ridiculous ways, through books of etiquette or those narrow convent schools where the most challenging subjects were needlepoint and how to instruct servants. Even more, Locke's philosophy suggested that women didn't *have* to be indoctrinated that way. Different education, or different attitudes in society, could let us break free from that narrowness.

(There was a powerful shift in society beginning here, sweeping up Emilie and many others. Popular fiction in the 1600s and very early 1700s, for example, before Emilie came of age, seems odd to our eyes: the plots are amorphous or random, while the heroes or heroines are often led by internal moral or semi-religious quests. But now, when Emilie was a young woman, a new sort of writing—the novel—was becoming popular. In 1728, the very year that Emilie returned to Paris with her two toddlers, the Englishman Henry Fielding produced his first play at Drury Lane. It was the start of a career that would peak two decades later in his novel *Tom Jones,* with its perfectly Lockean hero, so energetically shaped by the sensations and attitudes that society has on offer for him.)

Yet even Locke's insights had a depressing twist, for Emilie might remain locked in the wrong world her whole life long. Suppose social attitudes didn't change. Then even if we personally did better—even if we'd tried to get our minds "written on" in a sensible way—we would still be trapped inside societies that didn't let us live as we wished. Emilie needed to break from that, but how to find the strength? She was greedy for knowledge, yet couldn't go forward on her own.

And then her world transformed.

At age twenty-two, Emilie now met the most sought-after man in all of France. It wasn't Voltaire, but rather the one man Voltaire often said he wanted to be: Louis-François Armand du Plessis, the duc de Richelieu, ten years her senior.

If Emilie had wanted to make the women in her Paris circles dislike her even more, she couldn't have chosen better. Richelieu was a man's man, yet also one whom most women blindly adored. It was through him that she got the confidence crucial for the next stage of her life.

He was the great-nephew of the famous cardinal who'd helped establish the centralized French state; the Sun King, Louis XIV, himself had been his godfather. He'd inherited a fortune and been thrown into the Bastille three times before his mid-twenties—first at age fifteen by his own father for disobedience, then at age nineteen for dueling, and finally at twenty-three for plotting to overthrow the government. He was a renowned soldier—or at least successfully managed to give the impression he was one—and later led the victorious combined land-sea attack on the fortified island of Minorca, reducing the British Empire in the western Mediterranean (and making it fall back, once again, to what was felt to be the temporary stronghold of Gibraltar).

When Richelieu wasn't at the front he dressed cleanly, with only a minimal elaboration of the lace cuffs that Versailles drones insisted on. He was polite and quietly humorous, and—most wondrous of all—he listened at length to female confidences. Laclos probably modeled the character of Valmont in *Liaisons Dangereuses* on him, but in real life Richelieu was more scrupulous: he seems never to have slept with a virgin, or anyone underage.

Those were probably his only exceptions, though, as Emilie's friends all knew, for in the words of awed contemporaries: "He was woman's idolized lord. The coquette and the prude, the duchess and the princess—all alike yielded to him . . . never a passion, but much debauchery. He even has mistresses who aid him in his acts of infidelity, their jealousy stifled by their desire to please."

Most pampered court appointees did poorly in the high jobs they were granted, but the confident, direct Richelieu was excellent. At age twenty-nine he was appointed ambassador to Vienna, the capital of the most ancient branch of the vast Habsburg Empire. In four years he transformed French prospects during complex peace negotiations, and when he returned to Paris—in 1729, when the unknown Emilie was twenty-two and he was still only thirty-three—no triumph was beyond his grasp.

It seemed inconceivable at first that he would turn to this quiet, intellectual young woman. But Emilie's late father, Louis-Nicolas, had indirectly helped set it up. He'd known that the du Châtelets had distant family connections with the Richelieus, which ensured that at some point his daughter would meet this powerful man. Whatever Louis-Nicolas might have intended, when Richelieu did return to Paris Emilie had already stayed many times at his sister's house, and it was there that they naturally overlapped.

She was cautious at first, almost disbelieving what was beginning to happen—"I can't believe that someone as sought-after as you wants to look beneath my flaws, to find out what I really feel." To make it more intimidating, affairs were a serious matter, and were allowed only so long as the appropriate forms were followed. In Florent-Claude's own affairs, for example, he was always careful to sustain the external forms of Catholic marriage. This meant no holding hands in public and no staying the night at someone else's home while you were in the same city as your spouse. (Having more public affairs away from Paris was less of a difficulty, for one was showing polite discretion by being so far removed.)

The trick was to be able to hold two views at once. The married Louis XIV, for example, would always stop his carriage when he passed a priest, and bow with full sincerity—even if he was in the carriage because he was heading off for an afternoon with one of his innumerable mistresses. All of France worked that way. Censorship, for example, was not a matter of either/or. There was an intermediate category of "tacit" censorship, where a work was somewhat illegal, but not strongly so: the author could publish a few copies so long as he was discreet. (Even the king's chief censor, in a later generation, temporarily used his own home to hide copies of a work he didn't want to be generally circulated, yet which he didn't want to be entirely destroyed either.) Marriage was a matter of financial and social alliance between families, and so long as that was respected, the natural passions that humans felt could be fulfilled without destabilizing the system.

When Emilie began sleeping with Richelieu, everyone waited for him to drop this intense, albeit gracefully tall youngster and move to a more conventional partner. But he was having too much fun. As Richelieu would be the first of many powerful men to discover, Emilie was different from anyone he'd ever met. She still blurted out her sentences, and sometimes it was as confusing as when she'd been that child trying to get a word in past her visiting cousin ("My ideas were all mixed up last night," she wrote to Richelieu, ". . . I know I'm not eloquent"). But when she wasn't too shy or too excited, she was captivating. Two vastly wealthy young women from the court had once awkwardly grabbed pistols and fought a duel in the Bois de Boulogne after arguing about which one should get Richelieu. That level of behavior was beneath his dignity, and Emilie would never do such a thing. Which of Richelieu's previous conquests would have been able to intrigue him with the twists and turns of Locke, or—a legacy from that kind old dinner guest Fontenelle—lead him on to ideas he'd never suspected about the distant reaches of outer space? For now the truly astounding had happened.

Louis-François Armand du Plessis, the duc de Richelieu, was in love.

It couldn't last, of course, despite the increased thrill he found. Emilie was young and pretty enough, and also would have picked up from Florent-Claude's sisters, as well as from other female friends, knowledge of the appropriate bedroom techniques for these circumstances. With one's husband, formal sex in the missionary position was all that should be offered, but with a lover, the woman could be more inventive. Indeed, one aristocratic young woman had reported that she *only* engaged in sex in the female-superior position when she was with her lover: she respected her husband so much that if he asked her if she'd let another man mount her while he was away, she wanted to be able to reply truthfully that she certainly had not.

Nor was contraception a difficulty. The rhythm method was occasionally used at this time, but withdrawal was more common. With mutual trust, this could be satisfying enough. Aristocratic women of sufficient confidence, as the ever-diligent chronicler Brantôme had earlier recorded, took pleasure in "putting it in and frolicking until they are surfeited, but they do not receive any of the seed . . . for they do not wish to permit anything to be left inside them."

The problem, rather, was that Richelieu's attraction to Emilie had depended on her reversing the usual course he was used to, of women blindly glorifying him. Instead, with her extraordinary quickness and insight, she soon managed to assess his underlying feelings, his underlying self. Being Emilie, she also felt no need to keep her thoughts to herself. "Friends get to see each other in every way they are," she wrote. "I love you sad, happy, lively."

Soon, however, she began to see too deeply. It had been clear from the start that he wasn't going to be the man who could lead her forward into science. Now it was evident that their relation couldn't last as a mere sharing of passion either. She joked about it at first. "No, I'm not at all satisfied with your letter," she wrote with mock seriousness. "It's not that you're not charming, but . . . you don't speak about yourself enough." But then she got closer: "You write as if you have all the grace and gaiety in the world. But I see the melancholy you're feeling." And even later, most coldly dissecting of all: "I think we met too late for me to have a real place in your heart. You'll never love anyone unless you need them for your pleasure, or if they're useful to you."

The affair went on for a while longer, but no eighteenth-century French *galant,* conqueror of foreign armies—not to mention the majority of the court's favored mistresses—was going to forever remain lovers with someone who made him probe so closely into himself. He realized he couldn't quite match up, and broke it off.

Emilie then did another thing no other woman in France had managed. Richelieu wasn't the man she was looking for, but she was so graceful during the breakup that the two became lifelong correspondents and friends. In the years to come, he sent her hundreds of letters, sometimes superficial, sometimes thoughtful (and always poorly spelled, even by the relaxed standards of the time).

It was a happy enough ending, and Florent-Claude, as always, was friendly with his wife when they happened to overlap in Semur or Paris. But now that she'd had a glimpse of real passion she was even less content to be alone with her books. She was still excluded from the world of science researchers and exciting writers, still looking—despite Florent-Claude's kindness—for the partner who could help her enter this world she sought.

4

Exile and Return

Voltaire ended up in England when he was expelled from France after de Rohan's attacks. His arrival there was magnificent, as he explained to his friends back home:

> It was in the middle of spring [1726] that I disembarked near Greenwich, on the banks of the Thames. The sky was cloudless, the air cooled by a gentle west wind . . . The river was covered for six miles with rows of merchant vessels, their sails all spread in honor of the King and Queen, who were rowed upon the river in a golden barge, preceded by boats full of musicians, and followed by a thousand little row-boats.
>
> Close to the river, on a large green which extends for about four miles, I saw an immense number of comely young people caracoling on horseback round a kind of race-course marked off by white posts stuck in the ground. . . . There were young girls on foot . . . [who] were to be in a

footrace as well. . . . Some merchants to whom I had letters
of introduction got me a horse; they sent for refreshments;
they took the trouble to put me in a place where I could easily see. . . . I fancied that I was transported to the Olympian
games; but the beauty of the Thames, the crowd of vessels,
and the vast size of the city of London soon made me blush
for having dared to liken [Olympus] to England.

It was a great story, but about as accurate as his declaring to Beauregard that he really had written the scurrilous poems about the regent.
Voltaire was thirty-one but still needed to exaggerate and show off.
There were no music barges on the river that spring, he had no letters
of introduction to local merchants, and if there were footraces at
Greenwich, he wouldn't have been able to ask any of the locals about
them, for he didn't speak English.

What really happened his first day, or near his first day, was that he
trudged up to Highgate, on a hill north of London, where he'd
arranged for a cash transfer to be waiting. But when he arrived he
found that his banker was bankrupt. He had to go all the way back to
the grand boulevard of Pall Mall, where Bolingbroke's city mansion
stood, yet there he found that "My Lord and my Lady Bolingbroke
were in the country." Voltaire was broke, and no doubt sweaty, and
knew no one to help him. The Bolingbrokes' country house was impossibly far away. As he later admitted to the one friend to whom he
was always honest, Nicolas Thieriot, "I was without a penny, sick to
death of a violent flu, a stranger, alone, helpless, in the midst of a city,
wherein I was known to nobody. I could not make bold to see our ambassador in so wretched a condition."

It was at this point that Voltaire's luck turned. In Paris the year before, he had met a passing English trader, Everard Fawkener, back
from several years in Syria trading silk garments between Europe and
India. Most educated Frenchmen had snubbed Fawkener for being a
mere tradesman, but not Voltaire. He'd chatted with Fawkener about
his business, and the archaeological sites he'd poked around in Syria,
and now, in England, seemingly by chance—or with a little help from

Voltaire—they met again. Fawkener had a mansion in the bucolic wonderland of Wandsworth, a country town with its own windmills outside of London. Voltaire needed a place to stay. He knew that there were a number of French-speaking émigrés in London, and with his literary reputation he could probably find one among them to stay with. If he did that, though, he wouldn't learn much of England: he'd stay immersed in émigré politics, and émigré arguments, and an émigré's ever more out-of-date language. He was too proud to do that, yet he was also too proud to scurry back to Paris and beg to be accepted by the French authorities again.

Why couldn't he learn English well enough to become a great author in England instead?

Fawkener had no idea what he was letting himself in for. Voltaire invited himself over and stayed for a week, and then another week, and then another, and yet another: he was transforming into that horror of the English countryside: The Guest Who Never Leaves. But he had one goal—to learn English perfectly—and he'd found the ideal place to do it.

He began (*"thirty and one of july a thousand seven hundred twenty and six"*) by keeping a journal, carefully noting down verbs of interest. "*Mr. Scuttlars history,*" he slowly printed in English, "*. . . He cured his wife of the spleen, with a good fuking.*" Then Voltaire struck out the word *fuking* and above it thoughtfully wrote the shorter variant *fuk,* to be sure he got the spelling right. When he needed help in pronunciation he made his way to the theater at Drury Lane, where the prompter loaned him a copy of that night's Shakespeare script, so he could mouth the words to himself while listening to the actors speak them.

He kept on going to the theater, and he kept up his journal, and just three months after moving in with Fawkener, the no longer indolent Voltaire had it cracked. By October he casually wrote a friend the following note, in English: "I intend to send you two or three poems of Mr Pope, the best poet of England, and at present, of all the world. I hope are acquainted enough with the English tongue, to be sensible of all the charms of his works." He knew very well which poems were considered good, for he'd begun corresponding with Pope, and soon

Jonathan Swift, and Sir Hans Sloane, and Samuel Clarke (rector of St. James's, Piccadilly), and almost everyone else who counted in England.

Voltaire got so good so quickly that when he finally did move out of Fawkener's home, he could joke—also in English—with Bolingbroke's secretary, John Brinsden (who had two school-age children):

> Sir, I wish you good health, a quick sale of your burgundy, much latin and greek to one of your children, much law . . . to the other, quiet and joy to mistress Brinsden, money to all . . . But dear John be so kind as to let me know how does mylady Bolingbroke.

Since he was fluent in English, and the Bolingbrokes—both lord and mylady—were back from their summer country house, soon he was introduced everywhere in the bizarre country that was England. The distance of under thirty miles across the Channel meant a great deal then, for with no regular travel, and of course no television, radio, or magazine pictures, Voltaire had had hardly any clear idea of what to expect.

Personal servants, he found, didn't have to carry letters between individual homes for delivery within a few hours: instead there was a "postal service," more efficient than anything in France. He also learned that, at least in the wealthiest mansions, servants didn't have to carry water from room to room—there were miniature pumps and pipes instead, an arrangement that Paris entirely lacked.

He discovered strange, meat-avoiding beings called "vegetarians," who compounded their oddity by going for long brisk walks for their health. He found his way to the Royal Exchange, where there was the greater oddity that "the Jew, the Mahometan, and the Christian transact together as tho' they all professed the same religion . . . and give the name of Infidel to none but bankrupt." In France that would have been impossible, for non-Catholics were forbidden positions of power, and as seen, until recently when Protestants had been identified—often by informers—they had been tortured or thrown into slavery on galley ships.

Often around London there were fierce military recruiters with bearskin hats and rapping drums, with the king's authority behind them, but Voltaire also learned that there were some Britons opposed to all that. He made his way to the wooded isolation of Hampstead, and discovered even greater radicals, called "Quakers."

"The reason of our not using the outward sword," Voltaire recorded a leading Quaker there, Andrew Pitt, explaining:

> is that we are neither wolves, tygers, nor mastiffs, but men and Christians. Our God . . . would certainly not permit us to cross the seas, merely because murtherers cloath'd in scarlet, and wearing caps two foot high enlist citizens by a noise made with two little sticks on an ass's skin extended. . . . When, after a victory is gain'd the whole city of London is illuminated; when the sky is in a blaze of fireworks, and a noise is heard in the air of thanksgivings, of bells, of organs, and of the cannon, we groan in silence, and are deeply affected with sadness of spirit and brokenness of heart, for the sad havock which is the occasion of those public rejoycings.

How could this be? In France, no religion that opposed the king's militarism could survive. But in England there was far more freedom for minority religions than in France. Voltaire talked it over with Bolingbroke, and he read Swift's newly published *Gulliver's Travels* ("stick to the first [volume], the other is overstrained"), and he began to imagine a new way to work. He'd been a poet before, and willing to mock public inanities, but that had mostly been in scattered, merely clever remarks. There was no system, no consistent vision.

What if he could create a new form of writing to take his new insights further?

It couldn't be through poetry—it's too hard to carry logical arguments along that way—so he would have to find his new approach in prose. The letters he'd been writing to Thieriot could be a start, since letters seem an innocuous, nonthreatening style of writing. But their very informality would allow him to casually put across views that in fact he'd thought about a lot. If he compiled enough of these chatty yet analytic letters, building up on each other, he could develop a powerful critique of his home country.

He began editing his letters to Thieriot, playing with ways of drawing out the conclusions he liked. The more he saw of England's pro-business attitude, for example, the more he liked it. "I do not know," he tried composing, "which is the more useful to the State, a well powdered courtier who knows to a moment the hour at which the King rises and at which he goes to bed . . . or a merchant who is enriching his country, who gives from his office orders for [Bombay] and for Cairo, and who contributes to the happiness of the world." Voltaire realized this would be the way to show what else was wrong about the profoundly snobbish country he'd left behind.

There was a lot more to learn in England, about religion and business and science (although Newton had had the bad grace to die just a bit too soon to be interviewed by Voltaire). Yet as the months in England turned into years, in 1727 and especially 1728, his enthusiasm began to fade. Voltaire had been enjoying himself, and even had the good fortune that Suzanne de Livry had arrived in London, alone and lost and needing comforting. But there comes a time when every émigré has to face what it would really mean to be in exile forever.

Voltaire's English was better than ever, and he wrote poems in English and began literary works ("You will be surprised," he wrote in English to Swift, a year after he arrived, "in receiving an English essay from a french traveller"). But he recognized that he was never going to be able to write like Shakespeare, while in France he'd received acclaim for writing as well as Racine and Molière.

He began to spend time with other Frenchmen in London, at their coffee shops near the Strand. He missed the easy conversation in his native language. De Rohan was disagreeable but wasn't going to show his cowardice by attacking him again. Politics was changing, and there had been letters hinting that the court might be ready to discreetly overlook what had happened. Voltaire had been in England long enough. It was time to go home.

HE ARRIVED back in France in the autumn of 1728, a little over two years after leaving. For a few months he cautiously stayed far from Paris, going over his notes, trying to relax by horse riding and working at his tennis. His good friend Richelieu was still stationed in Vienna, and Voltaire wrote asking him to check with his contacts at court and in the police if it really would be safe to enter the capital. By early 1729 he received confirmation, and probably in April that year he went back.

There was no question what he would do first. "I was not born rich, far from it . . . [and] I saw so many poor and despised men of letters that I decided . . . not to add to their numbers. . . . There is always one way or another by which a private individual can profit without incurring an obligation to anyone."

His lessons in ingenuity went far back. Voltaire had been a student at the Jesuit school Louis le Grand in the hunger year of 1709, when a catastrophic winter saw wolves enter the outskirts of many French cities, and the failure of crops the subsequent summer caused mass starvation. The clerics who ran the school had managed to keep the students fed and scrounged enough wood for the stoves through one series of black-market machinations after another. Although Voltaire had not been taught any science or modern history, that example of practical skill from his teachers and others had done wonders in showing him how obstacles could be overcome.

He had the opportunity to use that now, right at the moment of his return to Paris. The city government had recently defaulted on its municipal bonds, which meant that there were a lot of wealthy individuals who owned valueless bonds. If the government left it at that, those individuals would be very wary of ever investing in future bond issues. To show good faith—and make up for some of the investors' losses—the city government now decided to offer a lottery, to which only owners of those now valueless bonds could apply. Since the angry bondholders wouldn't participate in an ordinary lottery (having been so misled before), the government decided to go further and add substantial extra

Lottery

funds to the total lottery amount. The government felt this was safe, since it expected only a few holders of the original bonds to invest, despite the sweetener of the increased payment per ticket.

What it didn't reckon with was Voltaire's ingenuity, aided by his new friend the mathematician La Condamine. Voltaire had been audacious and creative in literature. Now he applied the same skills to finance. What if someone went around and bought *all* the valueless bonds that were in default? It was easy enough, for the owners of the bonds were still so upset at having lost all their money in the city's original default that they didn't really believe the promises the city gave that there would be extra money in the lottery.

In fact, though, these bonds weren't quite valueless, for Voltaire—and La Condamine, and a very few others he brought into his syndicate—weren't blinded by that recent experience of financial loss, and so understood that the bonds were "tickets" they could use to enter the city's lottery. And since the city genuinely had added extra funds to sweeten the lottery . . .

The only possible way that Voltaire could lose would be if, by horrible chance, one of the original bondholders entered the lottery. To forestall that, he and La Condamine effectively bought every single one of the defaulted bonds. In other words, they bought, at a greatly discounted price, almost every ticket for a lottery that was guaranteed to pay out more than the total price of all its tickets.

They got very, very rich. Voltaire amassed a fortune that—combined with other shrewd investments—meant not only did he never have to worry about money, or ask an aristocratic "friend" for financial help, ever again in his life, but he was actually now richer than most aristocrats in France.

Now he was free; now he could do what he wished. But what was that? He couldn't really spend much time with Sully or his other previous hosts. They might be willing not to bring up the de Rohan matter, but they were never going to apologize for their coldness. And they had all been complacent—almost enjoying the joke—when his Rouen mistress, de Bernières, had ostentatiously gone to the Opera on the arm of de Rohan himself, just a few months after the beating outside Sully's.

There were other reminders of what he couldn't accept. With Suzanne left behind in England, he'd started up with the intelligent, breezy actress Adrienne Lecouvreur again. But then, scarcely a year after he got back, and with Adrienne only in her thirties, she seems to have been struck by typhoid and died. (Paris still got much of its drinking water from the Seine, into which a city's worth of raw sewage poured.) Voltaire had spent her last days trying to help her, but when she died he found that she couldn't be buried in any of the cemeteries she'd have wished for—since she was an actress, she was officially excommunicated by the Catholic Church in France.

Instead of a respectable burial, where Voltaire and her family could have mourned, her body was dragged away in a cheap municipal carriage and thrown into a shallow grave in an open field outside the city gates. Sizzling lime was poured over her corpse, and that was it: it was unsanctified ground, and no headstone or any other memorial was allowed.

How could this happen? In England in the same year, the great actress Anne Oldfield died, and in the British tradition was granted a richly attended funeral in Westminster Abbey. That was how Voltaire wished Lecouvreur had been commemorated. He wrote bitter lines of poetry about the injustice to Lecouvreur, contrasting it with what happened in Britain, and he called on future generations as yet unborn to remember that such a thing could once have occurred.

He recognized that the reason had to lie in some deep difference between France and England. On the surface, the two countries had many similarities: both had overseas empires and had suffered civil wars and great religious battles. Yet England respected its artists and thinkers—Newton had been buried in Westminster Abbey as well—in a way that France did not. The entire climate of opinion was different. Possibly it was linked to the greater tyrannical power of the French king, and the court's dislike of any competitors; possibly—in some way Voltaire couldn't yet grasp—it was linked to the more advanced developments in science over in England. But although he wanted to put a section on Newton right at the center of what became known as his *Letters from England*, the mathematics was too hard for him to advance on his own.

He fell back on poetry and drama. The fame from his *Oedipus* play and other writings had lingered, and he was still respected as an important writer in France. But that simply meant he had to spend boring evenings in the salons of Paris ("If you neglect to enroll yourself among the courtiers, you are ... crushed"). Was Bolingbroke right, after all, that he was never going to fulfill his promise?

The years went on, he was getting old—in his late thirties by now—and possibly he was getting disheartened as well. Despite the clove mouth rinse he used on his teeth, his gums were receding; he often suffered from terrible dysentery as well.

To save the effort of supervising a staff of servants and cooks and porters he moved in with a wealthy and shockingly unattractive widow, who luckily had no sexual interest in him (but enjoyed the reflected fame of this author's presence). When she died, in January 1733, he moved again, to a house near the river in central Paris. He was investing in the grain business, and also had been overseeing a factory to fabricate paper, and wanted to be near the dock where his barges arrived in the city. It was a life, but not a very interesting one. He had no one to fight against, but no one to live for either. He was in a rut.

And then, one summer evening, a couple he knew came visiting. They were bringing a friend: a young woman who divided her time between Semur and Paris. They thought the two might like each other.

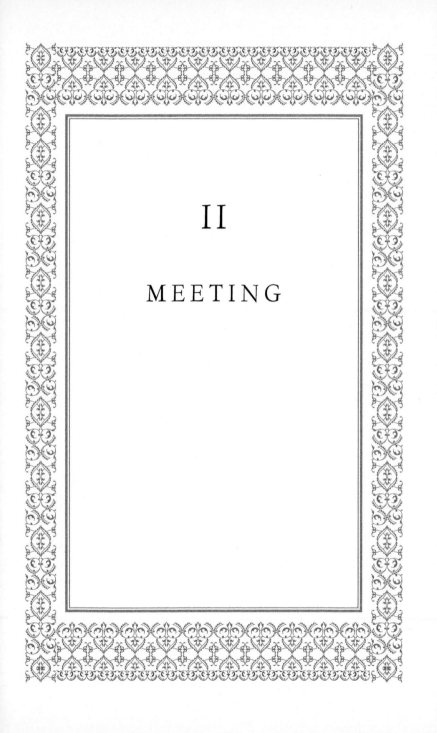

II

MEETING

5

Meeting ... and Caution

The friends and Emilie turned up, giggling and laughing, in this un-fashionable quarter of Paris just before dusk on a warm summer's night. Voltaire might have called down from his windows, but he couldn't invite his visitors in, for there wasn't enough food—without refrigerators it was hard to store fresh meat in the summer—and any-way his housekeeper would yell at him if he asked her to get something together this late. It was easier to go out.

They rode to an inn outside the city walls, they had chicken cooked in wine, there were candles everywhere, and Emilie sparkled as her words leaped around Voltaire's. He'd never even had a male friend like this, so what kind God had created this delightful woman, still just twenty-seven?

Voltaire kept it a secret at first. To the mutual friend who'd brought Emilie, he merely wrote a polite thank-you for the evening. But he and Emilie had become lovers almost immediately, and just a few weeks later he wrote a poem for Emilie:

. . . Why did you only reach me so late?
What happened to my life before?
I hunted for love, but found only mirages
    I found only the shadow of our pleasure.
You are a delight
    You are tender
What pleasure I find in your arms

At first she felt the same. Part of it was simply the sex: they spent nights at his house, and then—flouting all convention—even at hers. When they caught breath enough to realize how dangerous that was, they took off for two summer weeks to a tumbledown abandoned old château at Cirey, in the Champagne region 150 miles east of Paris, and far from the dreaded Semur. She had access because it had been inherited from her husband's family—who probably didn't know at this early stage that there was any affair at all—and there they went at it some more.

It was more than just passion, though. Each had experienced physical attraction before, a meeting of bodies. Now they were multiplying that thrill, swept up in this meeting of minds as well.

Back in Paris, late in the summer of 1733, Emilie and Voltaire tried to keep their hands off each other, at least in public. Florent-Claude was far away, with the army, and if they were discreet enough it would be easy for no one to have to mention the affair. But one time right on the street Emilie couldn't restrain herself: she was a mother now, she was married to a well-known noble officer, but she wrapped her hands behind Voltaire's neck and leaned forward and they kissed and kissed and kissed. What could she do? "God gave me the sort of soul," she explained, "that doesn't let me hide or moderate my passions." France's most talked-about poet was in love with her—and she was seeing what it might be like to be in love back.

When Emilie had tried to share her ideas before, the women in Paris had snidely attacked: "She was born with a fairly good mind," the acid Madame du Deffand typically commented, "but wishing to appear even cleverer, she preferred the study of the most abstract science to more agreeable knowledge."

With Voltaire, though, there was nothing to hide. She'd become fascinated by Newton, and in the time since her affair with Richelieu she'd learned more and more of his work. The old medieval worldview had planets orbiting through space simply because it was God's pleasure to make them move that way. Even her first hero, Descartes, hadn't been able to provide a well-justified mechanism for explaining how they moved. All he'd been able to propose was that there were invisible whirlpools in outer space, and that the planets and the distant stars—by some unknown means—swirled around in those whirlpools. It was so vague that he was never able to attach any exact numbers to that vision or make fresh predictions from it. That vision was still lauded by the French chauvinists who dominated the research academies, but Emilie realized it should now be left behind.

Isaac Newton, working after Descartes in the late 1600s, had taken a very different approach. To him, the planets and distant stars were giant billiard balls. Stretching outward from each one was the great gaping force of gravity. That force was invisible, but it stretched across the heavens nevertheless. Think of the way the hands of a big clock move. If you couldn't see the cogs and rods inside the clock—if the cogs were made of totally transparent glass—you'd find it a mystery that the hands moved. But once you saw that the cogs and rods were there, you would then understand why the hands moved. In outer space, the force of gravity played the role of those invisible cogs. The billiard balls of our planets and the stars were tugged along by these stretching lines of gravity.

If Newton had left it at that, he would have been little better than Descartes. But he'd been able to do exact calculations, predicting how the different celestial bodies moved, and that's what had convinced Emilie that he was right. Voltaire knew some of the secondary accounts of what Newton had done, but could only copy the figures that these popularizers had written out. Emilie, however, understood the new mathematical techniques of the calculus that Newton had used, and was able to use them to perform fresh calculations. She could show Voltaire, in exact detail, how our planets really did roll along like clockwork.

Voltaire was awed: he'd never had an intellectual partner like this, and bragged to his friends, telling the Abbé de Sade (uncle of the notorious marquis) that he must meet her, even though

> *I swear to you, she's a tyrant*
> *To be with her*
> *I have to speak of metaphysics*
> *(I'd rather speak of sex)*

There was an extra attraction. Today we think of Voltaire as famous, while Emilie and the Breteuil and du Châtelet families are barely known. At the time, though—as the de Rohan assault showed—things were viewed differently. In Emilie's world, only families that had been ennobled for at least three hundred years were officially allowed to go hunting with the king. If a family had made its fortune in business or law, as with Voltaire's father, they had almost no chance of being let into the top levels of government; they or their relatives certainly couldn't be given a commission in the army. It would be as if only Americans who'd had ancestors who came over before 1776 could be allowed top jobs at the Pentagon or in the White House today, while everyone else, however competent, had to stay put.

There was a slight amount of mixing in some of the Paris salons, where the fiction existed that sufficiently clever intellectuals from humble backgrounds could be treated as "equal" to the wealthy aristocrats who ran those gatherings. But that was only for the duration of the evening gatherings, and there were clear bounds beyond which any quick-witted impudence would be punished.

Emilie was breaking all that by being willing to sleep with this man who so clearly was from the wrong class. A few close friends might be tolerant, but almost everyone else from her background would be waiting, often eagerly, for it to fail. Only the most intense love can survive such pressure from without—and in the bliss of these first months, Emilie and Voltaire knew they were lucky enough to be in that group.

Voltaire was so delighted at finding someone who adored him—and whose intellect he admired so much—that his creativity rose to a higher level. He quickly added a key section to the Letters from England that he was preparing for publication. He'd always hated his older brother, a smug Calvinist-style rigid Catholic who was a member of the grouping called the Jansenists. Pascal had powerfully written that the Jansenists were right, that we are alone in a harsh universe, and that without blind submission to God we deserve to be terrified by our solitude. Now, however, amidst those long days entwined with Emilie, Voltaire was confident enough to refute him. The essay-like form of the Letters from England was ideal for this:

"Why be so horrified by our existence?" Voltaire inked in his tight, neat script. "To look at the universe as a prison, and all men as condemned prisoners about to be executed: that's the idea of a fanatic. . . . Why despair because we can't see God directly? It would be like despairing for not having four legs and two wings. . . . We can [simply] be . . . as happy as human nature allows."

We take this for granted today, but it was radical at its time. For centuries the Church had taught that fallen mankind had no right to be happy: this was not our role on Earth. Our purpose was to suffer, as the Savior had suffered for us. The aristocratic elite also would have laughed at the idea that mere ordinary people should aim to be happy. Ordinary people were, quite obviously, placed on Earth to work. Let the majority of people aim for their own happiness, and the system could collapse.

LIKE all new lovers, Emilie and Voltaire soon wanted to change each other. He told her she should spend less time at Versailles, and she explained to him that he should do more thoughtful work and spend less time on mere rhymes. He taught her English (and in a few weeks she was starting to read Milton in the original). She seems to have tried teaching him the basics of projective geometry. It was fun, it was delicious—but then, as the summer ended and the cooler days of late September began, something changed.

The rhyme Voltaire had written about metaphysics and sex had been a joke, but it was also a little bit true: Emilie was brighter than he was, as Voltaire was the first to admit, and his attention wandered as she inked out, during the discussion, the force lines and tangents that so fascinated her.

Did she know, he would happily interrupt, how it was that Newton had come up with his idea of universal gravitation in the first place? When Voltaire was in England he'd interviewed Mrs. Conduitt, the great man's niece, and discovered a sweet story Newton had told her: that Newton had been at his mother's house in Lincolnshire and had seen an apple fall to the ground—Voltaire was going to publish this in his forthcoming Letters from England; it would be the first time the story would see the light of day—and when Newton had seen that it had made him wonder: was the force that pulled the apple down something that stretched higher and higher, all the way above the Earth's atmosphere, to pull the moon tumbling along as well? And this was how he realized that one linking force spreads out through the whole universe.

But Emilie *had* heard the story, and from Voltaire: he had told it to her many times already. It was getting irritating. He was bright but had the attentiveness of a magpie, flitting from one anecdote to another. Unlike her, he couldn't use the insight about the apple to take any of Newton's calculations further. Indeed, she wasn't sure he'd ever be able to seriously explore what it meant.

At first all their arguments had been easily resolved—they would tumble into bed—but that September Voltaire got sick, with another bout of his recurrent dysentery. He'd been a hypochondriac at the best of times, but when he actually was ill he became impossible, always needing more attention, sometimes joking about it, but also getting short-tempered and cranky. Emilie was in her late twenties and very trim despite her children: a servant who later saw her nude described her as having the body of a fine Greek sculpture. Now she had a difficult, bedridden older man—he was thirty-nine—to take care of.

Everything that had brought them together was changing. He was no longer the confident, powerful man who would give her the support she needed to organize her own tentative thoughts, perhaps even to help her become one of the great writers and thinkers she admired so much. Yet she, in his mind, was failing him. His illness was testing her for signs of love, for the affection that comes across in tending an ill partner as a parent would, even when the partner has nothing to give back. Since each was failing the other, they got angry; they had arguments; they split up.

Voltaire didn't care. He was in the depths of hypochondriac misery, writing to an old school friend that he was dead to pleasure: Emilie's sexual demands had become all wrong, for "my machine is totally exhausted." His susceptibility to infection wasn't helped by the condition of the river Seine. Paris's population was several hundred thousand, and although there were workers who were supposed to cart away waste products in special carts, immense quantities of excrement and urine and vomit daily ended up in the Seine. From the city's large numbers of animals yet more sewage, as well as blood, intestine, skin, and tendons, also went directly to the river. (Refrigeration was scarcely existent, so slaughtering was local and daily.) Small quantities of water could come in bottles from rural springs, but although the city's fountains were supposed to be clean, those too often got polluted from the Seine.

Unfortunately, even in his illness Voltaire couldn't keep from bragging. He wasn't as weak in science as Emilie thought, he told her: why, he was very well acquainted indeed with one of the most eminent young mathematicians in France, an expert on Newton named Pierre-Louis de Maupertuis. They'd corresponded, they'd even met, and he could assure Emilie that Maupertuis was just the sort of vigorous young friend who appreciated him.

Which is how Emilie's second affair of 1733 began. Emilie didn't really want to find another man now—what she'd begun with Voltaire was clearly better than anything she was likely to find again. But once she'd opened up with Voltaire, she couldn't bear to return to her previous isolation.

Maupertuis certainly seemed plausible, at least at first. He'd grown up on the coast of Brittany, and his father had been as close to a pirate as sailed in the North Atlantic, heading a forty-gun attack ship that stormed English vessels on the open sea. But the son had also studied with Europe's leading mathematicians, in Switzerland and in London, and he'd just written a book on the higher mathematics of the universe—and best of all, having completed several years as a cavalry officer, he was far more muscular than the ever-complaining Voltaire.

It might have been a rebound relationship, but Emilie began by having her fun. She'd undoubtedly learned a lot about sexual satisfaction in her affair with Richelieu when she was twenty-three. The cover story she and Maupertuis gave for their trysts was that he was tutoring her in advanced calculus. She taunted him delightedly about that. "You must not want," she wrote him in January 1734, "to encourage your student, for I still haven't heard if you found my last lesson agreeable."

When they weren't in bed, they actually did talk about science— why should lounging naked with a handsome corsair's son get in the way? Maupertuis had recently been able to show that the immense gravitational attraction Newton wrote about would—if true—cause our fast-spinning Earth to squash ever so slightly as it turned, like a sheet of dough stretching lengthwise as an exuberant chef tossed it spinning in the air. He'd worked out exactly how much of this flattening there would be.

It seemed unimportant, but it wasn't, for there was a profound linkage with theology. If Newton's views were right, then the invisible stretching pulls of gravity were what tugged the planets around. But Newton's rules were so exact that he—and Maupertuis, and Emilie— were able to calculate exactly how gravity's pulls worked. These calculations showed that although the universe was like a giant clock, God was not a watchmaker who had set up our solar system and universe, wound the handles once, and then walked away. On the contrary. There seemed to be numerous cases of "slippage," where planets would tumble out of orbit unless some outside force reached into our universe to keep everything whirring at the right speeds. There was no guesswork in saying this. If Newton's mathematics and the laws of gravity were true, then this had to follow.

This is why Maupertuis's further calculation about the Earth's flattening was so important. What if someone managed to clamber across the uncharted ice above the Baltic Sea, reach the North Pole, and actually measure our planet's flattening? Then it would be possible to find out if this intervening God did exist! (Why? If the Earth was indeed slightly flattened as it spun, then that would be a sign that gravity operated exactly as Newton had described, and so—since Newton's gravity left gaps farther out in the solar system where only divine adjustment could keep the planets from tumbling away—God really was constantly reaching in and intervening to make thing operate smoothly.)

It was an immense change from Descartes's much vaguer vision of the universe, where all one could say was that, in some unknown, inexact way, planets and stars slipped around on spinning whirlpools. There was no way from Descartes's image to prove mathematically that those spinnings produced gaps that only a fresh force created by God could bridge.

This was unprecedented. For hundreds, thousands of years, theologians had either settled their arguments with volumes of dusty words or—when tensions grew too great—passed them on to religious warriors, who decided the truth on the battlefield, at the point of swords. Now there was another way.

If Emilie had met this Breton much earlier in her life, perhaps she would have decided to stay with him. But although he wasn't much older than she, he had already acquired the habits of a confirmed bachelor. It wasn't so much that he was selfish as that he was self-contained—and she needed more than that.

She realized she was missing what she'd begun with Voltaire, and began to keep an ear out for what he was up to—as Voltaire, once he finished sulking, now was doing for her. Each wanted the conversation they could only have with each other, and the passion of deeper contact too.

Emilie needed courting, of course, and by February 1734, Voltaire was feeling well enough to begin. He knew that he wasn't as educated in astronomy as Maupertuis, so he shifted that to his advantage, writing to Emilie:

> *The sublime Maupertuis*
> *eclipses my mere words.*
> *I'm not surprised*
> *Who wouldn't be overwhelmed*
> *by such eternal truths?*
> *But Emilie, what are these truths?*
> *How will you use them and what is their cost?*
> *. . . He's shown you the heavens*
> *he's uncovered their secrets*
> *. . . But where is your happiness*
> *Does he know that secret?*

For a brief while in late February she was seeing both men—Voltaire's machine was pretty much in order—but that wasn't sustainable, and soon enough she broke with Maupertuis and was back to the man she'd always wanted.

Just to ensure she stayed, Voltaire began another gambit. The year before, he and Emilie had decided that it was time their mutual friend Richelieu should settle down and get married. They'd started working on that together, introducing possible brides, dropping heavy hints to Richelieu that he was aging and this was the right course of action.

Voltaire decided that it would bring them together to continue that task. By plotting with her to get Richelieu married, he would keep this woman he needed.

6

Hunted

They couldn't tell Richelieu at first what they were arranging for him, since he was enjoying his bachelorhood about as much as any mortal could. There was also the complication that the woman Voltaire decided on for Richelieu was the young Elisabeth de Guise, from one of the haughtiest families in all of France.

The nineteen-year-old Elisabeth would be happy enough for the marriage to go through, of course—Richelieu was the finest catch a young woman could want. But the de Guise ancestors who had cheated, stolen, murdered, and prostituted themselves to acquire their great wealth had possessed the grace to do this many, many centuries before, which meant that their actions were obscured by a gentle mist of history. The Richelieu fortunes, however, were more recent, dating back only to the cardinal who had advised Louis XIII, scarcely a century before. Such variations within the aristocracy had developed over so long a time—and were encrusted with so much tradition and rules—that the oldest noble families had come to think that they were biologically superior to the newer ones. It was repugnant for them to marry someone outside their own caste.

Unfortunately, quite a few of the oldest families did have to overcome this distaste, partly because of some unfortunate inbreeding, which had not always produced the finest intellects in their midst, and partly because their self-pride prevented even the less dim ones from working in any profession or business, which meant—despite the tax benefits we saw—that many of these families tended to go broke.

That was what Voltaire knew would make this marriage possible. The de Guise family was very famous but also very low on funds, and through a series of loans and investments, Voltaire had conveniently come to own enough of their property that he could force them to let the relative upstart Richelieu in.

There remained the problem of getting Richelieu to meet the eager Elisabeth in private—and, for goodness' sake, to keep the pair from sleeping together before it was time—but by this stage Emilie began to understand what was really going on. Voltaire was putting Richelieu in moral debt by securing him a bride from a supremely respected family he couldn't otherwise afford. The two men had been schoolmates at the Jesuit-run Louis le Grand school, and they liked and respected each other—but they also had long shared an understanding that, in general, women were fair game. The marriage arrangement, however, would make it hard for Richelieu to start up any affair with Emilie in the future. How could he two-time the man who had enabled his own marriage? Voltaire was ensuring that Richelieu would not be a threat to his newly reestablished relation with Emilie in the future.

The wedding ("this dénouement of our intrigue") was going to take place on April 6, at the de Guise château in Montjeu, several days' journey from Paris. Emilie and Voltaire would be honored guests—for some reason, Maupertuis didn't receive an invitation—and since travel was so difficult in the intermittent rain and sun of a French springtime, the guests expected to stay, celebrating, for at least a month. Emilie became especially close to the exuberant young Elisabeth. There was drinking and dancing, and ever more music. It was an idyll—but secretly was under threat:

FROM JEAN-FREDERIC PHELYPEAUX,
TO THE CROWN'S AGENT IN THE REGION
ENCOMPASSING THE AUXONNE PRISON,
NEAR MONTJEU

*The King has deemed it appropriate to arrest Arouet
de Voltaire and bring him to the prison at the château
d'Auxonne. Inform me when you have carried this out.
He is not to be freed under any circumstance.*

Phélypeaux was the same secretary of state who'd sent Voltaire to the Bastille after the de Rohan affair. He understood that Voltaire had mocked him to everyone in society for years afterward—which would be insulting to anyone, and especially so to a man who'd fancied himself the court wit. But permanent governmental officials do not need to get angry to get their revenge. They just need to bide their time. Voltaire had now supplied the opportunity, albeit inadvertently.

His manuscript of the Letters from England recapped the nature of British society and thought, with sections on commerce, Shakespeare, Newton, and the like. All of it implicitly mocked France by repeatedly praising how things were done across the Channel. When Voltaire had described the Royal Exchange, for example, where investors were tolerant of each other's religions, since they only cared about successful business opportunities, it was a dig at France, where the king and Church insisted that there was to be no toleration of individuals of a different religion, however harmful to the nation's industry or commerce.

That was critical enough, but it now also had the explosive additions he'd had included in his exuberance since meeting Emilie, about the right for human beings to choose to be happy, rather than being dully obedient to the traditional calls of the Church and social superiors. In particular, in those writings against Pascal, Voltaire had proposed that we could achieve this happiness largely on our own, rather than needing the official clergy to help avert or diminish the sour damnation that Pascal's God would have wished on us. That under-mined the huge establishment of the Church, and even Voltaire rec-ognized that publicizing such words within France was much too dangerous even to try. The author of such heresy could be sent to the Bastille, or worse.

Unfortunately, Voltaire had left a few copies of his inked manu-script in the safekeeping of a printer near Brussels. That wasn't bright. The printer had a choice between keeping Voltaire safe by stowing the manuscript inside a strongbox and making a great deal of money by printing as many copies as he could, smuggling them into Paris, and ar-ranging to sell them surreptitiously. The printer thought about it, no doubt for at least several milliseconds, then realized where his own hap-piness lay, and began his printing and smuggling operation forthwith.

Phélypeaux's order was secret, and none of the guests knew of it at first. Communications were so slow, because of the rutted muddy roads, that even the king's local official didn't receive the *lettre de cachet* for several days. The happy wedding party went on. Richelieu had left shortly after the ceremony, since France was engaged in a military cam-paign on its eastern frontier, which had bogged down in a siege of the German fortresses at Philippsburg, near Karlsruhe. (The fighting was part of France's effort to keep Austria away from nearby Lorraine.) But Voltaire and Emilie stayed on at Montjeu with the other guests. The weather cleared, and they enjoyed brilliant sunny days. Voltaire charmed the bride, and Emilie was thrilled that her friendship with Elisabeth was becoming one of the closest she'd ever had. But then:

"My friend Voltaire," Emilie hurriedly wrote from the wedding town to de Sade (the uncle of the infamous marquis, as we saw in the previous chapter),

> . . . had just left us, to go and take the waters at Plombières . . . when one of the [king's officials] brought me a *lettre de ca-chet,* instructing him to go to [the nearby prison at] Auxonne and await fresh orders there . . . I'm sure Voltaire will get the king's orders soon, and he will have to obey. There is no

alternative when one cannot escape. I don't think he can be
warned in time.

It was quick thinking on Emilie's part. She knew that the letter to
de Sade was likely to be opened, and that was good, for Phélypeaux
was aware of Voltaire's constant hypochondria and would well believe
he had gone to Plombières. He hadn't, of course, but several days
would be wasted while government officers tried to find him.

The reason his escape was so important was that the police had
raided the printer's apartment in Paris. There they'd found bound
copies of the book, with Voltaire's name on the title page; his guilt was
thereby proven. The printer was thrown into the Bastille, but luckily
one of Voltaire's contacts had managed to get a message to Montjeu
before the arresting officials arrived. Voltaire had just had time to
escape on horseback. Emilie's job, they'd agreed, was to mislead everyone who came to get him.

Along with her letter to de Sade, she now also sent a letter to Maupertuis, suggesting that Voltaire might try to leave the country. This
too, she trusted, was information that Maupertuis might leak, or that at
least would be read when the government steamed open his mail.

But as for where Voltaire *really* was—well, she actually didn't know.

WHAT Voltaire ended up deciding was that none of the safe houses he
and Emilie had arranged among their friends would do: word would
get out, if not from the servants then from the hosts themselves, for
gossip in their social circle was almost impossible to stop.

But there was one man—and one group within French society—
Voltaire was confident could be trusted to hide him entirely.

Voltaire arrived in Richelieu's huge military encampment outside
Philippsburg in the middle of that 1734 summer, proud of his ingenuity. Richelieu normally would have applauded such a stratagem, but he
couldn't stand up to embrace Voltaire quite as steadily as he would

have under normal conditions. Although the German forces hadn't broken out of their fortress, there had been some other fighting, and Richelieu was wounded.

He wasn't going to talk about it, but Voltaire found everyone else around Richelieu's tent quick to explain. Stories varied, but the gist seemed to be that shortly before Voltaire arrived, Richelieu had been striding to a dinner for a fellow officer—or was he already inside the dinner tent?—when one of the other military officers, the hotheaded prince de Lixin, had accosted him. De Lixin was a relative of Elisabeth's who'd been especially disapproving of Richelieu marrying into the de Guise family. When he stopped Richelieu, it was late in the day, and Richelieu had come straight from the field after hours inspecting the trenches. His clothes were muddy, and de Lixin called out words to the effect of: In spite of this man's marriage, look at how much mud he still carries with him.

Richelieu knew that de Lixin had refused to join the rest of his family in signing the marriage contract, for he believed that Richelieu's lineage was unacceptable. What he'd called out now was deadly. These charges of social inferiority were as loaded as charges of miscegenation were in the American South a century and more later. But de Lixin wasn't done. Richelieu was an impostor, he repeated now. If Elisabeth de Guise slept with him, then she was, of course, a whore.

Why was de Lixin doing this? The wedding had already happened. Richelieu couldn't let the charges pass, not when they'd gone that far, but he also was a far better soldier than de Lixin. Everyone knew this. He had nothing to prove in fighting another man.

Possibly Richelieu tried to defuse it by quietly asking de Lixin to just withdraw his words. But de Lixin would not back down. He may have been spurred on by the soldiers in his own regiment, or perhaps it was just his fury at hearing of the elaborate wedding, with the great Parisian poet and so many other notables over at Montjeu. Certainly he was used to getting his way. The laws in France were written so that a young man from a family as prestigious as de Lixin's could beat up any ordinary person he wished for fun, with almost no chance of being punished. His youth, accordingly, had been spent like the most spoiled prep-school teenager imaginable, who knows he can push anyone else around in safety. If an ordinary person did fight back and strike a noble, then the penalty could be death. De Lixin liked fighting and had already killed one man in a duel.

Taking this attitude with Richelieu, however, was a different matter. After trying in vain to stop it—and perhaps de Lixin was drunk as well?—Richelieu simply called his closest officers to be his seconds.

The duel had to begin quickly, since the siege commander had at least ostensible orders to avert fighting among his own staff. Duelling had increased in recent years. Cavalry officers lusted for it, not least because they hardly ever got to use their swords in the charges they'd been trained for. (Those charges were becoming too dangerous when thousands of enemy infantry faced them with loaded muskets.) Also, more and more nobles felt they needed to defend their status, since ever more newcomers, such as Richelieu, were being brought into traditional, old-establishment ranks.

It was getting so dark when de Lixin and Richelieu began, in the loose soil around the trenches, that the other officers had to order servants to put up torches so that the two men could see. (One account has enemy troops in the fortress sniping at the French group crowding around the duelists; another account merely has the enemy guards and officers watching from the parapets as the bizarre French ritual began.)

The result was foregone. Richelieu quickly blocked this privileged man's furious attacks, then stabbed him deep in the chest. De Lixin bled to death, either directly from a heart wound or choking as his lungs filled with blood. But before the final strike, he'd managed to get a blow in on Richelieu, cutting him sharply—hence his convalescing as Voltaire arrived.

To have any of his other friends be slashed in a murderous duel would have been unexpected, but since Voltaire had known Richelieu for almost thirty years, he took this escapade in stride. He now explained to his old friend the slight problem with his *Letters from England* manuscript. Richelieu liked the humor of what he was proposing. It also didn't hurt that Richelieu and Phélypeaux hated each other. A military encampment under the direct authority of the king would be the last place Phélypeaux would look for one suspect author.

If Richelieu had not been wounded, he would no doubt have politely shown his friend around the sprawling base. As it was, Voltaire decided to wander a bit on his own through the rutted grounds. Since he was French and the soldiers were French—or allies of the French—he naturally assumed he would be safe.

The camp was huge, with more than seven thousand workers digging approach trenches and diverting streams, as the left and right wings of the French army stretched for acre after acre along the Rhine. They were cautiously working their way closer to the fortress, while also preparing for a surprise attack from the rear or the side by Habsburg troops who might try to break the siege of the fortress. Along with the troops, prostitutes, engineers, and carpenters, there were hundreds upon hundreds of supply animals and their handlers, scattered amidst the pitched tents or shacks. There was no canned food, so hundreds of cooking fires were spreading their smoke; there was shattering clanging from all the blacksmiths at work as well.

Hardly any of the siege force knew that Richelieu's personal visitor was alone in their midst. When this thin, constantly peering civilian was found wandering around, sentries arrested him. The penalty for espionage was immediate execution by hanging. Voltaire's protests that he personally knew one of the army group's top officers were scarcely believable to young, uneducated soldiers.

Luckily, the French army was very corrupt then (like those of almost every great country). Well-connected youngsters were made officers even when they were still in their teens. The sentries who'd grabbed Voltaire reported to a commander in their sector of the camp who was but seventeen. He had the authority to confirm the immediate execution, but as soon as he saw the prisoner, all was changed. The officer was the son of the prince who'd written an ode for Voltaire after the triumph of his *Oedipus*. His father had constantly lauded the great writer, so instead of the gallows, Voltaire was invited to a feast.

For the next month he enjoyed the hospitality of the siege camp, drinking and singing with the officers (including Emilie's husband), giving readings, and making up impromptu verses that everyone liked. Occasionally they had to pause. Prince Eugène was the enemy commander, and an aggressive soldier. Voltaire wrote to an acquaintance back in France:

> It seems that Prince Eugène will present himself before our trenches and pits tomorrow morning, about four A.M. It's the day of the Virgin, and it's said that he has a great devotion for Mary, which should help him against the Chevalier Asfeld [the French commander], who is strictly a Jansenist. (You realize, of course, madam, that you Jansenists are suspected of not having enough devotion for the sainted Virgin.)
>
> Naturally our troops are determined to destroy him, and are armed to the teeth. We have trenches, pits, and even a double fore-trench—it's a delightful new invention, well designed to snap the necks of the gentlemen who are now readying their attack. We'll see tomorrow who gains the victory. The 80 cannon in our camp are already beginning to fire. Here madam, you see human folly.

At Montjeu, Emilie had been distraught at missing Voltaire. "I've lost him," she wrote de Sade, "just when I felt the greatest happiness with him—and how I've lost him! If he was safely in England, I could bear it. But to know, with his health, that he could be held in prison . . . I'd never understood that closeness could produce such pain.

"I'll have to go back to Paris soon. I'm scared of that."

But when she did return to Paris late that summer, things got more complicated. She couldn't argue full out with her contacts at the court to revoke the *lettre de cachet,* for—the eternal plaint of the mistress—she had no official grounds to care about him. And when she did embarrass herself by trying, she found that he wasn't making things easier for her. The stunt of going to Philippsburg had backfired: when news did get out, Phélypeaux and the other ministers were furious for having been ridiculed. Voltaire's apartment had already been broken into—the same one where she and Voltaire had first met on that impossibly distant evening over a year ago—and his belongings torn open in a search for more evidence that he'd colluded with the printers of his book.

The printer had been interrogated and probably beaten while he was in the Bastille, but a further example had to be made. Prisoners were still subject to arbitrary torture, and the king oversaw a legal system that allowed certain offenders to be burned alive. Now, on June 10, the city's Parlement formally condemned Voltaire's Letters from England, for the book's heretical views mocking the one true path to religious salvation. The same day, at 11 A.M., the public executioner stood before the grand stairwell of the Palais de Justice on the Ile de la Cité, in the center of Paris. (It was in that very complex of buildings that Voltaire had grown up, for his father's notary duties gave him the right to lodgings there.) A great fire was lit, there was the stench of turpentine and billowing smoke, and then the executioner shredded the book and threw it into the flames.

Emilie was scared, but she was also infuriated at Voltaire again. This was the brutal, arbitrary world one suffered in France. Why hadn't Voltaire simply crossed the border into the far safer Switzerland or to Rotterdam, and stayed out of further trouble? Yet now he was nagging her in letters smuggled through friends to let him live at the tumbledown château at Cirey where they'd spent the delicious summer weeks a year before. She couldn't decide if he was utterly brave or merely a fool. She'd let Voltaire go to the château—but she was damned if she was going to join him there.

7

Decision

CHÂTEAU DE CIREY, AND PARIS, 1734–1735

Voltaire was so preoccupied that he didn't recognize Emilie was this angry, and at the height of that summer, the end of July, was happy when he arrived back at Cirey. Large portions of the main building were uninhabitable, with ancient, rotting walls and gaping window holes. He had ideas for poems and plays about the injustice of the king's servants destroying works merely because they threatened the conservative religious line; there were conversations he wanted to continue with Emilie on those matters and more. But that would have to wait.

The weather was still warm, and Voltaire studied what was left of the château. One approach to refurbishing it would be to patch up a single section—such as the rooms where he and Emilie had stayed before—so that he could survive a winter there. But that wouldn't induce Emilie to stay. He knew how much richer than he she'd been while growing up. Yet he had a chance to attract her here, since months ago she'd told de Sade—who no doubt had told Voltaire—that she couldn't bear all the petty gossip of Paris: she would rather end up in the countryside with Voltaire and perhaps a very few other friends.

To transform the ruin so it was attractive enough would be a huge job. But for the man who'd rigged the outcome of the entire Paris lottery as well as married off Richelieu, it was the sort of challenge he relished. (The château was also conveniently close to border roads leading east to Lorraine and north to the Low Countries, so he could readily escape from the king's police if needed.)

The first thing to do was get enough cash. Voltaire had made sure that Richelieu owed him money, but it wouldn't do to call on that loan quite so soon. Similarly for the loan to the father of the bride, who might feel perturbed at having lost his close relative de Lixin, even if the husband whom Voltaire had arranged for their family had been justified in stabbing him to death.

Yet while Voltaire was at Philippsburg he'd been more attentive to the gossip of the quartermasters than the noble officers had been. They had been brought up to pay no attention to the sources of whatever wealth they'd managed to obtain. Voltaire, however, had learned that there was a glut of wheat imports at the great harbor of Marseilles. Cirey was isolated—the nearest town was leagues away, and the occasional coach from Paris took up to a week to make it there. Even the main wine region of Champagne was well to the north, where the land was flatter than this forested waste. But ever since his return from England six years before, in 1728, he'd been developing contacts across France who could carry out the financial transactions he wished.

Instructions went out, by messengers on horseback, for his administrators to buy grain shipments from North Africa and ensure that the ships diverted to ports in Spain and Italy. The sale price would be higher than at Marseilles, where the local glut would have held down prices. But the merchants shipping the grain wouldn't know of the different sales prices available, so his original purchase costs would remain the same: only his profits would go up.

For more immediate returns, Voltaire remembered the thousands of men—and equally large numbers of horses and transport mules—

at Philippsburg. The siege had ended in a French victory, albeit with the commander suffering the misfortune of having his head separated from his body by an enemy cannonball. But the army was still in the field, and Voltaire sent out further instructions to purchase forage, cloth, and food at likely locations along the troops' supply path. Quartermasters in the field can't bargain. Here too Voltaire was buying cheap and selling dear. What he sold the army would bring in extra cash, and quickly.

It was ingenious, as always. But he'd become used to finding unsuspected sources of income. In all the time since his play *Oedipus* was produced, back in 1718, not a single poem or play or essay he'd written had been allowed to be sold openly in France. Without his business skills he'd have had to end up as paid flatterer for a famous aristocrat or official in order to survive—and his ambition was too great for that.

Now Voltaire could get to work. Relying on the advances from his sales of army supplies, as well as from his own reserves in Paris that he could still draw on (even though he would be imprisoned if he went there in person), he began to hire architects and experienced foremen. He didn't own Cirey, Florent-Claude's family did, but Voltaire was confident that in time they would come to an agreement about how much to pay him back for the improvements he would make.

Soon Voltaire's foremen were hiring manual workers for ditch digging and heavy construction; then they began to search out all the carpenters and masons and plasterers nearby villages could provide. He was pretty clear about what he wanted. There would be a great new wing, where he'd have his study and bedroom, and he'd entirely refurbish part of the old building—that would be for Emilie's arrival. As to the rest of the ruin, well, it would be enough to make sure that there was a big, usable kitchen. Guest rooms were much less important than ensuring that Emilie's window would be perfectly constructed and balanced, that she would have an attractive view.

That the dream he was preparing for her would come true.

All this work drew the attention of most local residents, which didn't slow Voltaire down too much, but it also drew the attention of the very few wealthy individuals who lived in the vicinity. There were two families in particular that counted, even though they were in different villages several miles away. Voltaire knew that any men in those families wouldn't have much voice—this was the French countryside, after all, where women ruled—and all his surviving correspondence is addressed solely to Madame de Champbonin and to the comtesse de la Neuville.

From the beginning he expressed his shock—his amazement— that two such cultivated women were to be found in this isolated region. He felt, he wrote to the portly Madame de Champbonin when she sent baskets of her favorite fruits, that he must be back in Paris, for never had he received such graciously apt offerings. And as for the quite young comtesse de la Neuville, did she realize that among all the ladies he had known at the court, there were none—or perhaps none that he could yet reveal the name of—who dressed as stylishly as she?

They were immediately on his side, which meant that their husbands and other male relatives were on his side—and this, as Voltaire would have understood all along, meant that there were no grumbles from any other scattered gentry about his bidding up the salaries for servants, let alone denuding one hamlet after another of able workers at this harvest time. Also, as it turned out, both Champbonin ("my little Champenoise," he soon called her) and Neuville were agreeable enough to have around. For when Emilie came down life might get boring—despite all their conversations—unless there was some possibility of local diversion, or at least outsiders to take extra parts in the amateur dramatics he liked to put on.

There would be one more gift to ensure that Emilie stayed. The Letters from England had brought him nothing but harm, yet theater was something with which he knew he was safe. There was a particular play he had been thinking about for a while, almost since he'd first met Emilie, and although he'd never done more than sketch it, now— despite the builders, and the neighbors, and the forges that he had to supervise being refurbished in the forests for charcoal—he vowed he would get it done before Emilie arrived from Paris.

He called it *Alzire*. It would be set in the jungles of South America, at the time when the Spanish conquistadors were beginning to administer the great Inca empire they'd conquered. (It was common to use distant societies for parables to safely criticize France.) His writing was deeper here than in any drama he'd done before, since he desperately wanted Emilie to respect him for it.

In this new play there was a virile young Inca leader, and the woman he'd go through anything to live with—that of course was necessary, to show Emilie how much he would do for her. But the play also carried the theme of whether good individuals can redeem a corrupt organization, for Voltaire hadn't made all the Spanish officials uniformly malevolent. To keep the multilayered story advancing, his hero would escape by galloping to Philippsburg—no, the Inca hero would escape by finding a breach in some Spanish fortress walls. And then . . .

Then what? "To be able to keep an audience interested for five acts, that's a gift of God," Voltaire complained in a letter to his friend Cideville.

He finally did work it out, and this question of whether a government could be reformed from within was central to the young writers who were increasingly turning to Voltaire as their guide. The issue was certainly topical. Not only was the Church utterly removed from the teachings of Jesus—with spoiled children of rich families being bought positions as bishops, as we've seen—but the basic administration was incompetent to a level that's hard to imagine today.

The secretary of state, Jean-Frédéric Phélypeaux, who hated Voltaire for his social ascent, had been brought into the government at age fourteen and later appointed director of the French navy despite having no naval experience whatsoever. This was not ideal for military success. At one important moment, when a French fleet was sent to Quebec to reclaim the fortress of Louisbourg after a successful British attack, Phélypeaux chose as admiral a young relative who had never been on the Atlantic. (Though in fairness to Phélypeaux, throughout the quarter century that he was navy minister he still was more able than most of the other aristocratic officers and administrators he had to work with.)

The aristocrats whom the king appointed to top jobs were incapable of collecting the government's own taxes, and sold the job to rich private individuals who filched as much of the revenue as they could. There were a few centers of independent power, as with the old Parlements in Paris and other major cities. But those groups too were encrusted with bias and a near-total lack of what we'd recognize as concern for the public's quality of life. The Paris Parlement in particular was run by near dynasties of religiously intense lawyers who believed that money was far better spent on radical preachers than on hospitals or public health measures. Dead bodies, for example, were kept in very shallow graves in churches across Paris. It was clear, as Voltaire wrote, that "This custom causes epidemic maladies every year, [because] the corruption resulting from so many bodies infects the air." But since it was a tradition, and holy, it wasn't going to be changed.

There were a few efficient technocrats within the government, but they tended to be midlevel civil engineers, especially ones involved in constructing roads and canals. They had some successes. A useful road alongside the Loire near Anjou was being finished, building on a route that had scarcely been improved since the twelfth century; plans and early construction were under way for an express service for mail, using relays of horses, linking Paris with the big western ports of Nantes and Brest. "It is time for France to start ruling, after having spent so much time trying to get something to rule," one supporter wrote (referring to the expansive wars Louis XIV had spent years on). Yet these planners constantly had to struggle for funds and were infuriated that their budgets were dwarfed by what was wasted at Court.

Several of these engineers came to share the attitudes of the thinkers and writers who knew that Voltaire had been writing mocking accounts of their government's incompetence for years. They didn't think of themselves as forming an "Enlightenment" yet, and they were certainly outnumbered by the ordinary readers and writers of cheap romances. But it was an important, waiting audience.

A few years earlier, they and others had enjoyed the aristocratic writer Montesquieu's ironic published account of a naive Persian visitor to Paris. What Voltaire was doing in the play he was writing for Emilie was taking that further: using details of a political tale (this time "far away" in the mountains of South America) to make clear the weak points in the French state's power here at home. He didn't go so far as to propose a full system of promotion on merit. But he knew that many listeners would like the idea that administrators already in place should at least take more rational and humane action.

August ended, and Emilie was still in Paris, which was fine, since the château construction was only just under way. But by September she still hadn't arrived. Champbonin and Neuville were more and more excited. To have a new companion in their isolated region! Voltaire knew the stay would only be for a few months this first time, and he had plans for what he and Emilie could do after, eagerly explaining to friends that the two of them could be visited later in Paris, since "I will be there in all likelihood toward Christmas." But then October arrived, the weather was cooling—and there was still no Emilie.

The two neighboring ladies were becoming suspicious that maybe Voltaire's new lady wasn't so keen to live here after all. Voltaire had to placate them as they waited. Champbonin—with her healthy appetite— was given a fresh boar's head; the taller Neuville was simply given more compliments on her beauty. If Voltaire was worried, he gave only a few clues. And then, halfway through October, in a rush and tumble of crates, after the bone-shaking, nearly weeklong journey from Paris, Emilie did arrive.

It wasn't a good visit. She'd spent the summer still upset about how much he'd put himself—and thus the possibility of their relation—in danger with his thoughtless actions: the untrustworthy printer, the stunt at Philippsburg; the subsequent book burning, and flight. Now in Cirey she tried goading Voltaire by pointedly writing to Maupertuis; she told friends that she felt profoundly alone, that she was filling her time till she could leave by reading Mr. Locke.

Voltaire didn't fight her. He was too proud for that. He watched her countermand his orders to the architects and builders: everything he was doing was wrong.

Champbonin and Neuville were beside themselves with eagerness to come over, and Voltaire automatically gave his usual graceful explanations for why they couldn't yet do so, promising that in just a few more days everything would be right for a visit. He even left Emilie alone for a few days, riding away entirely from Cirey on his favorite horse, but when he came back she hadn't changed. She returned to Paris, late in December, alone. She'd skimmed the new Inca play he'd written for her, but she made no detailed comments about it. Nor had they agreed when they'd meet again.

Earlier, before the icy visit, Voltaire had written to a friend: "I've been reading Locke again, and I'm playing with the idea of trying out his approach." Locke was an attractive guide for fresh writing, since—like Descartes, but even more independently of past religious solutions—he was known for proposing ways that calm thinking could reveal flaws in government administrations, as much as in the individual mind. Once such flaws were revealed, then there was at least a chance of them being fixed.

It was an appealing idea for Voltaire at this time, but his energy was fading. He knew what would help: "There's a woman in Paris, named Emilie," he casually wrote to a friend, "who outdoes everyone in intelligence. She understands Locke much better than me. It would be sweet to have such a guide."

But he was alone now, and it would just have to be different. There were working fireplaces here and there in the partially constructed rooms, and he would survive the winter. He had plenty of books.

And now he had all the time he could wish.

EMILIE arrived back in Paris, and for a brief while even tried a fling with Maupertuis again. "Let's go to Midnight Mass together," she wrote him on December 24. "We can listen to the hymns on the organ and then . . . ah, maybe I'll go home with you." But it was clear that neither of them was in love with the other. He treated her merely as a mistress and not as a potential intellectual partner: making her wait outside the Academy of Sciences but never trying to invite her in, breaking appointments and instead planning with his male friends the trip he had convinced the Academy to send him on, to measure possible distortions of the Earth's curvature in the polar north.

This was worse than having no man at all. She didn't really want Maupertuis—she was just using him as a stopgap while trying to decide about Voltaire—but the rebuffs were insulting. She started waiting at the cafés where thinkers went; she found herself breaking her own appointments with her friends; she seems to have started drinking. A police official who was having his informers keep an eye on everyone who'd been associated with Voltaire reported, "One more thing... Mme du Châtelet now seems to be doing everything she can to deserve the label of madwoman." One evening, infuriated at how coldly Maupertuis was excluding her from his plans for the polar expedition, she even took a carriage to the western edge of Paris, jumped on a horse she'd arranged to have waiting, and galloped on her own to the isolated house at Mt. Valérien where he was meeting with other scientists. She banged unannounced on the door late at night to be let in.

Back home in the light of day—bruised from the riding and having had a sudden night's sex with Maupertuis, with her servants bursting with gossip and her children loud in their rooms—Emilie realized she'd gone too far. It was not a way she could continue to live.

She had an important decision to make, but her female friends in Paris were too superficial to give wise advice, she knew that. Her sweet father, Louis-Nicolas, would have been ideal, but he had died years ago. Yet there was one other individual from her childhood whose kindness and insight she'd always trusted. She'd barely contacted him during all these years since, but there was no reason to think he'd be offended.

And Bernard Le Bovier de Fontenelle, now almost eighty years old, was always willing to help a beautiful marquise who was alone beneath the heavens, trying to decide her fate.

They went for a slow, hours-long stroll, in the summer dusk, right in the Tuileries gardens across from her old family home. He liked wearing a natty yellow waistcoat, and probably used a cane to help his slow steps. But he listened to his late friend's daughter, and he asked gentle questions, as if he understood the intensity that youthful passion could bring.

Voltaire thrilled her, but he could also break her heart again. Yet if she avoided him and stayed in Paris, all she could hope for was to find a somewhat better replacement for Maupertuis—and was she really old enough, in her late twenties, to feel that the hope of real love in her life was past? She wouldn't even have the chance of going on interesting trips, for Maupertuis and almost all other educated men were so smugly male that they'd never take her on their travels. There was so much she wished to do: she'd never been to the Royal Society in England, never shared ideas directly with important thinkers. A woman on her own couldn't travel abroad—but with a man who really admired her and was loving to her, maybe she could. She felt alive when she was with Voltaire, receiving hints of the intellectual inspiration she craved.

She and Fontenelle talked, and probably sat down for the old man to rest. In the end it was simple. When Voltaire was in form, he shone more than anyone she knew. In the poem he'd written to get her back after their first argument, he'd pointedly asked, referring to Maupertuis:

> . . . *He's shown you the heavens*
> *he's uncovered their secrets,*
> . . . *But where is your happiness*
> *Does he know that secret?*

Voltaire did know. She resolved to drop everything else from her life, take her children with her, and move. "Perhaps there's folly in my shutting myself up at Cirey," she wrote immediately afterward, while packing, ". . . but I've made this decision." With Voltaire, she'd be strong enough, finally, to create the new life she'd always sought.

III

TOGETHER

8

Château de Cirey

What happened when they first settled at Cirey is woven through dozens of letters and memoirs . . .

Mme du Châtelet has arrived, just at the moment when I received her letter informing me that she would not be arriving yet. Her coach was rough, and she's bruised and shaken, but she laughs and is charming.
 —Voltaire to Madame Champbonin, Cirey neighbor

Voltaire says I'm busy as a queen ant. But the lodgings aren't finished, and we still have 100 workers.
 —Emilie to Paris friend

Madame wishes to order a dressing-case from Hébert [the gold-smith] . . . who has moved and lives in the Rue Saint-Honoré. You must give him 1,200 francs in advance for the silver to make it. . . . Sell shares to get these 1,200 francs.

—VOLTAIRE to the Abbé Moussinot, his Paris purchasing agent

Now she is putting windows where I've put doors; she's changing staircases into chimneys, and chimneys into staircases. Then she is going to plant lime trees where I proposed to place elms, and where I have planted herbs she is going to make a flower-bed. . . . We have found the secret of furnishing Cirey out of nothing.

—VOLTAIRE to Madame de la Neuville, Cirey neighbor

There are whispers that madame forgets herself so far as to throw such handy portables as plates and forks at M. de Voltaire when she is roused.

—VISITOR recounting servants' gossip

I would add more, but I have to go hammer in some planks now. . . . Emilie says she would append some words herself, if the workers weren't keeping her so busy.

—VOLTAIRE to their mutual friend Cideville

Please remember to buy two small . . . tweezers. But we don't want the tweezers from the quai de Gèvres, only those sold in the Rue Saint-Honoré . . . To the parcel please add two little powderpuffs.

—VOLTAIRE to Moussinot, Paris agent

I spend my time with masons, carpenters, stonemasons—there's no time to think of anything else! . . . But however difficult I may be to live with—and I can assure you I've been almost as difficult for Voltaire as for you—visit us and you will see a strange phenomenon: two individuals who've spent three months together, and who love each other more than ever . . .

If someone had told me two years ago I would be living like this, I wouldn't have believed them.

—EMILIE to Richelieu

Would you please send the thermometers and barometers—I must insist very strongly on this. If I can have the thermometers made according to the modern method of Fahrenheit I should be very much
obliged to you. Would you also send a good air-pump.

May I now speak frankly? You must do me the kindness to accept
a small annual honorarium for all your help.

—Voltaire to Moussinot

First Glimpses

I stopped at Cirey. The architecture is surprisingly magnificent. Voltaire's quarters end in a gallery resembling Raphael's fresco of the
school of Athens, where scientific instruments of all kinds are assembled. The two of them are there. . . . One writes verse in his corner, the
other triangles in hers. I assure you it is like a dream.

—Charles-Jean-François Hénault, court official

Would you very kindly send me a hundred trimmed quills, two reams
of foolscap paper and two reams of large letter-papers. Also some
toothpicks, and three or four dozen little flat buttons for shirts.

—Voltaire to Moussinot

Cirey is four leagues from any other house. It's a terrifying solitude
where my uncle lives, though admittedly with a spirited woman . . . and
very pretty.

—Marie-Louise Denis, Voltaire's newly married niece,
    recounting a visit after the main construction was finished

Please have two good copies made of [the portrait]. . . . As soon as the
first is done, have it examined and retouched by La Tour. In the mean-
while send me the original well framed, well packed, and from the first
copy have a miniature made for a brooch. . . . Also, why not add a
dozen and a half oranges to the dozen and a half lemons.

—Voltaire to Moussinot

I only got there at two in the morning, covered in mud: the coachman had said that if I didn't get off and walk he'd have thrown me out! You can imagine my state. But the nymph [Emilie] greeted me very graciously, and soon Voltaire arrived, a candle in his hand. He's as elegant as if he were in Paris. (I think he powdered his wig for me.) As for her, well, she speaks so fast!

—MADAME DE GRAFFIGNY, excitable houseguest

Could you please send twenty pounds of wig powder, finely ground and ready to use, and ten pounds of wig powder suitable for grinding later? . . . It would be most kind.

—VOLTAIRE to Moussinot

Voltaire called a half hour before lunch, and said I could see his rooms now, since we were going downstairs to dine. Well, I didn't say boo! You go in through a little antechamber by the grand staircase, and then his bedroom—oh, what luxury! what expense! There are tapestries and mirrors and gilded paneling. It's all so clean I wanted to kiss the parquet floor! Then there's a grand gallery, forty feet long, with strange physics machines.

—MADAME DE GRAFFIGNY

I don't know, Voltaire said he had to go off and write, so Madame let me see her rooms (until then I'd only dreamed of them). Well, oh my God! Voltaire's rooms are nothing compared to hers! The main bedroom's wood-paneled, varnished in light yellow, with edges of the palest blue. Everything matches—even the dog's basket! I swear I could fall on my knees it's so gorgeous. The big window's curtains are embroidered with muslin—the view outside is wonderful. And her diamonds!

—MADAME DE GRAFFIGNY finds a fresh victim

Daily Life

Once I began to live in solitude . . . I was astonished at how much time I used to waste [in Paris], just tending my hair, or worrying about my appearance . . .

—EMILIE, unpublished manuscript

Yes, Hébert [the goldsmith] is expensive, but he has taste, and one must pay for that. So give him the 1,200 francs . . . but tell him the rest will only be paid when he delivers the dressing case. (Though he can have 50 more louis in advance if he really insists.)

—VOLTAIRE to Moussinot

The next morning, when Madame woke up, I went into her room at the same time as her chambermaid, who drew the blinds. While my sister [also a servant] got a blouse ready, Madame suddenly let what she'd been wearing on her body fall off, and was entirely nude. . . . I didn't dare lift my eyes to see. I have of course seen a woman change her blouse before—only never in quite this fashion.

When I was alone with my sister, I asked her if Madame du Châtelet always changed her blouse like this. She said not always, but that Madame wasn't embarrassed. She added that if a similar thing happened again, I should try harder not to stare.

—SÉBASTIEN LONGCHAMP, valet and secretary, memoirs

So after coffee, the goddess of this place [Emilie] got the idea to [leave me and] go for a ride; I wanted to accompany her, but wasn't sure because the horses didn't seem as if they had been very well trained. Then oh my gracious! When I saw the wildness of her stallions! I was scared—but I still couldn't decide if I should stay behind. Luckily the kind Voltaire was there, and he said it was ridiculous to force people to take pleasures which they found pains. He's always full of such good lines! Anyway, I stayed behind with the chubby lady [Mme

Champbonin]. We were a cowardly pair, and took our promenade on foot.

   —MADAME DE GRAFFIGNY

Then at four P.M. they sometimes meet for a little snack, but not always. Dinner's at nine P.M., and then they stay together talking till midnight. . . . They just don't want to be disturbed in the middle of the day at all.

   —MADAME DE GRAFFIGNY

Reflect on the advantages we enjoy. Your whole body is sensitive— your lips enjoy a voluptuousness that nothing wearies. We can have sexual intercourse at all times.

   —VOLTAIRE reminiscing

This morning M. de Voltaire was going to read aloud for me, but Madame was so carried away with a happy mood [from last night], that she began to giggle and interrupt M. de Voltaire, and parody what he was trying to read. He quickly looked at the text, and just as quickly began to parody it back against her. I was convinced no one could do this better, but it roused her so much that she came back with even more twists, until he was unable to continue he was laughing so much. . . . The lady said that for herself, she can't bear odes. Exactly, said Voltaire. He couldn't understand how any civilized person could read such ridiculous stuff! I think this shows pretty clearly that they're in love.

   —MADAME DE GRAFFIGNY

They're making fun of me now and . . . I think it's Madame's fault: She can be so imperious. . . . Why, when Voltaire came into Madame's room today to read out from his play, she told him he should wear a different jacket. But he said he didn't want to change it: that he'd be cold and would probably catch the flu. Madame repeated herself, and he stormed out of the room, saying he was ill, and to hell with the play . . . I left too.

... When we went back into Madame's room, Voltaire looked away from her, and wouldn't say a word. But then they began to speak with each other, in English for some reason—it's a language I don't understand—and suddenly everything was fine: Voltaire happily began reading his play aloud.

—MADAME DE GRAFFIGNY; she left only five weeks later.

Old Friends

By the way, is Maupertuis really going to the Pole? I think he's better at measurement and calculations than at being in love.

—EMILIE to Richelieu

Come on: you know Voltaire admires you, and he's worth being your friend. Don't jump directly from France to the Pole without stopping here.

—EMILIE to Maupertuis

Our vessel being provisioned at Dunkirk by order of the king, we set sail on the second of May, 1736.

—MAUPERTUIS, discourse to the Royal Academy of Sciences, on the Measurement of the Earth at the Arctic Circle

How many hardships accompany such an enterprise! What glory must not redound to the new Argonauts!

—FONTENELLE, speech on the departure of academicians measuring the Earth's curvature

This voyage would hardly suit me if I was happy ... but it seems the best I can do in my present situation.

—MAUPERTUIS to his mentor Johannes Bernoulli, Swiss mathematician

Can I really still write to you at the Pole? Voltaire says he would have liked to come—he could have been the expedition poet—but it would have been too cold and he'd have caught a chill. We'll drink to your safety, though. And do tell us about everything.

> —EMILIE to Maupertuis (letters were sent to Stockholm, then forwarded to outposts the expedition reached in northern Lapland)

It's not hard to drag and even to carry the flexible thin boats which one uses in the rivers of Lapland. We survived whirling rapids in these frail machines—at one moment lost in the water, the next tossed entirely in the air.

After [many adventures on] the river, we arrived at the foot of Mt. Niwa, and [following a stiff climb] we met two Lapp girls on the mountain, who were tending a flock of reindeer. They showed us how to avoid the insects that had plagued us (our food had instantly been black with them). The young women had simply built a huge smoldering fire. Soon we found ourselves comfortable in a smoke as thick as theirs.

> —MAUPERTUIS, discourse to the Academy

It says in the gazette that you were in danger of being eaten by mosquitoes. Perhaps the mosquitoes didn't feel the same desire that you feel for your Lapp ladies? Honestly, you can tell me everything. All the letters you write to Paris are apparently full of elegies for them.

> —EMILIE to Maupertuis

I will say nothing more of the rigors of traveling in the deepest snow as the winter came. The Lapps use curious long shoes—narrow planks of wood, about eight feet long—to keep from getting stuck. One walks on them, or rather glides. It's a manner of proceeding which requires long practice.

> —MAUPERTUIS, discourse to the Academy

I do ask you to continue to send me news. The accounts in your last letter made me worry for your safety.

—EMILIE to Maupertuis

When one has travelled, Madame, only from one's home to the Tuileries or to the Opéra, one has very limited ideas about all the wonderful things there are to see.

—MAUPERTUIS, letter sent from Arctic Circle

Now you've written from Stockholm to Madame de Richelieu, but she only wants your letters to brag about them. I genuinely want to learn your news—despite, that is, your pride, your vanity, and your infuriating flippancy.

—EMILIE to Maupertuis

I shall respond to the most spirited letter with which you honor me. The spring here is a bit chilly—the thermometers always give a reading far below what they'd reach in Paris even in the greatest winter. . . . But although the ground is bitterly cold, when I look in the sky there's a fabulous spectacle. Fires of a thousand different colors light it up, making ripples like drapes across the sky. . . . It is from such explorations, that we will understand the universe.

—MAUPERTUIS, letter sent from Arctic Circle

What They Began

All right, I have one more thing to tell you. That morning the nymph was reading aloud to Voltaire, a mathematical calculation for the size of the supposed inhabitants of Jupiter. The reasoning was roughly that since the eyes are in proportion to the body, and they knew the size of the pupil of the eye, and they knew the distance of the Earth from the sun, and they could work out the distance of Jupiter from the sun and so how much light it received . . . oh, I just don't know about something so useless!

    —What MADAME DE GRAFFIGNY also reported

And my good Moussinot, do also send a large reflecting telescope . . . It must be strong enough to detect the satellites of Jupiter clearly.

    —VOLTAIRE to Moussinot

The text was written in Latin, and yet she read it (aloud) in French. She hesitated a moment at the end of each sentence. I didn't understand why, then saw it was to work through the calculations on the pages. That's how fast she was. Nothing could stop her.

    —VISITOR to Cirey, 1738

9

Newton at Cirey

It's unsettling moving in with someone new, and even more so when you have children with you, let alone a husband who's a trained soldier, "friends" in Paris who want your relationship to fail, one ex-partner (Richelieu) who keeps on killing people in duels, and another who's decided to abandon you for the Arctic Circle.

Worst of all, despite all the social acceptance in their circle, and the way that Florent-Claude was content that his wife was safely with a decent man in this out-of-the-way château, the relation remained officially illegal. The punishment for adultery could include whipping and being beaten with rods through the streets. It was always the woman who suffered most, for in the French code of the time, "adultery is punished in the person of the wife, and not that of the husband." Yet given how much court officials were angry at Voltaire, he too could expect to be attacked if the law was ever fully turned against him as well.

Although in fact the two of them were likely to be protected by Emilie's family name, as well as by Florent-Claude (busy with his own extramarital relations at the army's frontier postings), there still was no certainty they would be left alone. Both she and Voltaire, accordingly, were ready to look closer at why it was that the nation they lived in had come up with such a harsh system. It was based on the Bible, of course—that's where the king and all his officials said their authority came from—so it was only natural that in these first months at Cirey, Emilie and Voltaire decided to examine the Bible.

It was hard for Emilie to get started at first. She'd spent a long time in Paris believing she could be creative, yet not doing much about it. "The yogis of India," she mused at Cirey now, "stop being able to use their leg muscles when they stay in the same position for too long without moving. We're like that too, and lose our ability to think afresh when we don't practice it. It's like a fire that dies out when we stop feeding it fresh wood."

Now slowly that changed, and their work was fun as only a shared adventure for new lovers can be. They had texts of the Bible in French and Latin, and they ordered commentaries from Paris, all sorts of them, and reports in English, and texts printed in Latin—especially those of Spinoza—and they began to collate them and read sections aloud to each other, starting at their regular 11 A.M. coffee. (Voltaire especially was partial to coffee, and sometimes a little quinine powder before snacks; Emilie would sip her coffee but preferred fresh fruit, though it's unclear if she shared Voltaire's great passion for rhubarb.)

After a while they began to assign each other a few verses of the Bible each morning, and they'd report on them in the afternoon. "I hardly spent two hours apart from him," Emilie remembered later, "and then we'd send each other little notes from our rooms."

By moving from Paris they knew they'd broken free of the traditional rules of society—not just about having this long-term relationship, but also in terms of the unspoken rules that said women could be chatty yet weren't really to be respected, or rules insisting that monks and bishops of the Church were in touch with the holy and so deserved whatever prerogatives they'd accumulated over the years. Now though, as they went through the books of the Old Testament, and then the New, they began to question the very foundations of those attitudes.

Until recently, they wouldn't have stood a chance. In much of the 1600s, there had been little notion of privacy for such important investigations. When a handful of dissidents in England did insist on the strange concept of "freedom of conscience," they ended up expelled from the civilized world to the distant reaches of rocky soil in the future Commonwealth of Massachusetts.

What Emilie and Voltaire were doing was creating a space where they could think for themselves—and doing this not in some primitive wooden shelter on the far side of the planet, across the Atlantic, but right here, in the center of the civilized world. It was a portentous accomplishment. The two lovers could cross the threshold to enter their château at Cirey, but the king—and the Church—could not. It was far different from the salons of Paris ("each presided over," Voltaire noted, "by a woman who begins to cultivate her mind as her beauty declines"), where no real science, let alone deep questioning of the established Church, was then being explored.

In their fresh investigations of the Bible, Emilie was especially good at catching illogicalities. If Noah had brought onto his ark all the animals of the world, she jotted, and yet he had lived in the Middle East, then how had he brought on board the animals that recent explorers had shown to live uniquely in North America? There were other problems as well: a sun that could stand still, a Red Sea that could part, and all the other impossibilities that we today are used to viewing as metaphors but which at the time were, with few exceptions, taught as mysteries that everyone was expected to take as fully true.

It was one of the fundamental acts of the Enlightenment, this questioning the bases of beliefs that had been held for centuries. There was a great bravery here, for almost every law and procedure in society ultimately depended on traditional religious beliefs. Rich young men, as we saw, could buy government posts and pocket the tax money that peasants and businessmen generated. This was allowable because the king decreed so, and the reason the king's edicts were to be followed was because the Church decreed they were to be followed. There was the same justification for keeping anyone from a working- or even professional-class background from being made an army officer: the king's edicts were that they were to be excluded, and the Church up-held what the king ruled. Undercut the Church, on however obscure a theological point, and the whole chain might come undone.

In fact, what Emilie and Voltaire were doing wasn't entirely nega-tive, for they weren't using the surface flaws in the Bible to reject every-thing about it. If they had, they would have been as closed-minded as the individuals they were critiquing. Years before, Voltaire had jotted down for himself what he felt about God, in the form of a prayer:

> *I'm not a Christian, but that's only to love Thee more closely,*
> *People turn Thee into a tyrant—yet what I seek in Thee is a Father.*

Emilie was religious too. They had a chapel installed at Cirey, and she attended regularly. Voltaire, ever uncomfortable with authority, didn't go as often, but in good weather he kept the doors leading out from his ground-floor rooms open so that he could hear the services. They both wanted their biblical study to lead further.

Again, Emilie was the quickest here. She'd made one start with Maupertuis and his realization (as we saw in chapter 5) that the amount of polar flattening in the spinning Earth was a mark of whether New-ton's theories or competing theories were right, and accordingly could be used to decide if Newton's corresponding views on how God inter-vened in our world were true or not. Now there was another way to an-alyze religious tradition: leaving science to the side for a while longer, and using the accounts of explorers and travelers to see how habits varied around the world. There was a powerful civilization in China, for example, yet from all accounts it didn't depend on anything like an established Church. There also were descriptions of societies where women ruled, or eagles were worshiped, or children were never chas-tised. She accumulated several hundred pages of manuscript queries from their coffee mornings, trying to work out what could be left once the hard-to-believe literal biblical tales were pulled away.

From her notes and general reading, she recognized that what was considered good and bad varied from country to country. It was, she wrote, "like the rules of a game. Just as a move may be considered a mistake in one game, and be allowed in another, so the terms virtue and vice will fit different acts in Paris and Constantinople." But what to do with that insight?

When she was younger she might have left that as a witty aside. She'd still lacked confidence ("Women usually don't recognize their own talents," she wrote, "or they bury what skills they have.... I know—for it's what I've done"). Here at Cirey, though, something was changing. "Since I've met a man of letters [Voltaire] who gave me friendship," she now wrote, "I've started to feel different.

"I've begun to believe I'm a being with a mind."

A number of writers had tried putting the travelers' stories together but often couldn't do much more than list how odd the world was. A few others did try to go further and use the apparent naiveté of an Oriental sage or a "barbaric" American Indian in Paris, to mock the over-refined manners of the Court, or expose the brutality on the street.

Emilie did even better. She began to wonder if there are deeper ideas, beneath the surface, that don't change from culture to culture, despite the different ways people behave. As one example, she noted, in all societies it seems to be expected that people should keep their promises. The golden rule—"Do unto others as you would have others do unto you"—also seemed to be accepted almost everywhere. Even ordinary grammar gave insights about what's universal. In no language that she knew of was there an imperative of the verb "to be able." The reason, of course, is that all peoples recognize that we can't order someone to be capable of doing something that's beyond him.

How to phrase her conclusions? Her writing had been stilted when she was young, but that was simply because she had no one to share her ideas with. Now, though, talking over her ideas with Voltaire in their long hours after morning coffee, she began to change how she wrote.

Within a few months she was inking it out gracefully: "There is a universal law for all men," she wrote, "which God himself has engraved on their hearts." The ideas and phrasing were so good that Voltaire recapped them in his later—long-unpublished—*Treatise on*

Metaphysics: "It seems clear to me that there are natural laws [with] which men throughout the world must agree, even against their will." This too was a fundamental step in Enlightenment thinking, for it helped create the very idea that there could be a universal social science, looking for insights about behavior that would apply to everyone, rather than—as previous history had generally implied—just be random curios of human action, to be pulled from one separate society after another.

Voltaire would have been willing to continue with these studies of society, even though they could never be published, but Emilie was restless. It was good to stumble along trying to find the universals in human nature, but Newton had traveled further and actually worked out the true universals in our physical world. What she decided now was that her next task should be to go through all Newton's work and recount that great achievement in fresh detail.

Her confidence—in criticizing the Bible, in promoting her own view of Newton—was a mark of a new sort of individualism. For example, people had written letters to their friends and family before, of course, but now that was happening more than ever. And in writing your thoughts in a letter rather than in a private, confessional diary, you're showing that you're proud enough, and confident enough, to expect that other people will want to hear what you're expressing about *yourself*. Emilie wrote an immense number of such letters, sharing her feelings about every conceivable topic with her close friends, and often with her favorite brother.

Even Emilie's signing a letter with a personal autograph flourish, representing her personality—something we take for granted—also matched this significant step. (Earlier letters had often just had an impersonal mark or printed name showing who had sent them, something that a scribe could put on just as well as the person dictating or writing it.) Hardly anyone had collected autographs before this period, but now that too began. It made sense, for autographs were yet another sign of this underlying individual personality.

In her choice of clothes, Emilie also insisted on the right to question received judgment. Her unpleasant cousin Renée-Caroline had always accepted Parisian style, and at one point was wearing dresses so wide that "I couldn't whisper to [my friends], since the hoops of our dresses made us stand too far apart." There were supposed to be tight bodices with innumerable eyelets to lace; layer upon layer of undergarments, with frilled petticoats on the highest level; hoops, and supports for the hoops; formal tucking of the outer surfaces of the dress, along with triple rows of embroidery at the sleeves; strict arrangements of tiny patches near the temples, close to the eye, or at the corner of the mouth, each signifying a different emotion. Emilie would have none of that. She greeted one startled guest with her hair up elegantly and a diamond brooch, but also just wearing a big taffeta apron over a simple India cotton dress: it was comfortable, and what she wanted, and so she felt no need to act differently.

Her furniture at Cirey matched this practice. Well before this period, many chairs weren't designed for comfort. They were built to show power and authority. It didn't matter how uncomfortable they were, so long as they held the sitter upright. Now, though, there was an increasing move toward soft, cushioned seats, or even padded armrests, which curved outward so that the elbows could rest comfortably. Emilie wasn't going to sit in chairs that stifled her ability to shift around and be herself. Why follow someone else's rules about propriety?

The portraits she and Voltaire commissioned—to hang on the wall, or as lockets for each other—were more of the same. Instead of having the artists draw a generic figure, representing wealth or authority or beauty, she and Voltaire at Cirey were confident enough to insist that the portrait accurately reflect their individual characteristics. By the time of d'Alembert and Diderot's massive *Encyclopédie,* two decades later, this led to the shocking definition that a portrait "is a likeness according to nature."

That was dangerous. When kings had been drawn in noble, idealized poses, it was a way of saying that the quirks of the human being who'd inherited the throne didn't matter, and indeed did not occur. All that existed was a perfect ruler. But if portraitists ever started showing bad skin or distracted looks, it would be natural to ask if those weaknesses were a mark of deeper flaws. The hereditary principle, however, depended on rulers being accepted, not evaluated. This is, for instance, what the parents of the young George Washington were ready to teach that child, over in the dominions of His Britannic Majesty in the North American colonies. But now at Cirey doubts were being raised about the whole notion of blind obedience to authority—and by two individuals, Emilie and Voltaire, who were so eloquent in their letters and their secretly shared writings that knowledge of what they were doing could not help but spread.

A whole network of correspondents was opening up to communicate this, and that too was part of a wider trend. When Emilie was a child, there had been virtually no newspapers in the world. A handful of noble or extremely wealthy individuals who had direct access to courts or merchants knew what was going on; others might try to scrape up gossip but had hardly any formal sources for finding out more. Now, though, a new form of publication—the "news gazettes"—was becoming popular, and these were often just compilations of the sort of letters coming from Cirey. (Today's newspapers are a direct descendant of those gazettes, with many news articles still presented as if we merely happened to overhear a modified letter—as with the label of reports "from our own foreign correspondent.")

Cirey was crucial to this new movement. Voltaire had always been respected as a clever wit, but now, with his more significant plays, and hints of these deeper explorations that he and Emilie were undertaking, he was being taken more seriously. That meant a lot, for there were so few significant thinkers in France or any other country. Only a few hundred books were officially published a year in France, and a similarly low number in North America. (Today in the United States more than 150,000 books are published each year: any one thinker is easily lost in that outpouring.)

People who received letters from Cirey accordingly tended to share them: sometimes just with a few close friends, but often formally recopying them, to send to even greater numbers of contacts. It was much like a primitive Internet: with information and opinions being fed in, then swirling from one node to another across Europe. If Emilie and Voltaire had merely been coasting in luxury—as rich people had since time immemorial—then this model of their self-created life, with its furnishings and clothes and portraits, wouldn't have mattered. But the research in science and theology and history they were doing was important, and showed the power this new sort of unconventional, strong-willed team could achieve.

It went even further. When people start to feel they should have the freedom to act as they wish in one sphere, it's natural to expect governments to respect them as individuals in other spheres. This was the attitude, after more vicissitudes in history, that led to such world-changing documents as Thomas Jefferson's Declaration of Independence, with its flamboyant listing of inalienable claims to life, liberty, and—as two independent Cirey residents would have enthusiastically understood—the pursuit of happiness.

VOLTAIRE accepted Emilie's proposal to go ahead with a shared study of Newton, not least because—although she didn't recognize it—he was feeling insecure in their relationship. It had nothing to do with Florent-Claude, of course, who was happy to allow this liaison to continue, even when he stayed over at the château on his occasional visits. He and Voltaire rode together, shared dinners, and no doubt gossiped about Richelieu's ever more complex courtships. There was no reason why the purely financial arrangements of a marriage should get in the way of their friendship.

The problem, rather, was that Emilie was young, yet Voltaire was old, over forty already (and as he explained in confidence to his good friend Thieriot, his weakening health was now such that "I fear I am not long for this world"). Life expectancy was short, and poor nutrition, contaminated water, incompetent doctors, and constant low-grade infections made people age much more rapidly than in wealthy countries today. Even if someone did reach their thirties or even forties, it was common to have bone loss from lack of fresh milk or cheese, bad teeth, damaged skin, breathing ailments, and much else steadily going wrong.

Voltaire had done a lot—all his plays and odes and essays and letters—but on despondent days he felt that all it had brought him was the stings of theater critics ("those insects who live for but one day") and the harassment of the court. To keep up with Emilie he'd need to move into fresh fields, and he had reason to think he couldn't delay.

A little earlier, Emilie had received word that her mother was suddenly ill. After Louis-Nicolas's death, back in 1728, her mother had left the family townhouse and moved to a smaller villa in the town of Créteil a few miles outside of Paris. Now, in August 1735, Emilie hurried there from Cirey. When she found that in the days it had taken her to arrive her mother had recovered, she no longer had any reason to be dutiful and, showing her true feelings, arranged to start back to Cirey the very next day. First, however, she sent a note to Maupertuis, saying that she'd be in Paris for a few hours. If he wanted to meet, she said, she'd wait outside one of his old haunts, at the Café Gradot.

She wasn't exactly propositioning him—all she went on to say in her note was that if he was there, they could then go to the Opéra with friends—and since Maupertuis was still sulking, he didn't reply to her note till it was too late to meet. But to avoid having to meet her, he had sent that reply directly to her at Cirey.

Voltaire didn't open the letter when it arrived, but the servants would have let him know whom it was from, whether he wanted to hear or not. Since it came so soon after her excursion to the Paris region, he would have to realize that there was at least some feeling still there. Maupertuis was boldly going to the far north to measure the Earth's curvature and see if Newton was right. Voltaire, as Emilie understood it, was merely planning to write a history of Louis XIV's France. That wasn't the true universal social science she'd glimpsed. When it came to a choice between learning how the universe was constructed and hearing anecdotes about a bygone court, it was pretty clear which one she would find more enticing. Voltaire was convinced he could write a more profound history than Emilie suspected, but he could tell she wasn't interested. Which meant . . .

"I've decided to give up poetry," he wrote to Richelieu. "Life is too short to waste my time merely hunting after sounds and rhymes." Over the years he'd reinvented himself as wit, professional houseguest, poet, playwright, diplomat/spy, expert on British society, financier, and much else. It was time for one more transformation. Maupertuis might impress the ladies by venturing to test one particular prediction Newton had made about the Earth's curvature. Yet Voltaire would now help Emilie write an account of everything Isaac Newton had done, presenting modern science in its full majesty. No one on the Continent had dared to do that before. What bright young woman would not be thrilled to share in such a task?

There were, admittedly, a few problems. Newton had written his great *Principia Mathematica* text in Latin, and although Voltaire proudly quoted Latin epigrams with ease, it seems he couldn't read the language as easily as Emilie. Even worse, Newton's great book was densely loaded with the most advanced mathematics of the time, and Voltaire's aptitude for mathematics made his Latin skills seem impressive. "I am," he admitted to his mathematician friend Pitot, "like those brooks that are transparent because they are not deep . . . calculations tire me."

But perhaps there could be an advantage in that. The year before, in 1734, Voltaire had brought Emilie closer by involving her with the shenanigans of getting Richelieu married into the de Guise clan. Now, if he was going to write the world's greatest account of Newton, he would need her help once again. This actually wasn't too bad, for he didn't realize quite how insecure she felt too. "There are," she jotted, in yet more unpublished manuscript pages at Cirey, "a few great geniuses, such as M. de Voltaire, who are capable of achievement in almost any field. . . . The rest of us have to look harder for useful work." She would be honored to work with him, even if she had to carry much of the analysis behind the project on her own.

They began with practical experiments, reconstructing procedures that Newton had described. It was cutting-edge stuff. The salons of Paris knew nothing of this, for society hostesses were not going to be able to follow complex Latin texts and advanced mathematics. But even the Academy of Sciences was largely opposed to it, or even unaware of the details: the majority of members were sunk in the older, nearly mystic astronomical visions of Descartes.

The trick was just to work through the stages carefully. In his book entitled *Opticks,* Newton had written that seemingly ordinary white light actually is built of numerous different colors of light, all hidden away within it. To confirm his experiments describing this, Emilie and Voltaire shuttered off an upstairs room at Cirey, making it dark enough to shoot single beams of white sunlight sharply into it. They put a prism by the window where the narrow beams of sunlight came in, and then saw that Newton was right: an exploding rainbow of colors really did burst from the light after it traveled through the prism.

Soon they installed a telescope in that room, and gazed out at night to examine the incredible rings of Saturn; they brought Emilie's son out into the open gardens to see how the full moon appeared to grow larger as it neared the horizon; they immersed a straight rod in water and measured how abruptly it appeared to become jagged as the light they viewed it by had to push through the denser water; they took sketches that the first modern astronomers had made of orbiting planets, and transformed those into the crisp numbers of Newton's powerful equations. The nights watching the moon were especially bonding: Voltaire sent notes to Emilie about that "brilliant light, so perfect for lovers"; it "lit our hearts . . . as it lit our love."

Voltaire was in his element. He'd always been a fast writer, once he got over his interminable delaying, and now, by mid-1736, when they finally had the builders away long enough for the hammering and banging to cease, he was flying. Everything made so much sense! When he'd met Emilie, back in 1733, he'd been so thrilled that he'd added his large section rebutting Pascal to the nearly final draft of his Letters from England. Pascal had believed that the world was fundamentally sinful, but Voltaire did not; as he recapped it at the time, "Pascal taught men to hate themselves; I'd rather teach them to love each other." Now Newton's vision, as Emilie was explaining it to him, also squared with his and Emilie's beliefs that the world was not fundamentally sinful. For the physical world wasn't a collection of accidents, with mountains or lakes randomly appearing in the middle of continents, and "we guilty beings deserving to inhabit the crumbling ruins" of our planet.

Instead, he and Emilie prepared a section showing the interconnected, meaningful cycles of nature: the snow on mountaintops came from clouds and moisture in the air, and will melt and replenish the riverbeds, which in turn will fill the seas, from which water vapor can evaporate to turn into rains for farming or more snow up on mountaintops. That's not the sign of a wrathful God, always wanting to terrorize His creations. The new science was backing up their philosophy and showing that Pascal's pessimism didn't have to be true.

Once again, this wasn't just a theological assertion, for they could see Newton's forces in exact action, leading to these harmonious results. The kindly Fontenelle had been unable even to imagine working out what gravity would feel like for any inhabitants or explorers on the planet Saturn—as a little girl Emilie had heard at her father's table how this, alas, was forever beyond our ability. But now, with the insights from Newton, she was able to work out the pull of gravity on Saturn, and the amount of sunlight that reached its great distance, and how much smaller our sun would look, glittering over its ring-bursting horizon. It had been a possibility waiting in Newton's work, but it's not clear if anyone in the world had worked through the details in exactly this way; certainly no one in France had.

Emilie showed Voltaire, on one foolscap sheet after another, how to go through the calculations. She stepped back from the final drafting, in recognition of his still superior writing skill, and Voltaire spent hours on end at his desk until, by the start of December 1736, his hundreds of manuscript pages were completed. It was cold out, there was icy sleet, and the winter was shaping up to be freezing, but Cirey had over a dozen fireplaces, and servants had put aside enough wood from the estates to keep them blazing. When they ate dinner, much of the research apparatus they'd used was stacked on tables and platforms around them: the magnifying lenses, telescope, prisms, a pendulum, and everything else. There was their automatic dumbwaiter to bring up food while it was still hot from the big kitchen downstairs, the butler who stood behind Voltaire to aid the elegant couple, shiny silver serving plates.

The finished work was called *The Elements of Newton*. Voltaire's name alone went on the title page, for that was the usual order of things, but it really should have listed them both. He knew whom to thank. At the start of their manuscript he penned the most graceful of acknowledgments, to "Madame La Marquise du Ch**," pointing out that "the fruit of your worthy aid is what I now offer to the public." Emilie was delighted: "My companion in solitude has . . . dedicated it to me!" she boasted to Maupertuis.

Voltaire sketched out a frontispiece that took the compliment even further. It showed Newton floating amidst a heavenly cloud, shining his insight down, while a graceful goddess—an attractive woman, with one breast tastefully exposed—holds a mirror to collect that light and redirect it to a humble scribbler, working at his desk far below.

It was ease, it was tranquility: it was exactly what they had envisaged life at Cirey could be. Emilie was finally content, with the man "to whom I happily subjugated my soul." Their ideas were spreading. Voltaire too was satisfied, in a way he'd never imagined before. "I spend my life, dear Abbé," he wrote to Thoulier d'Olivet, his old schoolteacher, "with a lady . . . who understands Newton, Virgil and Tasso, and who does not disdain to gamble at cards. That is the example I try to follow, though badly." But then, suddenly, in that freezing December:

> From Voltaire, to his friend Argental; 9 December, 1736
>
> *We have just left Cirey. It is four o'clock in the morning. We are at Vassy, whence I am to take post-horses. . . .*

There had been another order for his arrest, and this time it looked even more serious than before. Word from the court was that if he was caught and sent to the Bastille, he might never be let out. In the nearby town of Vassy, he and Emilie waited for first light for his coach to leave safely. "I see approaching me," Voltaire hurriedly scribbled to Argental, "the hour when I must leave forever the woman who . . . left Paris and all her past life for me. Yet I adore her. It's a horrible situation . . . [Emilie's] in floods of tears."

The coach was ready, and Voltaire left, on the road leading to the frontier. There were no passports, so if he got there before any king's officers arrived, he'd be able to cross. The snow was deep. A year before, Emilie had spent Christmas warm and giggling with Maupertuis in Paris. Now she got back on her own horse, probably Hirondelle "Swallow," her favorite stallion. What she'd created was being destroyed. If she was crying still, no one would know as the wind blew hard on her face. Cirey was nearly empty. The coach had quickly rolled out of sight, and Emilie rode back alone.

10

Dutch Escape

What had happened? On the surface it seemed straightforward. In his months of hard work on the Newton book, Voltaire had relaxed by writing a brief poem parodying the traditional story of Adam and Eve, playing with the idea that they wouldn't have had nail clippers or running water to clean with in their garden, and that in all that isolation the eager though not especially sparkling Adam would have ended up caressing Madame Eve. At the end of the little rhyme, he remarked how much finer was luxury of the sort he and Emilie experienced at Cirey. It was brief, playful, to Voltaire's mind entirely innocuous. But once again, he'd given ammunition to his enemies.

He'd sent copies of the poem to a few selected friends, but one draft had ended up purloined by a literary enemy, who'd copied it, added more potentially blasphemous lines that he said were by Voltaire as well, and then spread it among senior officials at Versailles.

Even that, however, shouldn't have been enough to get an arrest warrant issued against Voltaire. There had to be someone more powerful behind it. Emilie knew that the Versailles court felt threatened whenever one of the higher nobility lived in contentment away from the center of power. It was crucial—it was what the safety of the state depended on—to have them look only toward Versailles. The great prince de Condé, for example, at the age of just twenty-two had ended the Spanish military domination of western Europe when he led a fierce cavalry encirclement and directed artillery attacks in the Battle of Rocroi; years later he'd defeated the prince of Orange (the future William III of England), despite having three horses killed under him. Someone of that power who stayed independent could have sustained a dangerous center of opposition to the king. The luxuries on offer at court, however, as well as the unique chance of professional advancement there, managed to ensure that even Condé was drawn to a trivial courtier's life. The mighty warrior ended his years splashing in an ornate rowboat, seemingly content to row slowly around the ceremonial pools outside the king's chambers.

If country life could be made genuinely attractive—if the top nobles ever decided to leave this easily supervised clustering at Versailles—then who could say whether the centralized royal state would be able to survive? Government officials such as Phélypeaux had their ongoing personal reasons to hate Voltaire, but the example of his successful independent life with Emilie was a greater threat for them to defend against.

Even so, why the assault on Cirey just then? If it wasn't mere literary opponents, then who? "I need to know," Emilie wrote to Argental. She couldn't bear being responsible for having Voltaire forced out onto the sleet-freezing road. Knowing the truth would be the only way to get Voltaire safely back. But even with Argental making inquiries along with her, it could be months before they got to the bottom of the plot.

Until then, at least Emilie could be satisfied with the strategy she'd agreed on with Voltaire. It was Richelieu who'd managed to get advance word of the arrest to Voltaire, sending a fast rider to Cirey to warn them before the king's forces could arrive. This meant they'd had a few hours' grace, in which he could grab a few manuscripts and some gold coins. In that time she'd explained that it was imperative he travel with complete discretion. Voltaire understood. "The key thing," she recounted soon after to Argental, "is that no one knows he's in Holland. . . . Everything depends on his being sensible . . . and remaining incognito."

HE'D AGREED, of course, at that intense dawn parting in Vassy, but telling Voltaire to remain invisible when there was an audience to be had was about as useful as telling Richelieu to take a cold bath in preparation for a vow of eternal chastity. It was not going to happen. Voltaire managed to hold out for almost a whole day, explaining to the coachmen that he was actually a businessman named Revol. But he soon let the cover slip at one inn after another along the way, even before he'd reached Brussels, across the main frontier to the north. (Crossing the border was easy, but discretion was important, for there were no clear rules about extradition: if Voltaire was publicly irritating enough, pressure could be applied to get him sent back to France.)

When Voltaire did arrive in Brussels, there had been enough excited notice that the good burghers had prepared a thoroughly advertised production of *Alzire* (the play he'd written when first at Cirey) for the great author. It wouldn't do to disappoint the admirers of such a fine play, so "Monsieur Revol," the traveling businessman, was induced to attend its performance and wave to the crowd, accepting their cheers and compliments.

It was what Voltaire lived for, and although he'd never seemed to notice the lack of it at Cirey—or was it just that he hadn't complained about it?—now he was in heaven. After Brussels, when he went on to the Netherlands, the glory got even better, for his arrival was soon announced in the *Utrecht Gazette*. Again, he tried to be fairly discreet, merely supervising the printing of his new work on Newton, but he couldn't really be expected, could he, to turn away the great range of people—far more than he would have had a chance to meet in the isolated winter months in Cirey—who crowded to see him at the inns and private homes where he stayed. There were ambassadors, writers, businessmen—his investments could always benefit from up-to-date information—and even, in Leyden, a great sprawling dinner with twenty traveling Britons from the English court, who told him the unexpected news of how one of his latest productions had been received in London.

It was the play he'd written on the life of a young female slave, named Zaïre, caught between Islam and Christianity in her captivity in the Middle East. One Mr. Bond, in London, had liked the script so much that although he'd failed an audition at the Drury Lane theater, he'd used his own funds to rent another theater and put on the play anyway. Since Bond was sixty years old, he'd taken the role of Zaïre's beloved father, Lusignan.

The first night was going well, the audience compelled by the drama, when, just as the tension reached its peak and the Lusignan character was to die, clutching his beloved daughter, Mr. Bond emoted so powerfully that he did, in fact, die. Voltaire was delighted by this reminder of the professionalism of English actors and was even more encouraged when his English guests explained that, rather than it upsetting the cast, there was a great clamoring by London's actors to take on the role for the next night's performance. Everyone wanted to see the play, now advertised as the only one with "The Role That Kills!"

But there was something more than just stage gossip. In that play, Voltaire had given the girl playing Zaïre the lines "The way we're raised shapes our views. . . . I would have been a Christian in Paris, but I'm a Muslim here." It was a theme that increasingly intrigued him, for it was something more than just an argument about the relativity of manners or beliefs. The play was also reminding the audience that once we recognize how arbitrary is the world we've been born to, then we start to have the chance to reshape our own lives.

This was quintessential Voltaire: transmitting groundbreaking philosophy by means of a commercial play, so well written, with all the twists and pulls of an adventure plot, that it became a great popular success. But he wasn't yet done with the move from poetry to science that he'd begun with Emilie. For here, in the Netherlands, he saw that he had the chance to advance further still.

In the same city of Leyden, only 130 miles from the French border—but a world away in its openness to fresh ideas—he knew that there was an earnest, bemused Dutch lawyer who was even more ingenious in going through Newton's experiments than he and Emilie had been. For not only was the lawyer, Willem Jakob 's Gravesande, duplicating Newton's work, but he had found that with quite ordinary tools he was able to take those great findings further.

A central question for everyone following Newton was what it really meant to talk about the force or power that a moving object carries. It was clear that our moon had been spinning in orbit at a great altitude above the Earth for what must have now been thousands upon thousands of years without stopping. Emilie had studied similar observations for the moons of Jupiter and Saturn, and also of course knew that the Earth had been swinging in steady circuits around the sun for great lengths of time as well. What was the force that moving objects carried inside that let them perform these miracles?

The way the conscientious 's Gravesande was determining this was to build a tripod-like tower, the height of a man, and drop bullet-shaped ivory or brass cylinders straight down from it. What was underneath was important. If they merely hit against something hard, such as the fired clay tiles that the Dutch used to decorate their floors, the result would be a sudden shattering of the tile, with the brass or ivory cylinder rolling uselessly away after the destruction was over.

But 's Gravesande had something more important in mind than destroying nicely colored kitchen tiles. Instead, he put pans filled with soft clay right under the tripods. When the cylinders came falling down, they didn't shatter the carefully smoothed clay, but instead ended up simply stuck in the clay, with their tips embedded several inches down. The greater the height from which 's Gravesande dropped his dense little projectiles, the farther they pushed into the clay.

In a previous era, that would have been as far as his finding went, and it still wouldn't have revealed much about nature. Even Fontenelle hadn't known how to go further: he, like his master Descartes, kept most of his explanations at the level of general, nonexact description. But Newton had pushed for a mathematically exact physics. While 's Gravesande was only about Voltaire's age, he had made a pilgrimage to England a lucky several years before him, and so had been able to meet Newton in person. He'd spent time with other scientists and had even been made a member of the Royal Society. In his Leyden laboratory, 's Gravesande was carefully measuring how deep the different projectiles went.

This was the level of arithmetic Voltaire liked best. There was none of the calculus, trigonometry, or long cube roots that Emilie was so quick with and at which he always came in a slow last. One just took a measuring rod, stuck it into the little holes in the clay, and read off the result. Yet from that simple procedure, a startling truth about the "inside" of any moving object in the universe could be found.

What 's Gravesande had been discovering—as he happily shared with Voltaire—was that the force of a plummeting brass cylinder was not just a matter of how fast it was going at impact. Nor was it a matter of how much the brass cylinder weighed, nor even—another plausible guess—the combined figure one might get by multiplying its speed by its entire weight.

Instead, 's Gravesande was finding something extraordinary. As the speed of the cylinder went up, the force with which it whacked into the mud went up too—by ever-increasing and predictable amounts. If one translated it into the image of a farm wagon sent skidding along an icy road, it meant that when the wagon was going at a slow one mile per hour and the wooden brake was jammed on, the wagon would skid a certain distance, perhaps ten feet. But if the wagon was going at twice that rate, at 2 mph when the wooden brake was slammed down, the wagon wouldn't just skid twice as far. It would skid four times as far. If the wagon was going at three miles per hour and the brake was slammed down, it wouldn't skid three times as far. It would skid nine times as far. There was no randomness. Rather, this predestined rule was waiting.

Voltaire found that remarkable. When you've been holding a cylinder or ball or any other object and then let go so that it falls, some sort of force appears inside it and makes it act as if it had come quiveringly alive, with an independent life. But this independent life is not arbitrary, sending the cylinder slewing in any random direction, at some random speed. Instead, it follows this exact rule: the impact depends precisely on the square of the speed. A few other researchers had suspected this might happen; 's Gravesande was one of the first to show they were right.

And Newton hadn't known it.

Voltaire wanted fame. His poetry and drama were good, but he knew their survival depended on the whims of critics and actors; styles change and civilizations fall, bringing all the writings in their language to effective extinction. But science? It was written in much simpler language, be it the symbols of mathematics or just neutral, clear prose. Those particular writings might be as vulnerable to shifts in style or power as works of literature were. But the underlying laws of science were different. They could cross all boundaries of extinction, all voids of eternity and night. Voltaire realized that he was never going to come up with fresh ideas about how Saturn's moons orbited. That was perhaps something Emilie could do, but it was too abstract for him, too far away in space.

What 's Gravesande was doing, however, showed another way to lasting fame. There were experiments—*simple* experiments—that careful investigators could do right here on Earth. If those experiments were ingeniously planned and conscientiously carried out, they could reveal eternal truths that even Newton had never seen. Voltaire knew that he could be too impulsive, but he also knew he could be supremely diligent when he had to. This would be one of those times. He was working closely with his printers and clarified his text's last pages to assert:

> [Newton's understanding] of gravity is not the final result that physics will have. There are no doubt other secrets, ones we scarcely suspect . . . and they are just as important. . . . In time, with enough experimental results, we can find them.

This, Voltaire knew, would be his next task. It had been fun being feted by the crowds and seeing his plays performed. But he missed Emilie, and Cirey. That's where he could do his next stage of work—if, that is, Emilie was able to bring him back.

By NOW, in February of the new year of 1737, it was almost impossible for him to learn what she was doing. "I'm 150 leagues from him," Emilie had written their friend Argental, "and I haven't heard a word in two weeks. . . . His handwriting's easily recognized, so his letters are probably being intercepted." When she and Voltaire did get letters through, they had to restrict themselves to banalities, knowing that their words were being read by Phélypeaux and his enforcers at Versailles.

But to Argental, in a separate series of letters that she'd arranged to escape the censors, she now revealed something else. She'd finally discovered what was behind the order for Voltaire's arrest. "I know you'll find it hard to accept; the idea . . . that someone can be so capable of evil, but believe me: some men are capable of anything. Listen and you'll understand.

"I firmly hope I'm wrong, but if I'm not, then I'm really worried; it would change everything. We'd have to abandon Cirey, who knows for how long." And then to Argental she recounted the extraordinary story she'd just learned about. Her life wasn't what she'd thought it was.

For you see, she began, "my father had another daughter. . . ."

11

Michelle

Decades before Emilie had been born, a rich family of six sons had had a seventh child. That was in Montpellier, in 1648, and the wealthy father had been so proud of his lastborn that he'd brought the boy—it was Louis-Nicolas, Emilie's future father—to Versailles, even before he began his teenage years. The boy was unusually handsome and had none of the arrogance that children blessed with great beauty often acquire. He was courteous to everyone, and as he grew taller, in his teens and then as a young adult, his easy nature and golden looks made the still young king—Louis XIV—begin to grant him special respect.

Most of the young women at court would no doubt have been willing to be caught up romantically with the golden youngster, even if it wasn't known that he enjoyed the king's favor. With that advantage, though, he now truly had his pick of the nobles' daughters. But then, when he was twenty-three, at a ball given by a wealthy financier, he met a girl who was different from everyone with whom he had ever flirted. She was only fourteen—which made her too young for a physical relationship—and had only quite ordinary looks, being far less attractive than most of the women he'd met. Her name was Anne Bellinzani.

Since the handsome young man was charming and always polite, he didn't snub her, but gave her the time to begin a serious conversation. For most plain fourteen-year-olds, to be focused on by one of the most attractive bachelors at court would have been overwhelming: enough to make them giggle, or blush, or in some other way be less than articulate in response. But Anne Bellinzani seems to have decided on the spot that this was the man she would someday marry, and she confidently drew him aside so that they would have a quiet corner or settee on which to talk.

And talk they did, or rather, talk she did: about everything she'd read, and everything she'd dreamed of. There was poetry, of course, but there was also something else, something new at the time and suddenly compelling to the gorgeous yet scarcely educated Louis-Nicolas. Anne was fascinated by astronomy and all the fresh discoveries that were being made about the stars. Her own father had come from Italy and so knew of Galileo's discoveries with his new telescope that the universe above us was full of greater wonders—of moons that orbited distant Jupiter, of comets that could be charted in great detail—than had ever been imagined before.

The conversation went on so long that the dazzling young man for once forgot his manners. There were many other women at the ball, and they knew that even if a new flirtation was going to take up a certain amount of a young man's time, it was still right that before too long he should excuse himself, step away, and offer his services as a dancing partner. But Louis-Nicolas didn't do it. He wasn't going to dance with anyone else that night.

The first explanation the court gossips gave, as word went around over the next days, was that he was drawn to Mademoiselle Bellinzani's money. Her father had become a colleague of Colbert, the king's brilliant finance minister, and from that connection had become immensely rich. But Louis-Nicolas had his own family money, and if he was trying to curry favor with this girl's father, he was going about it very oddly. He spent very little time with the parents—as in a proper courtship one was supposed to do—but rather seemed to remain entranced by young Anne. She'd teasingly called out to him from her window one Sunday morning, when he was walking alone to church, and then broke all precedent by tossing down a book for him to read. They went to the theater and opera, and were seen at other balls, but almost everywhere they remained transfixed in conversation. She taught him Italian and gave him poems; she listened to the new thoughts he had, and she went on, whenever he prompted, about her deepest interests in the extraordinary fresh insights into the distant stars, as well as all the rest of the new science being developed to explain our sublunary world.

If he'd been less striking, the courtship might have led smoothly to the marriage for which Anne hoped. But almost as a habit, even while Louis-Nicolas continued his fascination with the young teenager, he engaged in a few of the affairs that were almost automatically necessary for the most dashing young men at court. Unfortunately, in one of those brief affairs the woman involved became pregnant. The pregnancy went badly, and she fell gravely ill.

The handsome young man married the dying girl—it was the right thing to do, and of course the king wished it. But the Versailles doctors insisted on bleeding her, and just a few days after the marriage she was dead. The unborn child died with her.

Anne Bellinzani was shocked that Louis-Nicolas had so unambiguously cheated on her. She was eighteen by now, and had always been impulsive. Now she was humiliated. She fled to a convent, but the court couldn't allow someone with a dowry the size her father could provide to do that. She was arrested inside the convent, brought back to court, and forced into a marriage of her own.

Louis-Nicolas was in his late twenties now, and chastened: he tried to get diplomatic postings far from Paris, so as not to have the pain of being close to the married Anne anymore. But he did return, and soon Anne was writing him flirtatious letters ("I'm the tenderest lover you'll ever have"), and angry letters, and sometimes simply intense ones.

They met in private rooms at court, and then—daringly, awfully—in her own home. "My lover," she wrote, "is dearer to me than anything in the world. He's dearer than my life itself."

In 1683—a dozen years after they'd first met—the finance minister Colbert died. This meant that Anne's father no longer had a protector at court, and all his enemies who wanted a part of his fortune could now make their move. He was arrested and lost his money, upon which Anne's husband began divorce proceedings. She and Louis-Nicolas just had to wait a very little while longer, and they'd be free.

But then, in 1686, she got pregnant by Louis-Nicolas. The timing was awful, for the baby was born before she had a complete legal separation from her husband. This meant that Louis-Nicolas couldn't recognize the child, and her husband certainly wasn't going to. It was a girl, and she was given only a single name: Michelle. When she was baptized no father was present or listed on the baptismal register. Instead, two beggars were dragged in and listed as her guardians. Almost immediately the foundling was sent away to an orphanage inside a convent. Death was nearly certain, given the poor care and epidemic diseases of the time.

Anne and Louis-Nicolas stayed together for almost two more years, but something had broken. In 1690 they parted a final time, by their own volition. In 1691 she withdrew to another convent, committing herself to a life of penance.

Louis-Nicolas had no heart for love after that, and in his despondency quickly married the first suitable woman with some money his friends pointed him toward—a fact recognized by Emilie's mother, Gabrielle-Anne, and a source of her unending bitterness.

For almost half a century the story had been hidden, only occasionally surfacing in furious whispers between Emilie's parents. No one but a very few intimates knew all the details, and even that knowledge seemed to be of fading importance, for everyone assumed the child had died. But then, in 1736, a notary came across some long-lost records, and out of professional diligence, or expectation of a reward, he followed the chain from baptism to orphanage to nunnery. The child had lived. He continued tracking the long-forgotten documents till he found an obscure fifty-year-old nun named Michelle, living in a Paris-area convent, and told her who she was.

EVERYTHING made sense to Emilie once she discovered this: why her father had been so proud when she'd shown her own first interests in science and especially in astronomy; why—even more—her mother had always been so angry, and especially so whenever her daughter had tried to gain favor by showing more of the scientific interest her father admired.

That past intrigue did more than just explain her early years. It also solved the mystery of the continued attacks on her and Voltaire at Cirey. It was a question of money. Michelle, the bewildered fifty-year-old nun, was bringing a court case to claim her share of the Breteuil family's huge fortune. Emilie, of course, would support her. But Emilie also had a most unpleasant first cousin who'd achieved eminence as the secretary of war to Louis XV himself. He was a Breteuil, as she was, which meant they all shared a stake in that Breteuil fortune. The rich cousin didn't want to lose any of it, yet realized that Emilie would take her newly discovered half sister's side. If he could threaten to destroy her idyll at Cirey, though—or give her a sample of the untouchable power he could muster against her—then she would have no choice but to take his side in the court case against this unwanted half sister.

The cousin had ensured that Voltaire's Adam and Eve parody went all the way up to Cardinal Fleury, who was the wily chief adviser to the king, and effective head of the government. Fleury's dislike of such impious writings gave Phélypeaux the chance to move against Voltaire once more. Being locked away, or just sent into permanent exile, would destroy Voltaire for good. It would also—as the war minister cousin wished—have the further advantage of sending this arrogant young marquise back to Paris in disgrace. She would be unable to resist his wishes after that.

It was a powerful plan, and might even have worked if the cousin hadn't gone too far. But he had decided it wasn't enough to attack

Voltaire from the outside, simply through sending arresting officers. He also wanted to undercut his irritating cousin even more directly. Why not wreck her marriage while he was at it? He had a word with Emilie's mother, Gabrielle-Anne, who was now quite recovered from her health scare of the year before, and furious as ever that her child was so different from what a proper daughter should be—perhaps even more furious that this intense shame from the past was coming back.

The cousin wanted Gabrielle-Anne to write directly to Emilie's husband, Florent-Claude du Châtelet, and with false naiveté say that she had just heard rumors that something untoward might be going on between her daughter and Voltaire and that, as a diligent mother, she was bringing this to the husband's attention so that he could, of course, discipline his wife as he saw necessary. In French law, not only were women legally the same as children (aside from the financial protection their families might have arranged for them in their marriage contracts), but they had no legal protection against physical punishment from their spouses. The distinguished and wealthy Monsieur Popelinière, for example, regularly knocked his wife to the ground and kicked and beat her, even in public. There was some murmuring at fine dinners where he did this, but no one was going to stop it.

That was when Emilie realized she could win. "The letter from my mother might have shattered any other relationship," she explained to Argental in relief, "but happily, I can trust the good intentions of M. du Châtelet." For what Gabrielle-Anne, the war minister cousin, and the tight-lipped Phélypeaux all had missed was the fact that her husband had frequently been at Cirey in the company of Emilie and Voltaire—and Voltaire, when he put his mind to it, was the most charming man alive.

The trick, Voltaire knew, was never to pretend an affection you didn't feel. Any intelligent person would see through that. Rather, you need to find what you genuinely do like about a person and then go ahead and share that.

Florent-Claude may have been distant at the start, but he had long had his own mistresses and—as we've seen—had also grown up in a culture that never expected a husband and wife to spend much time together. He recognized that Voltaire had been very generous in paying to rebuild Cirey, which by inheritance laws would likely end up being left to du Châtelet's own son.

Florent-Claude had taken long walks in the woods with Voltaire on his visits, together inspecting the many charcoal-fired forges on the estate; they'd gone hunting for wild boar and sometimes deer, and although Voltaire was not an especially dangerous shot, Florent-Claude with his years of military experience was comfortably better. Voltaire played with the du Châtelets' now ten-year-old son, bought him mechanical toys from Paris, and helped select the tutor for the boy; he had used his great pull in Paris salons to help Florent-Claude in everything else he wished. They really were friends now, from the heart.

And soldiers do not like it when someone starts picking on their friends.

Florent-Claude wasn't quite at Richelieu's level, but he too had been a powerful leader of men in battle. Also, Louis-Nicolas had thought ahead very carefully when he'd arranged Emilie's marriage. The Châtelet family had great powers in Lorraine, and Louis XV needed to ensure that the local nobility was on his side. As noted, Louis-Nicolas had given Emilie enough of a dowry so that whatever her husband turned out to be like—and Louis-Nicolas had suspected Florent-Claude was a decent man—the husband and this powerful du Châtelet clan would promote her interests in whatever serious problems might arise.

By the end of February the case was on the way to being solved. "M. du Châtelet," Emilie happily wrote to Argental, "is leaving [for Paris], firmly resolved to respond to the cardinal."

It worked. Cardinal Fleury wasn't going to upset one of the great families of this important frontier province, certainly not for something so trivial as some possibly forged writings from the pen of this noted poet. Nor did it hurt that Emilie's cousin was temporarily out of office (and would not be war minister again for several years). Phélypeaux was reined back.

Voltaire was free to return. The gentle, ponderous Florent-Claude had fixed everything. Cirey—the perfect retreat—could now be reborn.

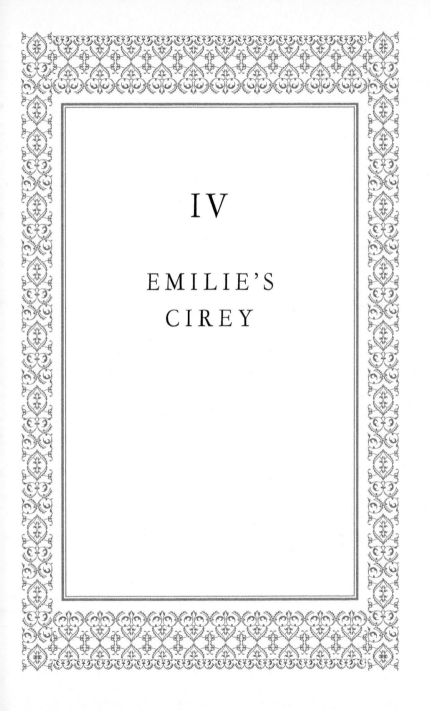

IV

EMILIE'S
CIREY

12

Voltaire's Fire

When Voltaire got back, he and Emilie were in love once more, they were passionate; the way he'd abandoned his incognito so quickly was forgiven. Each wanted the other near. "[She] means more to me," Voltaire explained to his loyal friend Argental, "than father, brother, or son." And also, most powerfully: "where there is friendship, there is our natural soil."

And yet, despite the words, despite the warmth, something was beginning to change. Emilie had forgiven Voltaire for his showing off on the road, but that didn't mean she'd been able to quite forget what he'd done. Those antics showed he could be weak—and had put them in danger until she'd taken control and fixed it.

That gave her a confidence she'd never had before, and one of her first steps was to get rid of the bane of her life: the tutor that Voltaire had insisted upon for her son. This was a ridiculous overweight abbé named Linant, whose first action, when he'd tumbled out of the coach that brought him down from Paris, had been to inspect the pudgy Madame Champbonin and the taller young Madame de la Neuville—

both of whom were eagerly awaiting the new arrival—and then almost immediately make a lunge toward the startled Neuville. It had taken Voltaire's best efforts—"he was quite carried away ... your beauty must have inspired so many gentlemen to forget their manners"—to appease her, and from then on things had become worse.

Linant was supposed to teach Latin, but he'd been too busy attempting to be a playwright—that's why Voltaire had taken pity on him—to actually learn much of Virgil's language. Voltaire suggested that Emilie teach Latin to Linant, and Linant would then teach it to her son. She countered that finding a better tutor might be easier, but Voltaire laughed, and charmed and wheedled until she gave in.

Even though Linant didn't do much tutoring, he went for long walks and complained to the neighbors about how boring he found Cirey. He complained even more when Emilie begged Voltaire to keep him from eating with them. (That was especially cruel, for the preparation for his future writing took a lot of mental effort, so it was only natural that he had a hearty appetite and didn't always have time for fussy etiquette when there were delectable grease-dripping drumsticks to gnaw on.)

Then Linant's sister arrived, ostensibly to be Emilie's chambermaid, but she succeeded in making her brother seem a paragon of efficiency. When Emilie complained again to Voltaire, he had a firm word with Linant, who admitted to Madame that he hadn't always been as diligent as he should have, but vowed that—as soon as his muse delivered—he would dedicate his future writings to her.

Voltaire was proud of how he had solved the problem, while Emilie was reduced to muttering to a friend that "I don't want him to dedicate his tragedy to me ... I want him to educate my son." Nothing whatsoever had changed.

Before the Dutch exile it would have stayed like that. But now? Emilie found that the brother and sister had been writing scurrilous letters about their stay at Cirey. Her tone changed, and she said that the Linants were going to leave. Voltaire still had a soft spot for them—he always did for underdogs—but Emilie insisted, and won.

The next change came in dealing with a young man Voltaire seemed to be readying to be his salvation if he needed a safe bolt-hole for a sudden exile again. This was Crown Prince Frederick of Prussia, just twenty-five years old. In the letters he had recently begun sending Voltaire, Frederick showed he was the gentlest, the most ethereal, of Francophile literature lovers. In elaborate, flowery letters he explained how much it wounded him that the barbaric French court had treated this living paragon so poorly. If only Voltaire would deign to visit the majestic lakefront mansion Frederick had set up well outside Berlin, then he would learn what true hospitality and security could be.

Emilie didn't believe any of it. In the previous century, Prussia had been brutalized by the Thirty Years' War, and up to a third of its population had been murdered or starved. The result had been a cowed civilian population, willing to do whatever the surviving military administration wished. The kingdom itself was only a recent creation, formed from a strip of what had been Polish territory, on a sandy, near-worthless stretch of land around the small town of Berlin. It was a garrison state, and the sensitive Frederick wasn't even its commander. His father, Frederick William, was king. This meant that if Voltaire ever went there, he would be under the father's authority—and Frederick William was not a normal person.

When he went out for lunchtime walks, he'd kick any women on the street he didn't like. If a clergyman was standing too close, watching one of the king's beloved guards regiments on parade, Frederick William would take out a thick cane and beat the clergyman to the ground. He regularly punched his son, dragged him by the hair, and choked him with curtain cords. When Frederick, at eighteen, had tried to escape with a friend, the father had caught them, made Frederick watch as the friend was murdered, and locked Frederick in the dreaded Küstrin fortress, on the Oder. Only at twenty-one, when the crown prince reached legal majority, was he trusted to be free—whence young Frederick's private mansion, which was as close to the outermost edge of Prussia as possible, but where he was still coweringly dependent on his father's strained goodwill.

Emilie knew that wasn't a safe refuge for her lover. In previous months she'd let Voltaire give hints he might take up the offer to visit there. Now she was ready to stop it.

Frederick wanted to send an emissary to visit Cirey, supposedly just to give him a flavor of the château. Emilie, however, suspected that Frederick would also get the emissary to seek unpublished writings, which Frederick could then use to show off at the Prussian court and prove how "close" he was with Voltaire. The most alluring writing was a mocking, semi-pornographic epic on Joan of Arc, which Voltaire had been embellishing for years, adding spoofs of contemporary political leaders being sexually humiliated or mocked. Its existence was the subject of intense rumor across Europe's high society.

When the emissary—tubby, cheerful Count Keyserlingk—arrived, he was delightful to everyone, exuberantly speaking any European language requested ("and often at the same time"). Emilie ensured that he was given fine dinners, and that there were firework displays, and that he got to see Frederick's name spelled in bright colored lanterns outside the château, beside the phrase "To the Hope of the Human Race!" He was even allowed to take back some of Voltaire's more innocuous drafts of history and poetry. But she placed the manuscript of Voltaire's Joan of Arc spoof in a heavy case, had that fastened with at least two sturdy English brass locks, and kept the only set of keys for herself.

Keyserlingk's return without even a fragment of the Joan of Arc poem was a little embarrassing to Voltaire, for it showed Frederick how much power Emilie had to decide what went out from Cirey. But Voltaire didn't mind, for he realized it would probably just make Frederick try to court him more intensively in the future.

In any case, both Emilie and Voltaire were turning their attention back to science. The Academy of Sciences in Paris had recently declared its prize competition of the year, to determine the nature of heat, light, and fire. It was a vague, unformed question, but it was one that previous researchers such as Newton had barely touched. Emilie was surprisingly eager when the prize was announced, and that further helped Voltaire think it was worth investigating. For months he'd been itching to try out that new style of hands-on research he'd envisioned at 's Gravesande's lab. If he gave the best answer to the prize question, maybe he would become respected worldwide as Sir Isaac's pragmatic successor.

Everything was ready. The grain shipments from North Africa and other ports had proved very profitable; the property investments were doing well; the loans out at 10 percent were being steadily repaid. (Ten percent was a high figure, but many noble families accepted it, for they had difficulties with more complicated calculations.) Using that cash, as the summer of 1737 approached, Voltaire now ordered all the equipment he wanted, from the finest instrument makers in London as well as Paris: soon more air pumps, giant focusing lenses, tureens that could resist strong flames, glass retorts, and everything else he might need began to be delivered by the coachman from the post station at Vassy. It was an expenditure that only a few very wealthy private individuals could afford, the equivalent perhaps of several million dollars today.

He also was more cunning in his approach than Newton. Over in England, Newton had almost always worked on his own, which meant he couldn't easily build on the findings of others. That may have been fine for theoretical work, but Voltaire was convinced it must have slowed him down in practical experiments. (The unfortunate incident when an agonized Isaac Newton had shoved a dull knife several inches long all the way into the edge of his eye socket—to measure the light flickers one saw when the eyeball was compressed—was something Newton perhaps would have avoided if he'd been as articulate as Voltaire and had simply quizzed others beforehand about what worked or not.) Voltaire now would give himself a much faster—and less painful—start.

He employed his cunning by asking Moussinot, his efficient financial agent, to make inquiries around the leading chemists in Paris, to find out how competitors were approaching the problem. Moussinot was to act as naive as possible. (The fact that he was an abbé and hardly anyone knew that he acted for Voltaire would make that easier.) Nor was he just to go ahead and blurt out his questions about the Academy's prize. There was a more indirect way, and when Moussinot began with the apothecary to the Academy of Sciences itself, Voltaire told him what to do. "Draw him into a conversation, by saying you wish to buy a half-pound of quinine," Voltaire advised. What merchant wouldn't be in a good mood after a large order like that? "You will [then] easily find out what the good [apothecary] understands of [the prize topic]. Send me what you glean. . . . You will of course keep my name out of it."

Most importantly, though, in his preparations he had Emilie. He didn't quite understand why she was more insistent now in deciding how to handle servants and foreign visitors, but that didn't matter. Deep inside, he believed that she still lacked confidence. It's true that she'd been willing to leave Paris and try a life of full-time investigations in history, religion, and science. But she was competing against great thinkers and, as she admitted, "I do sometimes wonder if I started too late." Voltaire managed to get her to put her own work aside now. She would help him in the calculations that Newton could do so easily. With that aid, Voltaire felt he could be equal to them.

Where to start? Objects changed when they got hot: some glowed, and some burst into flames; some got a thick chalky layer on their surface when they were heated red-hot, while others apparently did not. No one could work out the patterns. But had anyone ever taken the time to measure every aspect of heating with accuracy?

That's what Voltaire now began, and as he expected, Emilie was happy enough to help. Their sharing was even more spirited than the year before. They'd have the servants lug huge blocks of iron to one of Florent-Claude's forges in the forest, and there they'd heat it till it glowed, and then they'd measure its weight, more exactly than anyone had before, to see how it had changed in the glowing transformation.

It went on for weeks: iron was heated and cooled, and lead was heated and cooled; thermometers were plunged into half-molten metal (and when the first, insufficiently insulated thermometer burst in a shatter of glass, Voltaire simply wrote to Moussinot for a sturdier one).

They set small forest fires—servants standing near with buckets of water—to measure the rate of a fire's growth; they prepared a perfect cubic foot of wood, and set it flaming to see whether it expanded before it collapsed in ash. They even brought in glassblowers to create huge glass containers, big enough to fit one of those cubic feet of wood inside, and then—as an air pump was attached to the glass, and the atmosphere inside was gradually sucked out—he and Emilie, with Florent-Claude, and no doubt Emilie's son jumping around excitedly to see as well, took note of the result.

What they saw made no sense. Sometimes the metals that they heated gained weight when they got hot. That suggested some substance from the atmosphere was being pulled down by the fire and attaching to the metal to make it grow. But other metals didn't gain weight at all. There were even a few—however carefully they tried to calibrate the scales—that seemed to temporarily lose weight when they were heated up.

Voltaire wrote urgently to Moussinot for more equipment and instructed him to make more surreptitious inquiries among the various other experts in Paris, to find out what they were doing, and so learn methods that might help him fix these problems. But it didn't help: the weight figures kept on fluctuating. If Voltaire couldn't even tell whether fire made metals heavier or lighter, what chance did he have of gaining the Academy's prize?

Emilie was supportive, always standing with him during the day, and willing to do whatever calculations he needed. But it seemed that, as a woman, the heavy labor with all the forges and metal and fires was exhausting her. Often now she cut short their late-night coffees and chats, almost unsteady with tiredness as she left; when they met again, for morning coffee, she still appeared to need a good rest. Voltaire accepted that, and as a good hypochondriac, he was never kinder than when someone was actually suffering one of the many ailments he'd so vividly imagined for himself. It got worse for both of them as the heat of the summer built to its peak. The deadline was September 1, and now, in mid-August, he had to begin writing up his incomplete results as best he could. He was alone, the only one awake in the château as he sat at his writing table, working till midnight or beyond.

Or rather, that's what he thought. He wasn't alone in his writing at all. Emilie wasn't ill, and she wasn't asleep either. She was at her desk, over in her own candlelit rooms in the château. She'd seen that Voltaire was flailing in his experiments and she'd decided what she was going to do about it. She'd decided to enter the Academy's competition in secret, and on her own.

13

Emilie's Fire

Voltaire had never had a chance of succeeding. Metals do gain weight when they're heated, but not nearly as much as he'd expected. The effect is so slight that the scales he'd lugged to Florent-Claude's forest forges were far too crude to detect it, hence his randomly scattered high and low results.

From the beginning, Emilie had recognized that he was going in the wrong direction, but she also knew she couldn't simply tell him to stop all his heating, burning, and woefully inaccurate weighing. It would have been undercutting him; it also would have been bolder than she felt justified in being at the time. Voltaire was famous across the civilized world, and she was an unknown woman. Although this was his first attempt at original work in experimental physics, he'd succeeded in almost every other creative discipline he'd tried. She, by contrast, had never done any original work at all.

It didn't help that women were widely considered—even by other women—incapable of true creativity, with one male authority after another declaring they should simply be cheerful consumers of what their male betters produced. "I didn't want to be ashamed . . ." Emilie wrote about her efforts later. "When I got the idea to work secretly at night, I didn't even know if I'd submit my results."

Yet in the months before the prize competition was announced, she'd stood up to Voltaire over the exhausting Linants, and to Crown Prince Frederick over the Joan of Arc poem, and that had made her begin to feel differently about herself. In previous years, she'd needed Voltaire as a guide, to carry her across to the realm where she could try to be creative. Now, though, she'd seen that she could plan things, and envisage how they might turn out, and then—on her own—make sure that they happened.

Everyone who's going to try true creativity needs that self-assurance. Voltaire had achieved it with his *Oedipus* play at the age of twenty-four, after his year in the Bastille. Emilie had taken till thirty—but was ready now. She even had an advantage in her relative isolation in the countryside. Maupertuis had needed to hide many of his true interests in Newton at first so he could be accepted at the overly traditional Academy of Sciences in Paris. Here at Cirey she didn't have those constraints.

She got to work. "I couldn't perform any experiments, because . . . I wouldn't have been able to hide them from M. de Voltaire." But now the strengths she knew she did have—her easy ability to do long calculations and, even more importantly, to carry through chains of original reasoning—came to the fore. She couldn't use the solid instruments of wood and glass and metal that Voltaire had, so she would simply have to think her way through to the solution.

Her handwriting was messy at the best of times, but now, only able to start her thinking after a long day helping the increasingly desperate Voltaire, she scrawled. She let her wide writing slip down the right-hand edge of her foolscap sheets; she left drenching ink marks, but just blotted or scratched over them and kept on going.

She began with what she knew about light. It manages to rise up out of the sun and cover the immense distance to our planet in barely nine minutes. The only way it can do that is by traveling at fabulous speeds. She'd helped Voltaire with this very calculation when they were preparing their Newton book the year before, so she knew that streams of light from the sun pour down on us, and hit at a speed of close to 1 billion feet per second.

That's faster than anything we're used to. Put a big, half-pound charge of gunpowder in a cannon, and it can send a heavy shot hurtling out of the barrel at about 600 feet per second. Even that "slow" speed is enough to shatter anything it hits. Yet the light from the sun is hitting us a million times faster.

She started thinking about what this meant. If there were any solid particles inside those sunbeams—if light were made of miniaturized particles, as Voltaire and almost everyone else assumed must be the case—then they would utterly devastate life on our planet. Even if atoms of sunlight weighed merely $\frac{1}{15,000}$ of a pound, Emilie calculated, each one would hit the Earth with the power of a full-sized cannonball. You could go further. Even if they were a billion—even a trillion—times smaller, their shatteringly fast impact would still destroy all living beings on the surface of the Earth.

Voltaire should have recognized this, but he was blocked because every authority he'd read had assumed that light had solid weight. They'd ignored the problem of how dangerous it would be to us in that case as it smashed down on our planet.

Emilie, working on her own, was different. She had the imagination and fearlessness to go past currently accepted concepts. What if—she couldn't yet say for sure, but just as something to consider—the assumption everyone made was wrong? And then—this would really be striking if it was true—what if light was something that had no mass at all?

Voltaire would never acknowledge that, least of all from her ("I was disagreeing with almost all his own ideas"). It was a breakthrough for the time. But wasn't the image of light that weighed nothing the only way to explain how the sun worked? For if light did weigh something, how would it keep on lifting out from the sun? All its weight, inside the sun where it began, would make the sun so overwhelmingly massive—and produce such an overwhelming pull of gravity—that nothing would be able to fly out. But we don't see our sun as a dark void in the daytime sky. We see it as a brilliant glowing orb. That glowing is the sign of the weightless light stuff pouring our way.

It was warm at her bedroom writing desk this August, even so long after dark when she was now working, and that made it hard to stay awake. When it got too bad she plunged her arms deep in a vase of ice water. Other times she stood and paced up and down, clapping her hands together to stay awake. Then she'd return to her desk and the rows of candles and continue.

If light really did weigh nothing, then she could work out some of its properties. It had to be very different, for example, from the heat pouring out from her candles. If she put her hand near the rows of candles on the desk now, she'd feel their heat wherever her hand was. Heat spreads slowly, and it's impossible to control its direction. But light, she knew, could be aimed far more easily. Hold a curved mirror beside one of the candles, and if you blew out the others, in the near-darkened room you'd see a single beam of light shooting away from that selected candle, in something much closer to a straight line.

With that, she was ready for her great discovery. Many researchers had used prisms to scatter a beam of light into different-colored rays. They knew it came in different colors. Researchers also accepted that light was powerful enough to heat up our entire planet; everyone knew that as well. Yet she was now insisting that, in addition to all that, it was also entirely massless. That meant that it couldn't have any hidden particles inside to carry that great power. Yet if its great power couldn't be carried along by little particles, then . . .

Was light's great power transmitted by its different colors? This was as extraordinary an idea as anything Locke or Newton had thought up. She must have been mulling it over in some way, even if subconsciously, for a long time, but it all burst into clarity in these hurried late-summer nights. If only she could do the experiments to confirm this now! If she was correct, then perhaps those colors would also carry heat. The different colors of light might even carry different amounts of heat. But how could she check it when Voltaire was hogging all the thermometers that Moussinot sent down from Paris? And even if she did manage to spirit one away when he wasn't looking—and even if

Florent-Claude was willing to help—she still wouldn't be able to do the necessary experiments on her own.

To conduct her test she'd need to pass a single beam of bright sunlight through a prism. That would produce a rainbow splay of colors on the far wall of whatever room she was doing the experiment in. The upstairs room they'd shuttered off the year before for optical research would be ideal for it. Everyone knew that light had great power, as with its ability to create heat, and what she was proposing now was that different colors of light would carry different amounts of that heating power. To test it, all she'd have to do was hang a series of thermometers on the wall, and see if in fact the different colors of light made the different thermometers heat up differently. But it all depended on a bright sunbeam, and that meant she could only do it during the day. The setup would take hours, and Voltaire would certainly find out. She realized, with disappointment, that she couldn't do it. Her idea would have to stay untested.

In the final report she wrote up—sprinting to make the September 1 deadline—she was reduced to suggesting that "fruitful experiments could be conducted concerning the distinctive heating power" of different-colored light. It wouldn't be till more than seventy years later, in 1800, that the famous astronomer Herschel actually carried out those experiments at his home beside the giant forty-foot-long telescope he operated in Slough, England. His procedure was almost exactly what Emilie could have followed, and he used thermometers of no greater sensitivity than Moussinot had in fact sent to Cirey. For whenever one sets up a series of thermometers side by side and lets a prism burst of light shine on them, the sun's position will gradually shift. A thermometer that had been recording the heat of the red part of the rainbow will soon be left in the dark. But its temperature doesn't go down—even though there's no light we can see shining on it. Seemingly invisible light really could carry the power to do that. What Herschel's experiments led to—following, although unknown to him, what Emilie had foreseen at Cirey—was the realization that there are more types of light beams than we can see with our naked eye.

Herschel discovered infrared light, and other investigators at about his time discovered ultraviolet light, and in time it became clear that our universe is full of a tremendous range of "lights," only very few of which are visible to us. Photography, electromagnetic theory, and almost all of modern science and technology developed from or used that result.

Emilie was far from any of those great conclusions. But in those August weeks alone in her candlelit room after midnight, developing her reasoning in step after step, she prepared the paper that was a first, crucial step along that path. (She even put in a suggestion that there might be solar systems where suns glow with colors unknown on Earth—a further hint in the direction of Herschel a century later looking for types of light beyond anything previously known.) Voltaire sent his own paper off with a great flurry, amidst demands for proper sealing wax and envelopes, and no doubt elaborate instructions to the postal couriers. Emilie, however, had to send hers in without anyone knowing, and so probably either rode herself to the nearby town of Vassy or had her husband send it.

Then they waited for months and months as the Academy deliberated, and Voltaire asked everyone he knew what was going on. Emilie had to pretend that although she too wanted to get an early hint, it was only for the sake of supporting Voltaire. Maupertuis was back from the Arctic now, and her husband was one of the many dignitaries who met him, but she knew that noble families understood about loyalty. "M. du Châtelet," she proudly told Maupertuis, when it all came out the next year, ". . . kept my secret so well! He never said anything about it to you, did he?"

Instead, Emilie had to go through all the forms of daily life. There was a new tutor to try to find, and never-ending construction work to supervise, and the painter who insisted on putting scaffolding up in her bedroom to finish the mural on the ceiling, and the other painters, from Watteau's workshop, who wanted to put more touches on the panels beside her desk. There was the way the big mastiffs that slept outside would try to mate with the daintier house dogs that guests brought, and so she'd need to have a word with the groundsman, to keep the mastiffs tied up when the house dogs were in heat, and then a word with the guests, to placate them despite their thoughtlessness. There also was Voltaire spilling oil from the slide-projecting lanterns he liked to entertain guests with all over his hand, and needing to be succored, for the burn could—and he knew how easily this could happen!—lead to a grievous infection unless she ministered to it. It went on and on; it never ended.

"There's so much to do when you have a family, and a house to run," Emilie wrote, "so many unimportant details and obligations, that I barely get any time to read new books. I give up at how ignorant I am. If I were a man I'd . . . just get rid of all the useless things of my life."

Voltaire desperately wanted the Academy's highest acclaim, for that was the one thing that would justify his shift into science. Emilie, by contrast, knew she'd never get the top prize—"the originality of my ideas," she wrote, "would keep me from winning, aside from the other reason [i.e., being a woman]." A few science researchers accepted her at face value, but most weren't going to let a woman try to outthink a man. It reversed all the categories of nature: men, and especially upper-class men, were supposed to take command and explore things; women were not. If by awful chance a woman were to be seen to succeed, it would upset everything. Even so, to Emilie an honorable mention would be fine: "I wanted to stand out from the crowd, and . . . to be taken seriously by the judges."

Finally, in April 1738, the Academy announced its results. All submissions had been numbered, to reduce bias by the judges. By chance, Voltaire's had been logged in as number 7 when it arrived; Emilie's had been logged as number 6. Neither of them was given the top prize—anything linked to Newton's foreign and disturbingly new system was blocked by the old guard, which was still fond of the Frenchman Descartes's vague whirlpools—but both were given special commendations. "The one and the other [of those two essays]," the Academy's formal report stated, "demonstrate wide reading, and a great knowledge of the best works of physics . . . besides, number 6 is by a lady of high rank, Madame du Châtelet, and number seven is by one of our

best poets." (The top prize was actually divided. Part went to a minor French researcher, who merely repeated unimportant—though
patriotic—pre-Newtonian work; part, though, did go to the important
mathematician Leonhard Euler, who offered useful calculations on the
speed of sound.)

As other researchers began to read the papers, it became clear
which submission had been best. Maupertuis was becoming France's
best-known scientist, after his triumphant return from the polar circle,
and the Royal Society in London hung on his words. "Mr. Algarotti is
leaving for London," he wrote to James Jurin, a noted English mathematician, a bit later, "and I've given him this work to pass on to you. Its
author is a young woman, of the highest merit, who's worked on science for several years now, leaving the pleasures of the city and court
behind. She wrote it for the French Academy's prize—when you read
it, you will find it hard to believe they gave the prize to anyone else."

Soon there were positive mentions at the Sorbonne, and word of
Emilie's fame—and how she'd had to accomplish it—began to spread.
The international network of letters and research societies and impor-
tant friends was in full operation. Cirey—and the model of Emilie and
Voltaire's willfully independent life—became even more esteemed.

Before too long, Emilie's reputation had extended from researchers
to the top salons, and then to the less esteemed salons, and finally even
to provincial courts—including the one not far from Cirey in Lorraine,
where one voluble future houseguest resided. Addressing her boyfriend, who was nicknamed Panpan, Madame de Graffigny wrote:

> Oh my God, Panpan, I began to read the dissertation on
> fire that Madame wrote—the one Monsieur her husband
> bragged about. It is so clear! So precise! I apologize to
> Monsieur de Voltaire, but it's much better than his. . . . And
> when did she write this discourse? At night, because she
> was hiding from Voltaire!

14

New Starts

Voltaire tried to pretend Emilie's success didn't matter. He complimented her; he laughed at the way other researchers were ranked higher than themselves simply because those researchers had followed the outdated style of Descartes, which the Academy still officially supported. He had important work to do in science, he let Emilie and Florent-Claude know: there were the page proofs for the Dutch and a possible French edition of his Newton text, astronomical observations to make, other experiments to plan. The fact that Emilie had entered against him was of no importance, he insisted: merely a mark of her lively spirit.

Underneath, though, it had undercut his self-belief. "I am curious," he eventually wrote to a respected physics researcher, Jean-Jacques de Marain, "to know if I am on the right road. That is all I desire. I do not want approbation, but a decision. Am I right? Am I wrong? . . . If my memoir can show that I am not absolutely a stranger in Jerusalem, be kind enough to communicate it."

But neither Marain nor other specialists he quizzed were as fully encouraging as he needed. He'd received a high commendation in the competition, but that wasn't enough. Voltaire had always found it painful admitting errors, and as the weeks went on it became clear that he'd made numerous basic mistakes in using his expensively purchased equipment. Why hadn't he known that putting a glass thermometer, even one of toughened glass, into oil at the temperature of molten metal would burst the glass? Or that even when his thermometers hadn't broken, most of his readings had been invalid from the start because he'd sometimes recorded the temperatures of his thermometers when their bulbs were submerged, but other times when part of the bulb was exposed to the cooling air?

There had also been the embarrassing paragraph where he'd suggested—and, sadly, this was in the manuscript copy now out of his hands in Paris—that he'd found an entirely new phenomenon of nature. He'd reported that when he'd aimed a big focusing lens at a compass needle, lining it up so that sunlight poured through the lens and got concentrated, the compass needle would begin to move. Did that not show that light could create magnetism? Wits at the Academy pointed out, however, that this just showed that Voltaire's focusing lens must have been mounted on a heavy iron base. When ordinary iron is banged hard enough, it becomes partially magnetized. Voltaire must have been striking the iron base of his focusing lens. That's what had deflected the needle.

He was diminished in the educated public's view, and above all in Emilie's eyes. He began to doubt whether he should be dabbling in science at all. As a result, Voltaire responded as he always did under stress. He got ill, and insisted it was serious this time; he was unable to get out of bed, and had to be very carefully tended by everyone. Then, when he was able to croak out a few words and feebly gesture for writing paper and his quills, he started having his Paris agent Moussinot buy and sell things, expensive things: substantial bond placements, and thousands of acres of real estate. It reminded him of the power he still possessed. Only then did he do what he'd always known would lastingly cure him: he began to write.

His work in literature had placed him at the top in Europe, so a triumphant return to the arts would be the right therapy now. At first there were just little rhyming nothings to friends. Even before the Academy's results were in, one of these friends had written to suggest that Voltaire should get out of science, and return to literature, his true occupation. Voltaire replied in a little ditty:

> *My friend I'll do what you advise,*
> *Your counsel seems most sound and wise;*
> *Besides, it suits my inclination,*
> *That I resume my occupation.*

Voltaire made it clear to everyone that he was not exactly quitting science—that would have been cowardice—but rather that he was merely going to spend a little time relaxing in other fields. He began with drama, finding himself drawn toward a story where there's a noble yet cruelly misunderstood man, and a powerful woman who doesn't recognize the man's great strengths. She can't see how truly valorous he can be, but underneath he's actually a descendant of Hercules: that's how powerful he is. As he went on with the play there were twists and turns, with critical Parisian researchers, no, with critical ancient Greek warlords trying to undercut the hero and make him look even less worthy in her eyes. He slays some of them—he's really quite impressive with a sword—and maneuvers his way around most of the others, and at the end . . . what?

Voltaire was stumped: it was his fifth-act problem again, and writing a satisfying ending hadn't become much easier than when he'd struggled with his earlier dramatic effort to impress Emilie, writing the Inca play here at Cirey over three years before. There he'd finally found an easy way out, especially when his wishes had come true in reality: the two lovers had embraced and prepared to go off to the jungle to live in happiness forever. In this new play—called *Mérope,* and destined to become one of his most frequently performed works—something different was missing, but he couldn't tell what it was. He bothered his friends, to see if they could help, and when they couldn't bear continuing to try solving it for him, he put it aside. But he wasn't too disappointed, for now he was warmed up, getting back into his stride. Plays had been his strength for years, but if he was really going to show what he could do in literature, it would be more impressive if he invented yet another new form, as he had with the Letters from England.

There was in fact something lurking from that English visit. He'd loved Jonathan Swift's approach in *Gulliver's Travels* of recounting an imaginary voyage as if it were true, by pretending to have a narrator who'd seen it. He'd also had several dinners with Alexander Pope and had kept up with everything Pope had published in the years since. In particular, in 1733 Pope had begun publishing his long verse essay titled *Essay on Man*. Pope's content was clearly inadequate, and when the poem first came out, Voltaire and Emilie had laughed at how the poor Englishman had lived up to national stereotypes by forgetting to list passion as one of the motivating forces in life. But as a professional writer, Voltaire found it intriguing to see a tightly structured, very long poem that at least tried to carry through a systematic account of human nature in the world. It could be a great way to let out one's inner feelings.

Some of Voltaire's drafts for this new-style poem were a bit too raw. He tried a section on envy, which described how poisonous the feeling could be: how it's like a giant ogre imprisoned deep underground, swearing and struggling to tear its way to the surface. A copy of that section went to Frederick at Rheinsberg, who replied, most civilly, that it was perhaps a bit personal, and some refinements in phrasing might be in order. Voltaire toned it down.

Those cuts were easy, for Voltaire now had his strength back. He began to write afresh, moving away from his embarrassment at the mediocrity of his science research compared with Emilie's. (They'd both placed highly, but she'd come up with excellent findings without the advantage of his expensive equipment; he also recognized that she had no doubt been ranked lower than she deserved because of her sex.) He went on with his new poem—he called it a *Discourse in Verse on Man*—and now began to use the twists he'd always liked from Jonathan Swift, where animals can talk and size scales are reversed. He

Discourse in verse
Sur man.

imagined a sage overhearing a group of mice speaking, and what the mice say is that they are very happy to have such a charming world in which to live. All they need do is look before them to see that the palace they live in is clearly built for them: God has put big holes in it, so they can scurry in and out, and there are delectable chunks of food magically appearing on the floors of that palace—"created from the hand of nature."

The mice go on to praise the Lord, for even the cats that sometimes prowl in their palace are clearly put there just to instruct and correct mice, further proving the beneficence—the clearly mouse-centered purpose—of the universe in which they live.

Voltaire was writing fast now, examining the meaning of his own life, of course, and the draft poured out: after the mice he wrote in a group of sheep bleating that no, it is clear that the mice are deluded, and that in fact the world has been designed for them—look at all the nice humans who let the sheep stand in fields, and obediently feed them, and wash them, and lead them into safe paddocks.

It went on and on. Next there are humans who insist that they are the ones the universe is designed for (with winds designed to transport their ships, and stars in position to light their way); then there are angels, who insist that no, *they* are the true reason for creation, as the fine planets waiting for their angelic breath to rotate in orbit clearly prove.

Why stop there? The narrator wants to find out more of what this means: to understand the brevity of life, and the fading of human love. Voltaire's writing became beautiful as he gave dreams of his Emilie, or another wise alien visitor, soaring down to help, and saying that the fundamental secret lies in giving happiness to others. The narrator is desperate to learn how to do that. But this the visitor is not allowed to tell. It flies away, as kind as ever, to the realm where all answers lie. Voltaire, waiting below, can only watch it go.

What he wrote was new and quite revolutionary: commenting on the foolishness of man's grand self-perception, yet doing so not through hammering mockery, but in a tender, wistful story. Even so, as with almost all Voltaire's works of this period, royal censorship meant that it couldn't be officially published. It was circulated as if in an intellectual samizdat, among his friends and a few interested correspondents. The first parts were eventually published anonymously, with Voltaire publicly disavowing his authorship; later a more complete edition was printed abroad, to be smuggled back into France.

IN THE months after the Academy papers, Emilie paused in her own research, partly not to upset Voltaire and partly because she was finding it hard to get back the free time she needed to come up with a fresh topic. Instead, there was the new tutor to convince to come to distant Cirey for her son ("he's such a sweet-natured boy," she wrote imploringly in one request letter), and the funds to arrange for her half sister, Michelle. There was ever more construction, and tapestries, and temperamental cooks, and even an extra expenditure on Maupertuis's account, to help support the two young Lapp women who'd followed him down to Paris from his polar expedition and had no one else to take care of them when he was out of town.

It was a detail she could learn about in person, for with the Lapland expedition over, Maupertuis came to Cirey for a visit. Voltaire encouraged the trip, recognizing that although Emilie's ex-lovers might be tempted to revisit an old affair far away in Paris, they'd have second thoughts with Voltaire around and being graciously hospitable.

Maupertuis and his team had had time to go over their measurements and were convinced they'd proved that Newton was right, and the Earth really was flatter near the poles. Voltaire was delighted. He knew that the main critic of Newton in France was Jacques Cassini, head of the Paris observatory. He now merrily declared that "Maupertuis has flattened the Earth and Cassini."

Since Emilie didn't know what to do next, she fell back on several of the things she and Voltaire used to do that gave them pleasure. Right under the roof at Cirey was a cramped open space where they'd built a tiny theater, with just two small rows of cushioned benches for seats, and a narrow gap in front of the stage for the plank with candles that could be raised or lowered—this was the stage lights. Now she encouraged Voltaire to fill up their time with more performances there. The material was easy enough to obtain, for Voltaire had years of plays he'd written stacked up in his study ("our first rule is that we perform only what's been written here"). He would get to be the director as well as the male lead; Emilie of course was the female lead. Everyone at Cirey was liable to be roped in for additional roles: cooks, butlers, groundskeepers, and any other staff who were needed to fill out the script. (The pudgy Madame Champbonin was a regular onstage; the more beautiful Comtesse de la Neuville seems to have been too wooden as an actress or singer, and so was brought in more for stage ornamentation than for sound.)

The children loved it. On the day of performances, Emilie's son would join Champbonin's older son in racing around the château, putting up posters they'd prepared, which announced the night's title. Then after dinner there'd be the steep climb up the stairs from the top inhabited floor of the house to this hidden-away theater, lighted candles shielded carefully against the gusts from cracks in the roof. On winter nights Emilie and Voltaire and their guests would wear layer upon layer of coats, and if it wasn't too windy they could hear the wolf packs in the forests across the river. On summer nights it was the opposite: sweltering in this wooden attic, where all the day's heat had soaked in.

A final time-passing pleasure was an innovation Emilie had installed on the entry level of the château: a private bathing room—and one of the first in France. Having a bathtub for long soaking wouldn't have made sense in Paris, with all the excrement, urine, ligaments, and other items that poured into the Seine (and often polluted ostensibly fresher sources as well). But not only was the water cleaner in Cirey. There was also something more to Emilie's innovation. It had to do with privacy.

Previous houses had usually been designed without corridors, and to get to a particular room, you'd simply walk through any other rooms that happened to be on the way. Whether the individuals you passed were praying, dressing, cooking, chatting, or defecating, you'd see them as you marched along. That was normal: even Louis XIV at Versailles had been comfortable chatting with appropriate nobles while seated on his *"chaise percée,"* a chair that had a hole in the seat and a chamber pot beneath.

By the time Emilie and Voltaire had begun redesigning Cirey, though, they once again picked up on—and helped boost—a trend accepting the right to have more privacy. Their rooms weren't quite as demarcated as we're used to today—the corridor that went by Emilie's bedroom was only partly on the outside of the room, and rather seems to have gone partly past her bed—but they were changing in that direction. Her new tub and bathing room were marks of this transition. She'd installed comfortable sofas near the tub, for at least some visitors to sit and chat. When it came time for more hot water to be carried in and poured on her, she had no problem with an ordinary male servant doing the pouring. But her bath was not freestanding in a purely public space; it was in an attractively marbled room that could be closed off when she wished.

AFTER Maupertuis left, Emilie wrote to her scientific contacts, backing his work against the ever-critical Cassini. But she was also aware of Voltaire's sensitivity, and so made little self-deprecating remarks to friends who would pass on her words to him, suggesting that she'd certainly need help in understanding Maupertuis's complex explanations; she even sent an anonymous review to a Paris journal, lauding Voltaire's scientific work.

No one was fooled. She understood Maupertuis's calculations perfectly well—indeed, she had helped Voltaire through the stellar angle calculations in their own Newton book. And because of the recognition she'd received from her fire paper, as well as follow-up work she'd done, she was now active in the Europe-wide networks of scientists who corresponded with each other: letters were coming in from important researchers in Italy, Switzerland, England. It was irritating having to tend Voltaire's ego when what she really wanted was to be free to get back into her research. Everyone who counted in this science community was watching to see what project she'd choose next, kept informed by that constant stream of letters.

Their unspoken tension was interrupted by a visit from Voltaire's orphaned niece, whose late mother—Voltaire's little sister—had been the one member of his family he'd always loved. He and Emilie barely knew the niece, a young woman named Marie-Louise, yet now, in the spring of 1738, she'd married a government official named M. Denis, and was coming down for the honeymoon.

Something went very wrong. Marie-Louise recognized that Emilie was attractive, and it also became clear to Marie-Louise how young her uncle's lady was, only a few years older than Marie-Louise herself. Yet while Monsieur Denis might be able to give her a good life, it would never be anything like this: the fabulous mansion, the furnishing with gold and silver everywhere, the gardens and guest rooms, and the easy mentions of so many of Europe's cultural and political elite, as well as copies of their books and manuscripts.

Marie-Louise had once written to her uncle that she was reading John Locke. Clearly she hadn't meant that—it's unclear if she ever read anything more than a light novel in her life—but it had seemed fine to say in a letter. Yet here, if one referred to such a thing, Emilie was likely to sit her down and with apparent eagerness launch into a burst of words to discuss Locke's philosophy.

A monster of envy reared. Cirey was ugly, Marie-Louise declared in a desperate letter she wrote soon after, and it was surrounded by vile mountains (there are no mountains in Champagne), and, and—and just everything was wrong! "My uncle is lost to his friends . . . he's impossibly linked to Châtelet . . . no one can break the chains . . . he hardly sees anyone else . . . she does everything to enchant him." The tension was so bad that Voltaire felt a sudden illness coming on, and took to his bed. But transport for visitors was hard to arrange, and it was nearly a week more before Emilie could organize a coach and get the honeymooning couple to leave.

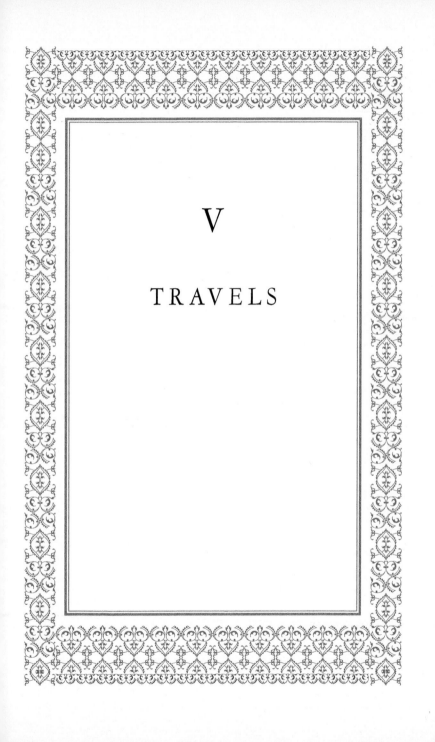

V

TRAVELS

15

Leibniz's World

For a while Voltaire and Emilie went on with their usual schedule, trying hard to make their old patterns work. But even though Marie-
Louise had been an unpleasant guest, she'd clearly been in love with
her new husband: whispering sweet words, probably staying close to
his side; delighting when Voltaire—briefly managing to stagger upright from his sickbed—had been charming to them both. The contrast with how Emilie and Voltaire lived together now was sadly clear.

Emilie was spending ever more time alone in her rooms, and even
though she carefully avoided discussing what she might be working
on, the hints Voltaire picked up—from the books she ordered and the
researchers she wrote to—made him think that she was abandoning
Newton and switching allegiance to the late German diplomat and
scholar Leibniz.

How could that be? Emilie herself had emphasized to Voltaire
that Newton was the greatest thinker there had ever been. And hadn't
Newton been proved entirely right by Maupertuis's polar trip? It was
the one constant that Voltaire could hold on to, even as his own efforts

in science were crumbling. Yet Leibniz had been Newton's mortal enemy; their quarrels had dominated European science for more than a decade before and after 1700, and Newton had become vitriolic whenever Leibniz's name was mentioned at meetings of the Royal Society. (The ostensible argument had been the matter of who had invented the calculus first. Leibniz had certainly published it first, and probably worked it out on his own; Newton, however, had the habit of keeping his great discoveries private, and insisted—plausibly—that he had created it first.)

Emilie was asserting her independence in her choice of topic. She suspected there were important areas in science *beyond* what Maupertuis had confirmed about Newton, and that these areas were still open to discussion. That's what she was going to investigate.

She was also offended by Voltaire's work choices. She respected him as a poet, of course, but now he was insisting on writing history, and returning to the manuscript he'd begun on the long reign of Louis XIV. Yet who cared about the arbitrary battles of one king against another? In her view, writing history wasn't the way to start a profound social science. She saw it as just a listing of arrogant royals engaging in one strutting contest after another.

They were tense with each other now, and Voltaire increasingly sulked, while Emilie became short-tempered. The gossipy Madame de Graffigny came for her none-too-welcome visit around this time, and after several weeks began nosing around among locked desk drawers. Emilie accused her of stealing illicit papers of Voltaire's that she could pass on to stir up trouble.

De Graffigny pleaded that she was innocent, and then suddenly Emilie started screaming at her, saying that she'd been giving her shelter for all these weeks—not because she liked her, God knows, but merely out of obligation. Yet in exchange she was being betrayed! Emilie was taking out her frustrations with Voltaire on this unsuspecting visitor. It went on, louder and louder, till Voltaire put his arm around Emilie and led her away from the terrified—though quite likely guilty—guest. There were only perfunctory apologies the next day, and finally de Graffigny left.

Yet even when a couple is irritable and exasperated by each other, they often don't want to go so far as to admit it explicitly. Voltaire half-heartedly tried his hypochondria again, but it got boring to stay in bed so much, and in any case Emilie saw through it. They tried their other usual evasion—of inviting lots of house guests to stay—and for a while they also splurged on gifts for each other, sending out orders to Moussinot in Paris for yet more trinkets, jewels, paintings. But Moussinot was so efficient, and knew the shops in Paris so well, that this was too easy. None of it worked, and they were both unhappy. They needed to do something else.

That's what gave them an enormous idea. Why not buy a brand-new house? It couldn't be another isolated château—there was no reason to lose Cirey as their main home—but if the court's censorship ever eased up enough for Voltaire to publish in France, then having a base in Paris would make sense.

There was one building in Paris so impressive that they both knew they shouldn't consider it at all. But there's a thrill in doing something you shouldn't. On the smaller of the two islands in the Seine at the heart of Paris, right where the Ile St. Louis narrows like the prow of a ship, is one of the city's most beautiful mansions. It was already a century old by this time. The architect was Le Vau, who had gone on to create Versailles. The interior decorations were by Le Brun, and he too had ended up at Versailles, becoming the chief designer of interior furnishings there. It was called the Palais Lambert, and for the first time in many years was now on the market. The owners may have thought they would get a good deal when some sort of rural military figure (Florent-Claude was involved, for the purchase had to be in his name, not Emilie's) and also a poet, however distinguished, proposed to negotiate with them. But Florent-Claude was a very sensible man—he'd efficiently led his troops in killing well-armed enemies—and Voltaire was so pleased at the possibility of negotiations that his health recovered entirely. He had been outwitting French aristocrats with his financial acumen for years.

The negotiations were carried out so deftly that it's quite possible the sellers felt they'd managed a good deal, even when they signed over the deed. Voltaire was happy to let them feel that, as it meant they wouldn't come back in a court case challenging the deal as having been unfair (as was often done if the sellers felt they'd been swindled). The absolute value was still high—it was one of the grandest houses in the most civilized city in the world—but he, Emilie, and Florent-Claude had ended up buying the Palais for just about 20 percent of what its original construction costs had been.

The negotiating was fun, and brought Voltaire and Emilie together in a way they hadn't felt for almost a year. Even so, and despite their huge wealth, the new house was a massive undertaking, and they were in danger of falling short. Luckily a potential source of new income came their way.

Florent-Claude had a relative—a very old relative, in poor health—with a complex series of land holdings up in Flanders, which was part of an inheritance battle between factions in the du Châtelet family that had been simmering for sixty years. The relative had visited Cirey recently and made it clear that he was not long for this world. If Emilie could accelerate the court's deliberation, then she and Florent-Claude would receive a great deal of money when the relative died, which they and Voltaire could use to finish paying off the Palais Lambert.

Thus their plan. Since they didn't want to argue with each other, after all the upsets from the fire experiments, they had decided that buying and fixing up an additional house would be a safe shared activity. But since the house was so expensive, and a trip to Brussels could help hurry along the inheritance court case that would give them extra money, they'd take the occasion to relax by traveling to the Low Countries. They both realized they needed more shared projects like this, far removed from literature or science.

It wasn't quite as expected, for the Flanders population, they soon found on their trip north, was not known for its intellectual curiosity. Spanish troops had spent over a hundred years closing Protestant schools, burning Protestant churches, and torturing very many Protestant individuals—especially any intellectually or politically curious ones—in the Flemish lands. Their labors had been intermittently interrupted by British, Dutch, and other northern troops, who'd repaid the favor by closing Catholic schools, burning Catholic churches, and torturing very many Catholic individuals—especially intellectually curious ones—whenever *they'd* had the chance. Fighting had ended since the Austrian Habsburgs had taken over twenty-five years before, but from it all most survivors had wisely concluded that venturing opinions, or reading too much, was not a wise course of action.

The result—as when Emilie and Voltaire stayed at a castle that had no books whatsoever—was to bring them closer together, since each saw how much they really did have in common. When they reached Brussels they decided to throw a fireworks party to see if that might attract some more interesting locals. Card games were apparently the main social draw in Brussels, so Voltaire, ingenious as ever, arranged fireworks that would light up to resemble playing cards, three red fireworks in a rough heart-shaped pattern suggesting the three of hearts, and so on. The plotting worked, and they did meet a few locals they stayed sociable with.

Once they settled, Voltaire took out his essays and poems and plays, but he didn't achieve much. He needed Emilie's enthusiastic support, but she was distracted, busy now with learning law, taking Flemish lessons, supervising legal strategy, improving her calculus, relaxing by writing a translation of Sophocles' *Oedipus Rex,* and attending church regularly.

Even that was just in her spare time. Her deepest focus was still on science, and she was excited about something big: deeper research into work started by that mysterious Baron Gottfried von Leibniz, who'd died in 1716, when Emilie was just nine. Many mathematicians on the Continent, as we saw, whispered that Leibniz was the one who'd invented the calculus, not the Englishman Newton. But more importantly, Emilie had heard that Leibniz had suggested a detailed way God could control the universe—and what was greater, he seemed to have proof. The difference between the two men was more than just a personal rivalry. Within Newton's system, there was no space for what Leibniz proposed.

Emilie wanted to understand what Leibniz had proposed. At Cirey she'd spent so long analyzing the Bible that she could no longer believe in the simple, literal beliefs she'd been raised with. But she was still religious. If there was a more complex, more subtle God, she was willing even to go beyond Newton to find it.

Leibniz, she found out, had taken a curiously indirect approach in his research. One of his most important examples began with what seemed an entirely innocuous question. If you dangle a chain from a high point and a lower point, what shape does that dangling chain take?

That seems straightforward enough. Think, for example, of the long swooping cables in a modern suspension bridge, such as San Francisco's Golden Gate. The cable stretches from the top of one tower down almost to the roadway before it then is lifted up to the top of the next tower.

That cable sags, of course, but it doesn't first sag straight downward and then take a sharp turn horizontally along the roadway. Nor, however, does it go in a perfect 45-degree line from its high tower till it's above the roadway, and then at that point suddenly tilt straight up. How to predict the intermediate curve it really does follow?

The way Leibniz and his followers went about this was to imagine tying lots of different ropes to the top of the bridge's suspension tower and connecting them all to the same point on the roadway. Some of the ropes are pulled so tight that they do stretch in a nearly straight line; others are left to sag so much that they almost hit the roadway; others are given an intermediate degree of sag. Now climb to the top of the tower and string a big round bead on each of the ropes. Let all the beads go at the same time. Imagine there's no friction.

They'll all start skidding down their different ropes, and they'll all take different amounts of time. The ones on ropes that sag nearly straight down will get the fastest start—they'll be falling almost vertically at first—but then they'll slow down as they reach the near-horizontal lower stretch of the rope. The beads that are on straighter ropes won't slow down so much near the end, but of course they won't get the same boost from being in free fall near the start.

There can be thousands, millions of possible ropes, yet only one will be the winner, leading its bead to the finishing line down on the roadway fastest. This curve of the winning rope, it turns out, is very closely related to the shape used by engineers on real suspension bridges. It's not mere coincidence. It's the shape that physical objects in our world really do take.

This was astonishing. Did God actually measure thousands or millions of possible paths and work out which one would let a bead slide down fastest, then use that as His basis for working out what the rippling tension in a real bridge's curved cables should be? To Voltaire the question would have been ridiculous. To Emilie it was wondrous. Maupertuis had hoped to find out whether God actively intervened in our world, by voyaging to the high Arctic. But that would just be a single, unique measurement: saying what our planet's overall shape was like, but not showing how to track God's hand as it actually intervened in ordinary events around us. Taking Leibniz seriously, though, was different. It meant believing that in some way God was sifting through these millions of possible measurements all the time, selecting for us the single one that kept the total time of this mythical bead's travel to a minimum.

These were the issues Emilie wanted to explore further. No one had synthesized the thinking of Leibniz and Newton before. Why couldn't she, showing how the best ideas of both their systems could be combined? It would be a step beyond her uncredited co-authorship of that recap of Newton's basic work that she and Voltaire had written at Cirey. Other researchers wouldn't consider undertaking the new syntheses she had in mind, for they were all, very distinctly, either in the Newton camp or in the Leibniz camp. But once again there were advantages in being excluded from the main science academies. Emilie was far enough outside that she could view them both objectively.

Voltaire wouldn't be happy with that—he worshiped Newton, and felt he had to despise Leibniz—but what alternative did she have? She knew that the insights she'd come up with from her fire experiments (about new forms of light) were too far in advance of her time to be followed up by the researchers she was corresponding with.

She'd been isolated long enough in her intellectual life before she'd met Voltaire.

She wasn't going to be isolated again.

Something important was going on. In previous periods, "time" had been something that the Church controlled: there were regular, recurring festivals, and regular, recurring daily prayers. Everything fitted within established traditions; nothing fundamental was ever supposed to change. When Emilie had been a child, her life had been planned for her in a similar way: there was to be a genteel yet trivial education in etiquette, marriage, and then subservience to a wealthy man. She was supposed to live as her mother had lived; any daughter she had was expected to live the same as well.

But a different sort of linear time was also making its appearance. In this new approach, events happened in a sequence that didn't circle back on itself, dully repeating from year to year, lifetime to lifetime. Instead, each day and each year might reveal something new. That's how Emilie wanted to live. There were hints of it at the time, especially with so many new technologies: big tapestry factories being created where none had existed before, new pumping engines that drained swamps or supplied water, new manufacturing processes. Careers and the relative positions of groups in society also seemed to be transforming more quickly than before. Amidst all that tumult, Emilie would start a new, self-chosen life.

There was another powerful idea. Our modern notion of optimism comes not so much from human affairs as from these early-eighteenth-century studies of how trajectories can take the "optimum" path (as with the Golden Gate bridge example above). Emilie was one of the very first people to use the word *optimiste,* and she did so in her mathematical analyses of these curves, in accord with her (and Leibniz's) belief that there's a beneficent deity behind the seemingly random events we see around us. An optimist was someone who believed that however complicated or random or odd a stretching curve might seem, if we had enough insight then we could understand the simple guiding principle from which it actually came. The concept then spread from mathematics to mean anyone who believes that such an optimal path can open up in life.

It was hard to keep these views entirely private from Voltaire, for although their rented house in Brussels was big, it wasn't quite as spacious as Cirey had been. Also, who could turn down his editorial help? Despite herself, Emilie let him read portions of the text she was working on. He tried to stick to just expository corrections and would neatly ink little queries in the margin ("explain more," "an example, please," "which means exactly what . . . ?"). But at times he couldn't help commenting on the work overall and letting Emilie know how inane he felt this genre of concerns to be.

To Voltaire, she seemed to be saying that there are many possible worlds, yet somehow, magically, we automatically are living in one that is perfect. But how could all the flaws we see around us—disease and torture and all the rest—be a mark of a perfect world? It was the opposite of what he'd been saying in his *Discourse in Verse on Man,* where he'd mocked the mice and other creatures that believed the universe *was* created for them.

Their relationship couldn't take this. Voltaire had always seemed to treat Emilie as an independent person, but now he responded as if deep down he still expected her to defer to him. Yet here she was attempting to surpass him, and discard what he'd believed. It was a betrayal. He was so upset that he began publishing public rebuttals of her work, scorning her for pretending that we lived in the best of all possible worlds. (His critiques were written as passionate technical arguments now, but in two decades he'd be elaborating the points in his philosophical fable *Candide.*) His writing hurt Emilie, for it was going well beyond their agreement to respect each other's separate study. But their argument summarized yet more key responses to modernity.

In medieval times, before modern science, it had been easy to accept that God shaped everything that we saw or lived through. There were no "coincidences," because there were no separate, freely moving causal lines to "co-incide." But the scientific revolution had changed that. Voltaire believed that almost everything we saw around us really was just the result of chance.

He liked that, for since the details of what we experienced were not all part of a complex divine plan, then we had the opportunity to reach out, intervene, and reform the world around us. In the medieval view, for example, God ordained when and where disease was to occur. In the modern view—as Voltaire saw it—disease happened because, for example, taxes were being misused and so clean water wasn't supplied to city slums. The French administration couldn't do anything about a divinely ordained disease, but it could certainly work to get more efficient government officers who would ensure that everyone had fresh water.

Emilie, however, was angry, convinced that Voltaire was willfully taking what she said the wrong way. Didn't he realize she was the last person who'd declare we could never make an effort to improve our lives? The world wasn't perfect—it would be inane to say that. All she was asserting, rather, was that before you began any course of action, it would be wise to look more closely at the subtleties of how things were connected in the world around us. Voltaire believed in straight, narrow reason to fix things. Emilie saw a world of more subtle interrelations.

The evidence seemed to be everywhere, once you knew how to look. Cynics might say that the universe isn't really arranged in the best way. Our eyes, for example, are so weak that even simple animals, such as hawks, can see much better. But Emilie countered that. Our eyes have a limit to their magnifying power, she wrote, but it's a limit that's *forced* on us by a higher good. For suppose somehow we had been granted eyes that were ten times or even a hundred times more powerful than now. We'd be able to see fine details, of course. But we wouldn't be able to see any overall topography or shapes. We'd be bewildered, unable to orient ourselves. What seems a limitation—the fact that our eyes aren't as strong as our best optical machines—is actually a strength. If they were that strong, we'd be as useless as a blinded Samson.

That, she pointed out, is what Leibniz was getting at. Clearly, we don't live in a perfect world. But that's because there *is* no such thing as a perfect world. Rather, every world that can possibly exist is going to have these sorts of trade-offs. Although our world isn't ideal, it might still be the best possible.

Voltaire didn't listen. Their arguments were getting worse—and then they both pulled back. This wasn't what they'd come to Brussels for. Maybe things would be easier if they tried Paris.

16

New House, New King

Although they arrived ostensibly to inspect their new home, Emilie and Voltaire's first stop was at Richelieu's town house in the Marais, where his young bride, Elisabeth, was bleeding from complications of pregnancy. From Emilie's years of experience with Voltaire's illnesses, she knew that the one certain way to make a patient worse was to let doctors near. The rusty hooked knives they brought, and worst of all, their insistence that home visits should begin with sharp open cuts so that the patient poured out more blood, were treatments Emilie knew Elisabeth had to avoid. Only when she improved did Emilie and Voltaire visit their new home, which they still hadn't seen.

They rode over the crowded bridges on the Seine, first passing across the larger island, the Ile de la Cité. This held the Palais de Justice, where Voltaire's Letters from England had been torn apart and burned by the public executioner. But that was years ago, and since Voltaire had carefully not said too much to Emilie about the possibly subversive history of Louis XIV he was secretly printing, she had no reason to worry that it might happen again. Then there was another bridge, connecting the big island to the smaller one, and then it was just a short ride to their house.

They loved it. Voltaire wrote to Fawkener (again in English) that it "is without doubt the finest [house] of Paris, and situated in a position worthy of Constantinople; for, it looks upon the river, and a long tract of lands interspers'd with pretty houses is to be seen from every window." With the Brussels arguments far away, he was content: "Upon my word," Voltaire went on to Fawkener, "I [could not] live without that Lady, who . . . understands Newton, she despises superstition, in short she makes me happy."

Emilie was content too. There was much less pressure on their relationship in Paris. Instead of facing each other with the utterly identical schedule of coffee, then work, then riding, then dinner, day after day, as at Cirey, now each had fresh things to tell the other. Voltaire had found out, for example, that their failed tutor, the pudgy Linant, had given up teaching, the poor man, and was trying to make a living as a writer. He was even planning to submit an entry for the king's prize essay competition. Since Voltaire and Emilie didn't want him to starve, Voltaire discreetly gave him some cash through an intermediary; Emilie, for her part, wrote letters of recommendation for the future tutoring jobs he would need after he failed to complete his prize essay.

Other arrangements would be more satisfying. Emilie had hired an advanced tutor for herself, the young Swiss mathematician Samuel Koenig. But soon she had outgrown what he could teach (and Voltaire's nerves couldn't take overhearing her explain that fact to him much longer). The most distinguished possible replacement would be Johann Bernoulli, in Basel, but he was past his best work and too old to move to Paris. His son, however—somewhat less than creatively also named Johann Bernoulli—had supplanted him as perhaps the leading active mathematician in Europe.

It would be invaluable to have him in Paris, not least because Emilie had heard that he too was keen on extending the now increasingly forgotten, fascinating approaches of Leibniz. Unfortunately, Bernoulli junior showed little interest in leaving his comfortable establishment in

Emilie du Châtelet. The Largillière portrait.

Voltaire. Also by Largillière.

Louis XV, age five.

The Bastille, 1789.

The Comédie Française, where many of Voltaire's plays were premiered.

Frederick the Great.

Richelieu in old age.

Madame de Pompadour, by de la Tour.

Isaac Newton, shortly after finishing his *Principia*. The Kneller portrait.

Card playing at Versailles. The picture is from late February 1745; Emilie was likely to have been there that evening.

Château de Sceaux, where Voltaire began his philosophical fables while in hiding.

Voltaire and his niece, Marie-Louise.

Château de Cirey. Voltaire's doorway is straight ahead; Emilie's rooms are on the right.

Stanislas's gardens at Lunéville, 1740s, where Emilie met Saint-Lambert.

Saint-Lambert.

Catherine, Marquise de Boufflers, Emilie's
supposed friend, who turned against her.

PRINCIPES
MATHÉMATIQUES
DE LA
PHILOSOPHIE NATURELLE,

Par feu Madame la Marquise DU CHASTELLET.

TOME PREMIER.

A PARIS,

Chez { DESAINT & SAILLANT, rue S. Jean de Beauvais,
LAMBERT, Imprimeur - Libraire, rue & à côté
de la Comédie Françoise, au Parnasse.

M. D C C L I X
AVEC APPROBATION ET PRIVILEGE DU ROI.

Title page of Emilie's final work, completed just days before her death.

Basel. But Emilie's work was going so well that she was confident in every activity she began to plan, and her six years with Voltaire had done wonders in showing her the many ways of getting around such obstacles.

She realized she'd need to get Maupertuis to back up her request to Bernoulli. If she was charming, and even flirted with Maupertuis a bit, that wouldn't hurt in getting him to help. "Here you are back in Paris," she wrote Maupertuis a few days later, "yet I had to find it out from someone else. Ah, this is very bad. . . . But do come and see us at the Opéra, in M. de Richelieu's box. Madame de Richelieu is counting on you dining with us today." Maupertuis tried to hide, by ignoring the invitation, but Emilie kept at him—"Despite your prodigious indifference, sir, Madame de Richelieu again requests you to dine with us today." In a few days he relented, of course, and wrote the encouraging letter she wanted to Bernoulli.

With that opening, Emilie could now turn directly to Bernoulli: "I hope, sir," she wrote to him in Switzerland, "that you would like to stay with us, and for three years at least. (I flatter myself that you will find Paris agreeable enough to stay longer.) . . . You will have an attractive apartment in my new house. . . . I suspect that I could also arrange for you to be admitted to the Academy of Sciences."

Through it all, she and Voltaire were now out and about in society. They were the most sought-after couple in Paris: elegant, articulate, and—for most—still powerfully mysterious. The fact that she was still married gave an extra thrill. Emilie had left the city five years earlier barely known. Now almost everyone who counted had heard rumors that she was a woman who'd learned Latin, English, Italian, and a good bit of Dutch and Greek; translated Virgil, as well as English social critics; written commentaries on the Bible; done all the technical work for a shared exposition of Newton; performed original research on fire and light; accumulated one of Europe's leading research libraries; and made Cirey a research center for important thinkers. Most of all, she'd created a unique way of living, and become—despite having been excluded from all the official, males-only institutions—a respected correspondent with top researchers in England, Italy, and France. It was the most unconventional of lives, and despite all the problems, she and Voltaire relished it.

In Paris those five years before, Newton and science generally had scarcely been discussed in popular circles. Now, though, helped by the flurry of letters and manuscripts sent out from Cirey, as well as the visitors Emilie had invited there, that had changed. As one observer put it: "All Paris resounds with Newton, all Paris stammers Newton, all Paris studies and learns Newton." Everything she'd been promoting was beginning to take.

Voltaire enjoyed the socializing too, after the years away in Cirey, though he sometimes pretended otherwise. "Paris," he wrote, as if resignedly, to Madame Champbonin, who was hanging on his every word back in Cirey, "is an abyss, where one loses repose and the contemplation of one's soul. . . . I am dragged in spite of myself into the stream. I go, I come. I sup at one end of the town, to sup the next night at the other end. . . . There is not one instant to oneself."

Several of the main thinkers who would carry the next stage of the Enlightenment forward were already in Paris, albeit still just young men in their twenties, hovering on the edge of the salons. For them, Voltaire was a god. They all wanted the liberty that not depending on the whims of rich patrons would give them. And here was this most debonair man, fresh from his proudly independent life with Emilie at Cirey, showing them it could be done. Even more, the elaborate understanding of modern science he'd developed with Emilie made his insights irresistible.

When discussion turned to the soul, for example, the visitors from Cirey might point out that Newton had shown that the universe was constructed in such a way that we could never know what the underlying nature of any object really was. All we could accurately do was describe its surface behavior.

This was an astonishing thought, for it led to heresy of the most extreme sort. If we couldn't presume to understand the inner thoughts of others, for example, then we'd have no reason to torture them to ensure they shared our religious beliefs. The essence of the French state, however, was that the king and his officers were at one with the Church. If someone was suspected of running a Protestant religious service, that person was to be tortured and brutalized with the state's full support. Protestant vicars were hanged; individuals attending Protestant services had often been arrested, beaten, and—as we saw— sent to be slaves on Mediterranean galleys. There was no private realm into which the state couldn't delve.

That's why the sensual pleasures at Cirey had been so important. They suggested a world in which surface pleasures could be valued as well as the individual choices behind them. It was the opposite of the official state position, which held that invisible sins were what should be valued, and that if sinners weren't led to redemption by the proper path, they were to be crushed.

Although Voltaire could be self-centered and loved to take over conversations, the young men who were making their way in Paris were now watching him use these science-based insights to go beyond his usual mocking remarks about the old institutions that most Frenchmen had to live under. For Voltaire now wanted to be more than a critic.

He wanted to change the world.

The question was how. Voltaire had long since realized that he was getting out of his depth when it came to research in science. (He'd never admit it to Emilie, but their debates in Brussels had made those limits even clearer than before.) Yet he'd loved the style of thinking that science gave him.

What if he used that, and examined politics with the crisp, un-biased approach of Newton? It would mean peering at the French or British monarchs as if getting a fresh view of them through a telescope. Those monarchs, for example, were used to saying that they deserved our deference because their authority descended from the distant past— in the case of the French monarchy, from Charlemagne himself. But Voltaire asked why that should matter.

The satellites of Saturn, he had learned in detail from Emilie, spin as they do merely because they follow the rules of gravity that every other object in the solar system follows. There will have been many quirks in their past—the details of how they were formed—but that has no bearing on the rules about how they operate now. That was the approach Voltaire could use: ignore what the king's ancestors had once done and instead ask the important question of whether the king *today* is efficient and fair enough to justify our deference.

This was yet another fundamental step in the Enlightenment. (It is, for example, the core argument in the Declaration of Independence.) Voltaire had already written increasingly powerful hints of this, in his verse and prose and theater. Now, excited by the acclaim in Paris, he was ready to go even further.

The question was how to ensure that a state's rulers actually took these best, efficient actions. For the British colonies in North America it might be possible to imagine that ordinary people should indirectly decide this by being given a say in how their government was administered. But even there, and despite so many independent farmers and a certain tradition of self-governing Protestant sects, it was still considered unreasonable to let all adults vote equally. In France, where education and class differences were even stronger, pure democracy was clearly out as a solution.

The obvious alternative, of giving the nobles in France more power, was also not going to work. They'd just use it selfishly. The Parlement of Paris would be no better, for it was composed of reactionary lawyers and officials like Voltaire's late father, who were as selfish as the old-style nobles, yet even more envenomed by being looked down on by the established nobles. It would have been ideal if Voltaire could influence the centers of power at Versailles, but he had no sway over the court officials and mistresses who currently controlled access to the king.

Instead, Voltaire decided on young Crown Prince Frederick, in Prussia, as the ideal vessel to carry out his will.

The young man was clearly insecure—as seen even in the way he constantly asked Voltaire to correct the embarrassing poems he tried writing in French. Such insecurity would make him easily manipulated. And as soon as Frederick's already elderly father died, the young man would inherit a powerful kingdom. Voltaire would use him to carry into the wider world the reforms he and Emilie had discussed for so long back at isolated Cirey.

17

Frederick

In June 1740 Frederick's father did finally die, which meant that the young, timid Frederick was now king, and Voltaire could begin his plan. He arranged with the top official in the French foreign ministry to be allowed to leave Louis XV's kingdom and garner what information he could about Prussia's future intentions. That ostensible spy mission—combined with an attempt to influence the diplomatic alliances Frederick chose—was what would convince the French government to let him leave. On a deeper level, though, he wanted to get close enough to the new king to be able to influence his policy for domestic reform as well.

He began by writing to Frederick, trying to console the youngster at the shock of losing his father:

"Your Royal Highness, there is one thing I would dare to take the liberty of asking," Voltaire wrote paternally. "It is whether the late king, before he died, knew and loved all the merit of my adorable prince."

Emilie still had her doubts. She wasn't sure if Voltaire's plans would work, and knew how much she'd miss him if he was away for weeks or perhaps months. Yet she also could tell how much Voltaire wanted to go on this mission—and he could be immensely persuasive when he wanted. She'd not wanted him to go to Prussia back in 1737, and he understood that. Frederick hadn't even been on the throne then: his brutal father was. But that had changed. And, Voltaire now asked, couldn't a son be different from his father?

It was an artful argument. Emilie couldn't tell him this was out of the question, for she knew how much he had hated his own father, the narrow-minded notary, and how he had tried to create a life as different from his father's as possible. And anyway—as Voltaire was quick to point out, when he saw her resistance wilting—Frederick was in fact showing signs of carrying out everything he'd promised in his letters and other writings so far.

His father had recruited regiments of giants, selected from across Europe, and had wasted a great deal of tax money keeping them equipped. Frederick had already disbanded those regiments. He had banned torture from any civilian courts in his kingdom; he had declared freedom of religion (at least to Christians); he was in the process of ending all censorship.

There was a final argument for going. Emilie had argued in Brussels that God could order the universe to produce the best possible arrangement. Well, would it be fair to stop Voltaire from trying to help that along? Prussia was small, but its army was powerful. Frederick himself had explained that he had nothing to do with that crude army—when he'd been imprisoned after trying to escape his father's cruel kingdom, at the age of eighteen, its soldiers had taunted him as he tried to practice the flute and read French literature in his cell. Voltaire was convinced there were hotheads within the Prussian military who would try to take advantage of this untried boy—unless he got firm, worldly, wise advice fast.

Early in November 1740, Voltaire left The Hague for Prussia. Crossing northern Europe in winter wasn't easy. When Voltaire's carriage broke down, the first peasant he tried to hail for help thought he merely wanted to share a drink; the next one fearfully ran away. Voltaire, one male traveling companion, and the driver were alone by a broken carriage on a rutted winter road in Westphalia. It was cold, and dusk came very early. Voltaire wasn't dressed for the weather: he had on his velvet trousers and thin silk slippers.

To a man who'd dreamed of being a spy on secret missions that would preserve the peace of Europe—and guarantee himself the appreciation of the French court—this was sheer heaven. He was confident now, proud at how well he could handle any problem. He managed to get himself a horse and rode through the cold to the nearest town. The sentry asked his name. "I am Don Quixote!" Voltaire proudly called out. The sentry had no idea what he was saying but duly let this Frenchman pass. Voltaire continued all the way across frozen Westphalia, and finally, after more than a week, he made it to the king's idyllic lakeside retreat at Rheinsberg.

Frederick was in ecstasy. He had a number of handsome young men around him, and even a few émigré French scholars—and now there was his hero, Voltaire. Frederick stayed up as late as he could, playing the flute, trying to talk about all the ideas he'd had in philosophy and literature and science. When he showed Voltaire several small Watteaus he'd purchased, the mood was warm enough that Voltaire could be honest and explain that they were cheap copies ("Germany is full of fakes, the princes being easy to cheat").

As the days went on, Voltaire tried to guide Frederick's strategic choices and pick up all the diplomatic gossip he could. He also found himself talking about Emilie perhaps more than he'd intended, for many of the handsome young men at the Court were there neither for their diplomatic skills nor for their scholarly abilities. In writings that were to be kept strictly private, Frederick jotted down his dreams. "I admire [Voltaire's] eyes, so clear and piercing. . . . I would kiss his eloquent lips, 100 times." Voltaire was willing to do a lot for his country, but Frederick was gay, and Voltaire was not. With a certain amount of deft footwork, he intended to remain that way.

Frederick was willing to accept that and would excuse Voltaire as the hour grew late, whereupon—again in the new king's private recounting—he and the other young men "lost money at cards, danced till we fell; whispered in each other's ears, and when that shifted to love, began other delicious moves." But once those interludes were over, the young king would return to whatever room Voltaire was in, easily sitting at the end of his bed—or he'd call Voltaire into his room—and there they'd go back to talking about life and literature and about the damnable problems of aggressive military leaders as well.

In this sharing mood—in this continuous house party—who could resist bragging about his new life and putting down his old one? Voltaire made dangerously mocking quips while he was there, and when he was back in Brussels and Amsterdam, in interludes between other visits, he continued to make them, in highly confidential writings prepared for Frederick's eyes only. He wrote about Emilie that life with her was "like living in a chapel; I have to return to her rules—it's an obligation, and I'm loyal to it . . . But staying with her, have I lost all my happiness, and life with my King? . . . I hate her lawsuit." He called her "that woman"; he complained that he had to sigh like a fool when he was in her presence.

It was satisfying to have the Prussian king's eager attention this way, and Voltaire liked to please—besides, it would help his secret plot to obtain the new king's favor—so he went on in yet other letters to mock Louis XV's chief counselor, Cardinal Fleury ("that played-out old man") and to praise Frederick's acumen, even lauding him for out-witting France's own diplomatic sratagems. Frederick had it all in writing, but Voltaire was convinced that didn't matter, that everything he shared was safe.

But it was a trap.

On the northwestern edges of the ancient Austro-Hungarian empire, not far from the Prussian heartland, was the rich, beckoning province of Silesia. A new, untested empress was on the Austrian throne, and although Prussia had formally guaranteed her rights of succession, Frederick was going to change that now. He knew that if he killed enough of the young Austrian empress's garrison troops quickly enough, and then invaded, the entire land could be his. While Voltaire had been watching the handsome drunken youngsters at the court beside the lake—and while Frederick had been joining with them at night—he'd also been getting up extremely early each morning, sending detailed instructions to his regiments and commanders. Their obedience was total, for the image he'd presented of being an uncertain, tremulous youngster was only for foreign consumption. To his troops, he was a monster.

When one soldier had tried to desert from an elite regiment, he'd been arrested and beaten. Then the soldier's ears were torn off. Then he was beaten some more. Then his nose was pulled off. "Troops must be more terrified of their superiors than of the enemy," Frederick coolly wrote, and did everything he could to make it so. The most minor disciplinary faults led to furious beatings.

Nothing that Frederick had presented to Voltaire was true. Just a few days after Voltaire started on his way back to Brussels, Frederick's massed troops stormed into Silesia. The army had been taught to march in a hideous fashion, with each soldier's forward leg kicking so high that the thigh was parallel to the ground, and the foot was stretched out flat. To keep their balance the soldiers had to swing their other arm sharply across the body and stretch their jaw forward in a way that pulled their face into a taut grimace. This was Prussia's distinctive *Paradeschritt*—what appalled outsiders termed the "goose step." It was the opposite of every lesson Voltaire had wished to give. Yet Frederick had created a true Newtonian machine, free of those illogical historical accretions that courtly politics had hitherto entailed.

Frederick was a superb strategist, which is why he'd engaged in this long plot to destroy Voltaire's relationship with Emilie and get Voltaire so mistrusted at the French court that he would be forced to accept refuge in Prussia. It would give a cover of respectability to his chilling military attacks. The teasing, male-bonding remarks that he'd lured Voltaire to put into writing were merely the final stage in the trap. Keyserlingk was a trusted emissary. Frederick started using him and others to leak Voltaire's words where they would do the most damage: making Voltaire hated at the French court, and—since Frederick had long recognized how important Emilie was in holding Voltaire in France—getting him rejected by Emilie herself.

Voltaire spent weeks getting back from his second trip. There were snowstorms across central Germany, and when he tried finishing by a sea route, the North Sea was wild: his boat was sent slipping sideways, repeatedly smashing into the onrushing waves. He arrived in Brussels exhausted and freezing; he had an infection in one of his eyes, making it hard to see.

Emilie was less than pleased, and let him know she had seen the leaked letters as much as anyone. Over the years she had spent untold hours lobbying through her family's aristocratic connections to get Versailles officials to allow him to travel freely, to protect him from arrest, and to have the censorship officials leave him alone. Even on his latest trips she'd kept up work on the Palais Lambert. Yet how had she been treated in return? "I've been cruelly repaid," she let him know. But Voltaire was just as furious. Did she know how irritating it had been to be followed by her pleading letters when he was trying to run an important diplomatic mission? And actually, did she have any idea how bored he was by her inane court case or her ridiculous science? She certainly wouldn't know what it felt like to have written a masterpiece—his *History of Louis XIV*—and have it suppressed.

Everything was collapsing. They'd had an agreement: they were to live in Brussels until the court case was over, when they would move to Paris and their grand home on the Ile St. Louis. But if he was banned from Paris after his embarrassment in Prussia and having been found to say traitorous things about France, how could that be? Already she was being made a laughingstock because of him. One wit said that there should be a clause in any mortgage Madame du Châtelet signed from now on: when Monsieur de Voltaire let her down, she shouldn't be obliged to keep up the payments on her own.

Almost a decade before, Voltaire had fallen in love with the dream of who Emilie might think him to be. He'd always imagined he was great: as good as his cherished mother had believed, not the failure his father had always insisted he was. Emilie had been crucial in that, for he respected her so much that her approval was the most important support in his life. Yet now she'd seen him humiliated—and it was his own fault. Either he could stay close to her and accept her accurate evaluation of how badly he'd judged Frederick, or he could lash out and convince himself to scorn her, so that he wouldn't have to face her reminder of his flaws.

He chose the coward's way out. It's cruel for a man to reject his lover, yet in his anger and embarrassment that's what Voltaire decided to do. He still cared enough about what other people thought that he had to do this properly. A dignified poem saying that he was too old for her would be just right. He'd get sympathetic tuts from his friends, while showing Emilie his anger.

He wrote her a long poem, accordingly, pretending to be distraught at being past the age where he could have sex with her again. The lines that leaped out from it were:

> *... I'm dying, you see*
> *I can't be your lover*
> *I'm old ...*

Emilie was furious. It was a travesty of everything he'd penned for her at their first meetings in those sweet months back in 1733, when they'd been unable to keep their hands off each other in Paris, and in Cirey, and every inn along the way. Also, the poem was false. On Voltaire's final trip, Frederick had suggested stopping on the way back at a castle where he would meet Frederick's sister Ulrica, who was young and buxom and most exuberantly heterosexual.

Voltaire had stayed there for weeks, writing erotic poems for Ulrica about their nights together. He was aware that Emilie knew this, for copies of those poems had been circulating widely. But he was hurting her on purpose now.

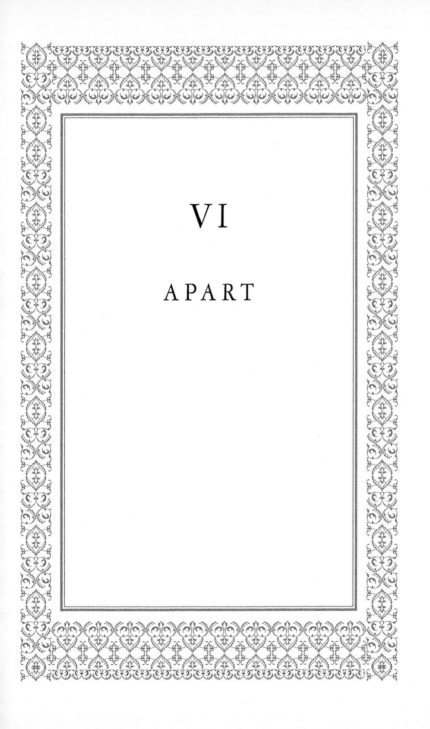

VI

APART

18

The Wound in My Heart

From a servant in Voltaire's household, one year later:

> *[Monsieur de Voltaire] is in an appalling temper, behaves to the Marquise with the utmost unkindness and makes her cry all day.*
>
> *The day before yesterday they had an argument that lasted much of the night. Voltaire expected to dine alone, and had a small table laid. Mme du Châtelet had come back to dine with him, and wanted them to use a larger table. Voltaire stubbornly clung to his, and when she insisted, he said that he was master in his own house, that he had been made subservient for too long and several other harsh things.*
>
> *These rows, which occur frequently, are mocked by the whole household.*

Emilie was falling, falling. She lied to her friends about what was happening, but that didn't change how she felt. "Nothing degrades you," she jotted to herself, "as much as an effort to regain someone who has closed his heart to you." Voltaire was horrible to her, cold and in an embarrassed withdrawal that seemed as if it would never end.

She started to gamble again, but from the turmoil, the constant disparagement, her skill was crumbling.

There had always been a different view of gambling between people raised in the middle classes and members of the older aristocracy. For the former, such as Voltaire, it was a dissolute waste of time, the very opposite of the sensible planning that was needed to take them forward in life. For aristocrats such as Emilie, though, it was a mark of how independent they were, how little they were tied down to such trivialities as paid labor and dull routine.

That hadn't mattered in the old days, before the disastrous Prussian trips. Although Voltaire didn't gamble, he'd been proud of how good his companion was. "The Court's ladies," as he'd noted, "playing cards with her in the company of the Queen, were far from suspecting that they were sitting next to Newton's commentator." But now, her concentration ruined, and desperate for the sensation that only playing for high stakes could give her, she began to lose huge amounts. All Voltaire's years of suppressed resentment came out at all the little marks of class superiority she'd shown through their relation: her utter confidence with servants, and in addressing nobles; the automatic entrée she'd always had to the grand homes he'd had to struggle to get within.

A little earlier he'd written, supposedly half joking: "If [Madame du Châtelet's] . . . superiority allows her to lower her eyes to me, it will be a noble deed, for she is very lofty. She has to blink her eyes in looking down to see me." Now he could take his revenge. At one particularly desperate moment she wrote him (the words in italics are in English in the original):

> *Dear Lover,*
>
> *I'm so sorry for choosing to write you rather than speak about this, but it turns out,* dear lover, *I'm really quite desperate for 50 louis to pay my rent this month. I'll also need 12 1/2 louis more, to cover more gambling debts, and to leave me with a little something to live on.*

*I'll only use it at the end of the month…. I can pay you in rent on
the house, or, if you prefer, here is a receipt Monsieur du Châtelet sent
me that luckily I haven't spent. Keep it, and loan me the money, and
I won't use what you give me in expenses. We can begin a new
account. You'll do this if you can, won't you?*

Voltaire turned her down. She tried other friends, with increasing,
humiliating urgency. Only when the bailiffs were going to remove her
possessions did Voltaire begrudgingly pay the debt.

Richelieu's wife, Elisabeth, had died—from another burst of
bleeding, this time that no one could stop—and at one point Emilie
thought of starting up that affair again. But this too failed, embarrass-
ingly, with Richelieu being too kind to take advantage of her now. "I
don't know," she wrote Richelieu quickly after one such incident, "why
I told you that at Fontainebleau. I couldn't stop myself."

She entirely stopped doing science. It was disheartening, for with
her research in Brussels she'd been on the edge of real creativity, her
work bringing her ever more into the mainstream of original thinkers
across Europe. When one of the old guard at the Paris Academy of Sciences had criticized her, for example, not on any valid grounds but just
out of paternalism, she'd fired back a nearly book-length rebuttal in
just three weeks, putting him in his place. But that audacity had depended on her having Voltaire's respect. Now that was lost. She would
pull herself together enough to reply clearly to the letters that continued to come in—from members of the Royal Society in London, from
important researchers in Italy, and elsewhere—but she couldn't concentrate enough to start anything fresh.

When she was exploring in science, she'd felt connected to the
universe. That was gone now. The solitude, the silence, was total.

VOLTAIRE was falling too, for, having excluded Emilie from his life, he
no longer had the support he'd always needed to get the confidence for
important writing. To make up for that, he engaged in what he later

termed—when he finally got his senses back, several long years later—the only entirely wasted period of his life. He'd always despised the French court and the useless hangers-on who populated it. Now, though, he did everything he could to join the king's minions at Versailles and rise as high as he could as a mindless, powdered courtier.

Being Voltaire, he justified it with some plausible reasons. He'd managed—barely—to avoid being arrested in France after the catastrophe of his Prussian trips, but that had been because the French government official he'd insulted the most—the aged Cardinal Fleury, long-standing chief adviser to the king—had had the good grace to die early in 1743, before any court actions could be taken.

Fleury's death had also opened up fresh possibilities at court. The boy-king Louis XV had spent his whole life being looked after by Fleury, and now—with Louis in his mid-thirties, and that elderly protector gone—poor Louis was at a loss. Even by the undemanding standards of European royalty, Louis was known for being a dolt, only with difficulty grasping what was happening in the world outside his palaces. The main body of nobles couldn't be counted on to help him, for Versailles was a hothouse of vendettas. Sarcastic posters were sometimes left anonymously on the outer door of the king's own rooms; even his predecessor, the far more authoritative Louis XIV, had once had the heavy tasseled drawstring from a curtain heaved over a wall partition, to land—amidst laughter and the quick scurrying away of feet outside—almost on his lap.

This meant the bewildered Louis XV turned ever more to his trusted mistresses for advice about what to do. Whoever controlled the mistress controlled the king. Voltaire hadn't been able to carry out his ideas for bringing Newton's crisp, decent universe down to Earth in the inhospitable precincts of Berlin. But if he could get his hands on the levers of power here at Versailles, perhaps he could redeem himself after all.

One of the most powerful individuals to take advantage of the void at Court had been Voltaire's old nemesis, Jean-Frédéric Phélypeaux, the man who'd seen Voltaire imprisoned in the Bastille during the de Rohan incident those twenty years before (and had tracked him to Richelieu's wedding for the abortive arrest in the Letters from England incident ten years before). Phélypeaux hated commoners such as Voltaire—especially commoners who overreached themselves—and he had succeeded in encouraging the insecure Louis to choose the sexy, malleable, and most definitely aristocratic young Duchesse de Châteauroux as royal mistress.

But Phélypeaux made a tactical mistake. One day in August 1744, while inspecting the troops on a hot day in Metz, the king fell ill, became terrified he'd die, and began to confess to his priest. He couldn't have a mistress during this deathbed confession (for then he'd suffer eternal damnation), and so young Châteauroux had to pack everything she owned and leave, fast.

She'd always been hated by ordinary people, and the mob began gathering around her carriage even before she'd finished packing: there were jeers and probably clods of dirt thrown after her as she hurried off. Phélypeaux was one of the first to tell the king how much he'd always despised that ridiculous woman, whose sexual antics had so dangerously threatened the royal soul. Unfortunately, the king had merely been suffering sunstroke—he scared easily—and within a few days he was better, the confession forgotten, and Châteauroux was back.

It was payback time. Châteauroux let everyone know she had a list of all the courtiers who'd made the very, very serious mistake of turning against her. In what everyone took to be desperation, Phélypeaux personally rode to Châteauroux's house, on the Rue du Bac in Paris. It was early in the evening of Wednesday, November 26, 1744. He was carrying certain documents with him, or perhaps it was something else, for he kept it in a closed case that no one else could examine. She made him wait downstairs, but when he finally was allowed through, he accepted her suggestion that they meet in her bedroom. The door was closed tight behind them. They were alone for a very long time.

To this day, no one knows for sure what happened in there, but when Phélypeaux came out, he seemed quite content. So did she, for she now explained to her supporters that this great official had told her how wrong he'd been and begged her total forgiveness. The next morning she was all set to return to Versailles, but she wasn't feeling well. As the day went on, she felt worse and worse. Soon she was "screaming with pain and at unknown horrors." She died soon after; the rumors of poisoning began almost immediately.

Phélypeaux had gone too far, however, for now there was no royal mistress at all. This meant Voltaire's access to power wasn't blocked anymore. If he could get his own choice of mistress selected, perhaps that would help erase from Emilie's mind the embarrassment of his frozen, bedraggled return from Prussia.

He and his old school friend Richelieu worked together. There was an exquisite young woman, tall and quick-witted, whom they realized the meek king would be awed by. Even better, her grandfather had been a mere fishmonger—she was born Jeanne Poisson (Jean Fish)—and that low heritage meant that everyone else at court would look down on her so much that she'd be unable to make alliances. Richelieu and Voltaire, accordingly, would be her sole protectors and thus the chief beneficiaries of her rise. Voltaire also recognized her as another outsider like himself, eager to rise from an imperfect background to power at the court.

Getting Poisson into the king's bed wasn't too difficult, for the men of the French royal family had a lack of restraint that made Richelieu look like a penitent. (When Louis XIV once had to wait while one of his upper-class mistresses got ready, he'd impatiently gestured to her maid to get undressed: he'd have sex with her first, while he was there.) Through a mix of bedroom skills and conversational ability Ms. Poisson soon became his official mistress, and at that point all Voltaire had to do was become more trusted by the king, so as to properly use the power that this new woman's access gave him.

The opportunity came in a military campaign that looked set to take place soon in the Low Countries, beyond the northern border of France, in this spring of 1745. (The ostensible reason was revenge for earlier losses against Austrian forces in central Europe, and a French attack on scattered Austrian possessions near Brussels seemed an easy way to do that. The Dutch and English sent forces to block that, how- ever; they didn't want France expanding near them.) For this military assault the king wanted to show everyone how virile he was, and so decided to actually join his armies in the field.

Voltaire and Richelieu knew how catastrophic that could be, so Richelieu traveled along, staying near the vast group of guards, cobblers, cooks, seamstresses, laundry staff, wig powderers, valets, and miscellaneous fops who traveled with His Majesty. Tough British troops were already landing, and joined with their Dutch allies as the French army was marching north. On the morning of April 11, 1745, near the village of Fontenoy, the battle began. Soon after the shooting started, the French infantry were in serious trouble. To help them, the French cavalry—officered entirely by hereditary nobles—raced forward. Their horses smashed into and killed a great number of French foot soldiers as they galloped forward; then, once the pampered nobles saw how fast the British were firing, they turned around and hurried to their starting point again, trampling and smashing more of their own infantry.

The king was scared, and his generals were dithering, when Richelieu abruptly pressed his spurs into his horse and galloped forward past everyone in the command group. If he could get closer to the battle, he could see what was going on. He collected a group of French marines and with them managed to move to the very front. He was soon forced back by British firing but had seen that there was a weakness in the British formation. Because of the English success, they'd been pushing further and further forward into the French lines, which meant that they were "as tightly wedged . . . as a square peg in a square hole."

Richelieu got back to the king and—at least in the version Voltaire recorded—explained that a sudden attack by French artillery would startle the British. Once that happened, a cavalry charge against their flanks would destroy them. The king's generals, however, were explaining that there was a very nice bridge over the Scheldt River that was quite close behind them, and with all the dry straw that their sappers were stacking under it, the king could safely escape, then burn the bridge behind him.

It was the moment when a commander shows his mettle. Louis

sweated. Where was someone to tell him what to do? Everyone was yelling at him. Richelieu looked as if he might draw his saber and kill one of the other French officers; the weather was very hot; there were horrible shooting and screaming noises not far away.

Somehow Louis recognized that Richelieu was repeating something. There were at least four French cannon available that he'd seen on his ride back. Could he order them into action? Louis still wavered, but Richelieu seemed very upset now and kept on repeating, in an increasingly intemperate tone, what he was saying. Finally Louis realized that if he agreed, perhaps Richelieu would shut up.

The king gave in, and Richelieu immediately wheeled around. With one set of commands, he had the cannon readied. With another set of commands, he had got every trooper who could ride to form up right away. The British troops, who'd been steadily advancing, now saw the French forces directly in front of them majestically separate, like the Red Sea before Moses. In their place, four uncomfortably large and loaded cannon appeared, aimed straight at them. The cannon blasted, and Richelieu led the charge. Irish troops, fighting with the Catholic king of France, were especially powerful in supporting him. The British lines were smashed, and the battle was quickly over. Soon there was nothing more to do than bayonet the wounded British troops who couldn't run away, and tug useful boots or coins from the inert or twisting bodies.

It was a victory for Richelieu and the ordinary French soldiers, but no one could admit that. Voltaire was beginning to realize what he had let himself in for. To continue his climb at Versailles, he now had to prepare a booklet titled *The Battle of Fontenoy, as Won by Louis XV,* in which he lauded His Majesty's cool, nearly superhuman determination. This wasn't what Voltaire had had in mind when he'd wittily explained to his young listeners at the Paris salons how the plans for political reform that he and Emilie had begun at Cirey might come to pass.

Ms. Poisson wasn't as useful as hoped either. Although she would sometimes daringly leave out one of Voltaire's subversive manuscripts, that was just to irritate the older, class-conscious women at the court who looked down at her. Her fortunes depended on the king's favors, and she certainly was bright enough to recognize that. It didn't matter that Voltaire had helped lead her to those favors. On the contrary. If Louis felt he had won a great victory, then her job was to make clear to this outsider Monsieur de Voltaire that this was exactly how he must present it.

Then it got worse. The king's ostensible victory at Fontenoy—and the confidence that Voltaire's praise brought him—tempted His Majesty to another feat of arms. His great-grandfather Louis XIV had repeatedly seen his plans for European domination thwarted by the dreadful English. Now that they were on the run, why not go all the way and invade their country, or at least install a puppet government that France could control?

The king had enough sense to quietly suggest that Richelieu should handle such minor logistic details as actually organizing and then commanding the assault troops. But the invasion would serve the greater glory of France, and the king was the same as France, sort of—there were theorists who wrote about these confusing matters—and anyway, somehow it would accrue to his credit.

At first the plan went well. In July, the Catholic claimant to the throne, the energetic twenty-four-year-old Charles Stuart, was landed in Scotland with promises of French support to come. By September he'd taken Edinburgh; soon he was marching on England. Pamphlets had to be prepared to get the English population to surrender, and Voltaire was the man to do it. There was a certain conflict of interest for Voltaire, in that it meant supporting the rights of what he had always described as a vicious, Church-ridden near-dictatorship (France) against a constitutional polity that for years he had thought was the greatest hope for the future of mankind (England). But if the outcome offered a chance of glory and an important role at court, isn't this what he would have to do?

19

Recovery ... and Escape

Emilie recognized that Voltaire was destroying himself, but part of her recovery was to distance herself from everything he did. She started something of a journal—a manuscript she sadly entitled "Happiness"—to collect her thoughts on what had gone wrong. She had a lot to reflect upon.

"For ten years," she wrote, "I was happy, in the love of the man who subjugated my soul. I passed those years, alone with him, and it was always enough. . . .

"I've lost this happy state," she went on. "What happened to make me see it was terrible: the wound in my heart bled for a long time." But now she accepted it. "Nothing will bring back lost love. I've learned that at least."

She made a list of what she was content filling her time with. Some were little things, like fine meals or singing—she still had that lovely voice—or the marionette shows she always could laugh out loud at. But mostly for the depth she needed—and the affirmation as well—there was science.

There was something about 's Gravesande's old experiment with the falling cylinder that kept pulling her back. Voltaire had been convinced that what 's Gravesande found was just a random fact, simply stating what happened when rounded brass chunks slammed into trays of Dutch clay. Emilie, however, still approached it differently.

If you measured the energy those falling cylinders carried at impact, even Voltaire and the diehard Newtonians would admit that something about that number never disappeared. When a cylinder falls into clay, the cylinder soon stops but the clay itself gets deformed and shakes, passing on that shaking to the tray it's in, which no doubt passes it to the floor it's on, which probably ends up making the entire Earth shudder the slightest bit extra in its orbit.

Emilie couldn't bear that: "what worries me now is free will. At heart I feel free, yet if the total amount of energy in the universe never changes, wouldn't that destroy free will? I mean, if we start to move, we must be creating some energy that didn't exist before. But if we're not allowed to do that—because it would add to the fixed amount of energy in the universe—then we can't choose to move. So then we're not free!"

Slowly, and especially in correspondence with the Italian Jesuit Francesco Jacquier, Emilie realized what the task that would give her life meaning would now be. Newton was the greatest thinker of all, but he was exceptionally difficult to read. In many respects he wasn't even the first of the modern natural scientists, but rather was the last of the medievals, for the great *Principia* he'd written summarizing his ideas was cast almost entirely in centuries-old geometry. Hardly anyone could use it directly. Researchers across Europe were slowed by having to depend on often only partially understood secondary accounts.

What if Emilie transformed Newton's *Principia* for the new modern era? Then the deepest answers she was looking for could be better explored, and she would have all of Newton's analytic tools to help. She'd made some desultory efforts on that before but had been too lethargic to take it forward. Now it was different. Her task wouldn't just be to turn Newton's Latin words into French. Instead, she would *also* turn his strange, immensely complicated geometric proofs into the form of more modern calculus—and would add her own commentaries, explaining how she thought his work could best be carried forward.

That itself would be an immense undertaking—the *Principia* had taken Newton himself years of intellectual effort to produce—but Emilie was beginning to feel she could go further and add important original areas.

In the past, she'd depended entirely on Voltaire's respect. But he had worked himself into such embarrassing straits at Versailles that— at least for now—his lack of support didn't mean so much. Emilie knew she was still quicker in reasoning than almost anyone she'd met; it had been great being feted for her research on fire and light. She could be proud of the work she'd led with telescopes and prisms and geometrical diagrams; the systematic study she'd made on the early books of the Bible, and what that meant for faith today; the translations and commentaries she'd also found time for at Cirey on economics and politics. The response she continued to get from foreign academics and thinkers across the Continent added to that.

She'd grown up in an aristocratic world, where making an elegant effort was all that counted. Yet she'd been drawn toward Voltaire and his more practical, middle-class world, where actual, solid achievement was what counted. That's what she was proud of, and what she was going to do more of, even if it was on her own. The difficult years were ending. She was taking control. European science would advance— and so would she.

VOLTAIRE knew he was stuck, but found it impossible to get out. Ms. Poisson had risen as high as he and Richelieu had hoped, but that simply made her more independent. Indeed, she was now increasingly known by the name the lovesick Louis had granted her, and had become the famous Madame de Pompadour. Since Voltaire and Richelieu had known her from the start, when she'd been viewed with suspicion, she was even more distant to them than to other courtiers, who'd been her enemies at first but whom she needed to convert into allies now.

The invasion of England had also failed, through a combination of Charles Stuart's Scottish followers being too cautious and Richelieu bungling the arrangements for the invasion (not helped by his ongoing arguments with Phélypeaux), even while the invading troops were waiting in the French ports.

Voltaire did get a wondrous promotion by the standards of Versailles, for he was granted a permanent suite of rooms of his own—an honor that aristocratic families had been known to barter their own daughters for. Since it was located at the top of an important and much-used stairwell, this meant it had an equally important and much-used large open toilet directly below. The odor of great half-floating islets of aristocratic excrement was hard to mask, even with the heavy orange-scented perfume candles used desperately for that purpose. Voltaire was reduced to writing to court officials in the humble third person: "Monsieur de Voltaire . . . begs the director-general of the buildings kindly to order . . . that a door be added to the public privies which are at the foot of his staircase, and that if possible the spout of the neighboring gutter be diverted so as to flush them."

Soon more honors came in, and there were even whispers that the king might appoint him Gentleman in Ordinary of the Chamber. The honors come with large cash stipends but also meant that Voltaire was requested to arrive outside the king's apartments often by 8 A.M., to push in with other honored gentlemen and assist in the king's formal waking: the lifting of the royal covers, the holding of the royal shirt, and for a select few the brushing of the royal wig. In perhaps the greatest indignity of all, Voltaire even found that Phélypeaux was now his friend, writing him kind notes and discussing—as one fellow professional to another—details of print runs for the really quite wonderful odes, proclamations, dramas, histories, and other documents that Voltaire was churning out in his new posts.

This wasn't anything like the application of Enlightenment ideas that Voltaire had been looking for. Before his Versailles stint, he and Emilie had been at the heart of Europe's new "republic of letters":

a meritocracy where decisions were to be made not on the basis of blind authority, but rather on an open, humane response to the facts.

At Versailles, however, truth was determined in a different way. What the king wanted was true, and what his top advisers wanted could also become true. Science didn't matter. The hierarchy at court determined what could be thought and what could be said.

Everything was crumbling. Voltaire had begun an affair with his now widowed niece Marie-Louise—incest between uncle and niece was much less abhorrent in Catholic countries then than it is now—but although that was thrilling for him at the start, she was a bit more cynical about it. When he managed to hobble up from the privy at the bottom of his Versailles stairwell, change out of his soiled dressing gown, bathe, shave his scalp and chin, dab on the clove oil he needed to keep his gums from hurting too much, have his manservant prepare a properly powdered wig, and make it all the way from the court for a romantic event at Marie-Louise's apartment in central Paris, he found that this voluptuous young lady often seemed distracted. (To one of her more appreciated lovers at the time she wrote: "I can barely believe, dear heart, that Voltaire is coming to dine with me again tonight. . . . I can't get out of it.")

And then after the flirting and the sex, when he had to talk to her, he realized what he'd always known. It was Emilie who had been right about Frederick, just as she had been right to warn him against getting pulled too far into Versailles. She understood him. No one would ever replace her.

THE question was how to get her back. It was especially hard, for he was too proud to apologize, and she certainly wasn't going to sleep with him after what he'd put her through. But they both knew they still had too much of a shared past to ever be content living entirely apart from each other: the years of daily talk, the dreams they'd shared at Cirey and after.

They began, tentatively, taking trips that threw them together more intensely than they'd been for years. In the summer of 1747 they spent weeks on end as guests in a château about seventy miles from Paris. Both went through the forms of working, and the other house-guests were upset that they didn't see this mysterious couple for hours on end during the day, for both were busy in their own rooms. At the end of the visit, servants found that Emilie had pushed together a great number of tables in her rooms to make a big working area for her writing desk, her stacks of manuscript pages, and the big folio sheets she needed for the cascades of calculus lines she needed to develop. Her inner resources were strong enough to make her creativity come back. Voltaire, by contrast, had done nothing more than make minor editing changes on a potboiler of a play he'd been niggling over for months. After all his years spent at Versailles, he had become utterly empty.

He knew he needed to get Emilie's full respect back if he was ever going to recover his skill. But what powerful event would allow him to convince her he was on her side enough to deserve it?

In October 1747 the court undertook its annual move from Versailles (ten miles west of Paris), to the old palace and hunting lodges of Fontainebleau (beside a forest forty miles southeast of Paris). Voltaire had to go along, for although he was cautiously trying to get closer with Emilie again, his main lodgings, and efforts, were still at the court. Emilie for her part now decided to come along too. She had friends there, from her family connections, as well as from the socializing she'd done on her own in Paris. There also was gambling she could look forward to, for her skill had now come back; there was no doubt the pull of familiarity with Voltaire as well.

Voltaire had a new chief servant now, Sébastien Longchamp, and it was with great, punctilious exactness that he oversaw the arrangements. Longchamp ensured that all their baggage was brought and unpacked, as well as the most important manuscripts and books, sufficient ink, quills, and fresh paper. It was also his job to see that fires were made in their respective rooms, that there was good stabling for the horses, and that the junior servants were well lodged. The logistics were complicated, but Longchamp lived to serve, and was so utterly without curiosity that he was ideal at his job. It all went without trouble until they'd been at Fontainebleau a few days, as Longchamp recorded:

> When I finished consuming my repast I returned to the rooms, and began neatly copying the manuscript Voltaire had left for me. The hour was achieving a lateness, but I was not worried for I was quite aware that individuals of Monsieur or Madame's social rank often remain out late.
>
> They arrived back at the time of 1:30 A.M., and it occurred to me that they were in a hurry. I would go so far as to say that they looked anxious. Madame informed me that they had to leave immediately. I was to rouse the servants, and get the horses ready.
>
> I responded to her requests with alacrity, and I chose to first wake the coachman, informing him of the necessity of harnessing the horses. I then attempted to assemble the other servants, but there was insufficient time for this further task. As soon as the horses were ready, Madame du Châtelet and M. de Voltaire climbed into the carriage, with but a single chambermaid, and only two or three of their many bags. They immediately left Fontainebleau. It was dark, for the hour was still well before dawn.

What had happened? Emilie had known that several individuals at the court who liked to gamble for very high stakes were likely to be there that week. To be ready for those high stakes she'd brought a great deal of cash—400 louis—with her from Paris, and it seems she'd puzzled out a new strategy she thought she could use. On her first day of gambling, however, something had gone wrong, and she'd lost all the 400 louis. Voltaire had quickly given her 200 louis more, and that disappeared too.

She spent the next morning going over what might have happened, and when gambling began again, probably in the late afternoon or early evening, she had more funds in hand: 380 louis that she'd had sent from Paris, much of which she'd had to borrow at high interest.

It was rare for a woman to bet using any intricate strategy, let alone a woman who, it became clear, could very quickly compute changed probabilities as each game went on. The betting continued, and her winnings went up and down; as the evening grew late, there were dense rows of glowing candles, for light as well as to help in heating the big room. Cold air gusted in through cracks in the walls; there was talc and perfume from everyone standing so densely crowded around the players. Voltaire, well dressed as always—his latest bout of dysentery was cured, and his wig preparers had perfected their technique—was standing immediately beside Emilie, keeping an eye on her, and the cards, and the other players, as well as on all the courtiers he knew so well.

By midnight she was somehow losing more, and had to borrow extra funds on her word of honor; by 12:30 A.M. something serious was happening, she was losing a fortune; by about 1 A.M. she was down the immense sum of 84,000 francs—the equivalent in purchasing power of perhaps a million dollars today. It would be hard for that to have happened if all the other players were honest. Voltaire had known not to interrupt her while she was playing, but now, as she was breathing deep, taking in the enormous figure, he leaned close. He needed a great gesture to impress her and support her, to show that he was back with her.

They'd become used to speaking in English when they didn't want the servants to understand what they were saying. Possibly he gave a final quick glance around the room before whispering to her, in English: what did she expect from playing with cheats?

It was a dangerous accusation, even if true. He and Emilie were in the official rooms where gambling had been authorized by the queen, and only the highest aristocracy was allowed to play here. If someone had been cheating, then it was someone who lived within the very top circle of court society.

By saying those words, he'd joined his fate with hers. She'd lost a fortune, which was serious trouble, but he'd insulted the queen and top courtiers, which put him in even greater jeopardy. He could be jailed or exiled for that.

If he and Emilie were very lucky, no one would have heard, or if they did, they wouldn't have understood his English words. But Emilie now saw that one of the courtiers had registered what Voltaire said. A murmur began, spreading from table to table. She quickly looked to him. They wouldn't make any fuss or say a word, but they would turn and walk out of the room without delay.

That's how they ended up riding quickly to their main lodging, where Longchamp was, and having him rouse the coachman so that they could flee before anyone with powers of arrest could be woken and sent to intercept them. Longchamp stayed behind to gather the rest of their bags and would only leave for Paris once day broke.

The carriage was going fast when it left Fontainebleau, but the road was rutted, and a wheel suddenly broke. The carriage skidded on one corner; it didn't turn over, but the horse could drag it no more. The nearest town was still at least a mile or more ahead. To their relief, a wheelwright soon appeared out of the dark, drawn by their driver's torches. (The arrival wasn't as much blind chance as it might appear, for hundreds of nobles and their carriages were at Fontainebleau, which meant there was an influx of wheelwrights and other mechanics to tend to them all. It's likely that a few industrious repairers made sure the ruts at corners coming into nearby towns were kept especially deep, to ensure regular business.)

Their carriage, now fixed, continued on its way into Paris, and arrived, pushing into those muddy streets, before midday.

20

To Sceaux

Emilie's first job, when she got back, was to start repaying her enormous debts. There was no way she could earn the money in time through investments, or even by remortgaging her family's various properties. But she knew that Voltaire had made a fortune after his return from England by ingeniously seeing a flaw in the Paris lottery. Emilie now took a leaf from that and began using her imagination to search out other financial opportunities that no one had recognized, and obtain the cash she needed that way.

What she realized, after just a few weeks, was that there would be a great demand in France for some organization that could supply decent streams of cash at reasonable interest rates. Large workshops and trading companies needed that, but there was no stock market and no well-developed bond market to supply it.

Now she thought of another way. Taxes in France weren't collected directly by the government—as we saw, there was no civil service capable of that. Instead, the king let a few private individuals collect taxes, for a high fee. After those individuals had collected enough to pay that fee, they got to keep the rest.

She couldn't take over that role, for the individuals who had the rights to it wouldn't let go. But those tax collectors themselves often needed money to organize the large private bureaucracies they required to collect taxes from across the nation. What if she offered to pay them for the right to get some of that money they'd earn in the future? Since hardly anyone was aware of this opportunity, she could buy what they'd be earning in the future at a low price. Once she had the tax collectors signed up, she could then tell the court gamblers (whose money she'd "lost") that she'd pay them back by giving them some of that future money when it arrived.

It was a modern form of derivatives, and she didn't even need to keep it running until she had the full 84,000 francs she owed. The Fontainebleau cheats knew they'd gone too far, since they of course had also been violating the royal honor by rigging the games played at the queen's table. In exchange for accepting partial payment as a settlement, Emilie quietly promised that she wouldn't use her family connections to start an embarrassing investigation into how they'd arranged their cheating. The whole maneuver didn't cost Emilie anything, for the tax collectors were so dim that they had accepted the promise of a fairly low amount of money for the right to their future earnings. When those earnings did start coming in, months or years later, Emilie would get a profit.

It would take a month or more for her to complete all the contracts, and in that time Voltaire remained in danger of arrest. To avoid that, the two of them shared another secret. Voltaire had been in the carriage when it left Fontainebleau, and even when its wheel was fixed. But when it had arrived in Paris the next morning, he'd been nowhere to be seen—to everyone but Emilie and a very few trusted friends, it was as if he'd vanished from the face of the Earth.

What they'd agreed on during that night ride was that the carriage would stop on an empty road outside Paris. There Voltaire had stepped down, intending to go into hiding until Emilie cleared the gambling debt. There was little question where he would end up, for he knew who could be counted on to shelter him in any argument with the court.

Back in the reign of Louis XIV, the king's most revered mistress had a son who was so playful and so outgoing that the king came to like him far more than his petulant, spoiled legitimate children. Louis XIV kept the boy near, and recognized him as the duc du Maine.

When he was twenty-one years old, du Maine married the one other person at court who felt as strongly as he that the king's official children didn't deserve to continue the royal line. This was the young granddaughter of the great prince de Condé, that warrior who'd almost taken over the throne in the civil wars of the mid-1600s but had ended up rowing harmlessly around the royal reflecting ponds. Yet he hadn't been as content as he seemed, and rather had been biding his time while passing on to his granddaughter the belief that one day she should redeem his line.

When that child married the Sun King's favored but illegitimate son, a center of opposition to the official court was created. The du Maine couple had to wait, but in 1717 the regent who'd snatched power after Louis XIV's death began to move against them. The duc du Maine wasn't sure how to fight back, but his wife was different. No offspring of a Condé was going to accept this further usurpation against the rightful heirs. The duchesse—although a tiny blond pixie of a woman—explained to her husband that they were going to take over the government.

For such a task it helps to have a safe base of command, and this the young du Maine couple had par excellence, having been granted a magnificent château at Sceaux, a few miles southwest of Paris. There were forests and lakes surrounding it, turrets and arches and secret passageways within. The duchesse du Maine orchestrated furtive meetings and the assembling of printing presses. There were messages in invisible ink among the conspirators, double and triple agents, and intense coded communications with the Spanish court (whose military forces would help in the takeover).

The plot was revealed, however, and the du Maines were imprisoned for several years—a stint that for the duchesse included a solitary cell in the prison fortress at Dijon. When she was released she went back to Sceaux, and a little later her husband joined her. Before the plot, when they'd been France's unofficial anointed couple, they'd had weeks on end of entertainment, with fireworks, orchestras, and entire theaters invited for their dozens of ebullient guests. Now, after the collapse of their plot, no one with any interest in advancing at court could be seen visiting them.

The couple waited in their isolated palace, and when in time the duc died, the tiny duchesse waited some more. Season succeeded season; decade followed decade. There were a handful of loyal visitors from the old days, who stayed for months in scattered rooms here and there, but as the years went on and they died off, there were fewer and fewer times when the once grand palace was lit up as before.

WHEN Voltaire stepped out of the coach that he and Emilie were escaping from Fontainebleau in, he'd waited till sunrise, then calmly walked to the isolated town of Villejuif. He was old enough to remember the tiny, forgotten duchesse du Maine from her glory days, and had kept in occasional touch over the years. He knew that if she was at all like the rebel she'd been those decades before, she'd take the side of anyone persecuted by the court.

From Villejuif he paid a peasant to go to her now, and soon got the reply he wished, including detailed instructions. Voltaire hired a horse in Villejuif and, once the hour was late enough, began riding to Sceaux.

It was freezing as the twilight came, but the duchesse had been adamant about the rules he needed to follow. Under no circumstances was he to be seen in daylight. The last paths through the woods and lakes around the château were especially hard to follow in the utter dark, especially with snow on the ground. When he emerged from the woods, finally in front of the château, he was frozen, exhausted, and deeply famished (for he hadn't dared to show his face at any inn or tavern in Villejuif).

The château had a huge banqueting hall, but when Voltaire met the trusted elderly retainer who was waiting for him, at a grilled porthole near the entry, it was clear that the duchesse's plans had only begun. Although there was hardly anyone in the château, there *might* be a leftover guest somewhere or other who would notice any sign of an arrival late at night. Under no circumstances would she let the important "personage"—for Voltaire's name was not to be mentioned— take that risk.

In the old days, when Sceaux had been used for important missions, the duchesse had built a secret stairwell. The servant led Voltaire along that now, skirting the empty rooms. Only at the top floor did the silent servant lead him out and show him to the room the duchesse had arranged for him. It didn't face the woods or lakes, for any spy the king sent with a telescope might see him from there; instead it overlooked the château's inner courtyard. But the shutters on that inward-facing window were still closed tight, to guarantee secrecy from any stray guests on the lower floor. The servant had led the way with a candle.

The duchesse had to greet her guest—it was the one inviolate rule of country house arrivals—but climbing secret stairwells in stone fortresses is tiring enough for lanky, aging poets, and she was seventy and not in the best of health. Nothing, however, was going to keep a proud Condé down. Voltaire heard a creaking, grinding sound break the stillness of the night. The duchesse had long ago had a lift-like contraption installed in the château, run by a combination of counter-weights in the lift shaft and sturdy servants tugging away on the ground floor. In this ingenious device, the tiny duchesse now ascended to the honored guest's floor, then walked the cold corridors to his room.

Voltaire was close to the wondrously inviting bed and had only to take off his wig and jacket and curl under the thick stuffed quilts to fall into the sleep he no doubt craved (for he hadn't been to bed since the night before the card-cheating scandal). But the duchesse knew the proprieties for welcoming a guest, and there were further instructions— she'd had decades to prepare—about how the escapee was to be protected. He could be assured that no word would leak from her lips, but there would have to be code names—the duchesse had always liked being called "director of the Honey Bee Society." And then there was the schedule to be agreed on, and arrangements for food, for her poor visitor must be starving—though this, Voltaire, listening to her weave her intricate vision, yet knowing the rules of established country house etiquette, would have to respond was ridiculously far from the truth.

21

Zadig

When Voltaire woke the next day, his misfortunes had only just begun. Under normal circumstances a servant would be waiting near, to be instructed to open the shutters. The duchesse du Maine, however, had decided even natural sunlight would be too dangerous. Her guest was in hiding from the king, and she knew what that was like.

Voltaire was going to live in the dark, for there was too great a danger of him being seen otherwise. What if a guest or one of the untested servants from the main body of the château saw some movement from this window, even during the day?

The duchesse understood, of course, that he was a writer, and that he had certain needs. That's why "Museo" (for direct names still had to be avoided, and this seems to have been Voltaire's assigned code name) would have seen so many candles stacked up in the room. He could use this period of seclusion to write her a story.

It must have made the privy-bottomed, converted kitchen rooms he'd left at Versailles seem like heaven. Even if most of the courtiers and visiting ambassadors there were superficial, there had always been several individuals around—as with Richelieu or the quick Ms. Poisson—well worth talking to. But here the creaking of the ramshackle lift going down meant that the duchesse was leaving him for what might be days on end. He couldn't bring his niece Marie-Louise over from Paris, since she could keep a secret about as long as Voltaire himself could, and in any case she was far too used to luxury to ever accept this single room. Emilie was out also, for this bare single room would make it clear that his noble, supportive words at the gambling table hadn't been quite as successful as intended. Instead, as Longchamp recounts:

> I received the following day instructions to find Monsieur de Voltaire at a new residence he had taken up, at the Château de Sceaux. It was impressed upon me that the strictest confidence must be practiced about this. I was to transport to him the small portable writing table in which we had always placed his unfinished manuscripts.
>
> The instructions were for me to arrive at 11 P.M. exactly, and I was, if I might say, precisely on time. Madame du Maine's guard met me at the gate, and led me up to a small apartment, hidden on the second floor.

But he wasn't to be let back home. Servants were nearly invisible and their absence rarely noted. He had more news: "It was there, I found, that I was to spend nearly two months with M. de Voltaire."

It's possible that there have been two individuals less suited to sharing a single room—one thinks of Cain and Abel—but the historical record is silent on them. Longchamp would perch eagerly on the edge of the bed or on a chair in their dark, candle-gloomy room and wait for Voltaire to give him rough manuscript drafts to recopy. Voltaire, unable to write anything with him there, would pace, or peer through gaps in the shutters, or sometimes escape into the upper hallways when du Maine's gatekeeper wasn't watching, but before long he'd have to come back to the room, where the ever-polite Longchamp would be stiffly waiting, an angel of creative death amidst the candles.

When Voltaire couldn't bear it any longer he'd probably tell Longchamp he didn't have to sit waiting at the writing table, but since there's no record of Longchamp ever reading anything or otherwise entertaining himself, this would just make things worse. "I slept a great part of those days," Longchamp recorded, "for it is true that the lack of activities to help with was a difficulty for one such as myself. I am chagrined to admit that to alleviate my tedium I sometimes [consumed my sole meal of the day very slowly], continuing till one or indeed even two A.M." There was no escape for either man, since they had to wait at Sceaux for however long it would take Emilie to set up the financial instruments she was devising to pay back the gambling debt.

Sometimes Voltaire managed to send Longchamp away on furtive errands into Paris—for which, by the duchesse's rules, Longchamp would have to leave before dawn, and return only late at night. But that just made Voltaire's isolation worse ("I saw that my absences bothered him as well," Longchamp observed).

Eventually there was no alternative. Voltaire had to start writing, even if it killed him. But what? The château was an ideal place to look back on the failure of his life. In over thirty years of effort he'd written about Oedipus, English governance, Inca lovers, Newton's laws of gravitation, the nature of envy, and military battles; he'd received ovations at the Comédie Française, galloped across Westphalia, and entertained at many, many dinners. If he was despondent, he'd say his accomplishments added up to nothing. If he was even more despondent, he'd say that his bare life experience was the only thing he actually did know about.

Which . . . raised an interesting possibility. Why not take some of the old manuscripts from that portable writing table the ghoulish Longchamp had brought, and work on them, writing totally afresh if needed, but this time writing not in formal meter, or for any audience at the court, or the Science Academy, or even at Cirey. What if he wrote just for himself—and only *about* himself?

And so he began. There was an old tale he'd once started, on the adventures of a young Middle Eastern noble. In itself that manuscript had been too random, just a series of disconnected episodes. Now

Voltaire pushed that to one side. He took out a fresh sheet of paper. The royal censor who'd tormented him for years, under Phélypeaux's eye, had been an old literary hack named Crébillon. The new tale, the one Voltaire would write without any care for how it was received— for it would be private, and composed just to break the grinding tedium of this candlelit room—would begin with a direct tease at Phélypeaux's censoring apparatus. His quill dipped into the ink, and he mimicked almost exactly the pompous way Crébillon and other minions phrased their proclamations—but with a twist:

Approbation

I the undersigned, who have passed myself off as a man of learning and even of wit, have read this manuscript, which, in spite of myself, I have found curious, amusing, moral . . . and worthy of pleasing even those who hate literature. So I have disparaged it and assure the authorities that it is a detestable work.

Now he was off. He'd reenact his own life's odyssey from Cirey on! The tale would begin in tranquility, with the hero starting in an isolated, perfect kingdom. He couldn't call it Cirey—the cover name would be Babylon—and he'd call the hero Zadig (from the Hebrew for "just man"). There would be a woman Zadig loved, from the highest social levels—the Emilie character—and she would have once loved him too. But when he made a mistake she would be too judgmental and drop him. Only much later, when she realized that he wasn't flawed, would she want him back. There would also have to be a Marie-Louise character, from a far more humble background, who somehow ends up betrothed to Voltaire/Zadig along the way.

Those twists were fine, but he was aiming for something richer now. Voltaire had always wondered how random anyone's life really is. What if Zadig's quest now incorporated the problem of whether our life's events create a coherent meaning or not? That way, Voltaire's fictional character would be trying to understand his life for him.

Longchamp's days changed. There were a lot of candles now, and a lot of copying, for "all the time that Monsieur Voltaire was not asleep—and I assert that he slept only five or six hours at most—he now spent writing." It got so busy—for when Voltaire was flying, his quill skidded in a blur of scribbled words—that they brought yet another servant to live in their tiny room, to tend to the chores that the frantically recopying Longchamp now no longer had time for: the stoking of fireplaces, the careful carrying of full chamber pots, the occasional errands into town.

Voltaire had Zadig get caught in one after another of the seemingly arbitrary twists that Voltaire had experienced himself. It was never clear whether the twists would turn out for better or for worse. After being forced to flee Babylon, for example—and seemingly having left an innocent woman in peril by his escape—Zadig is sunk in despair as he journeys toward exile in Egypt. At that point Voltaire deftly shifts perspectives, drawing on all the feeling for astronomy that he and Emilie had shared in their first years together:

> *Zadig set his course by the stars. The constellation of Orion and the brilliant star Sirius guided him toward the pole of Canopus. He marvelled at these vast globes of light which to our eyes appear to be only feeble sparks, whereas the Earth, but an imperceptible point in nature, appears to our cupidity as something so great and so noble. He then visualized men as they really are, insects devouring one another on a little atom of mud. This true picture seemed to annihilate his misfortunes, by retracing for him the nullity of his own being and of Babylon. His soul flew up into the infinite and, now detached from his senses, contemplated the immutable order of the universe. But when later, returning to himself and looking into his own heart again, he thought how the woman he'd left [Astarté] was perhaps dead for his sake, the universe disappeared from before his eyes, and he saw nothing . . . but Astarté dying, and Zadig miserable.*

There's no answer to the problems of life, for before we can fix on one conclusion, more events always get in the way. "As Zadig gave himself up to this ebb and flow—of sublime philosophy, and over-whelming grief—he was advancing toward the frontiers of Egypt. His faithful servant was in the first village, looking for lodging." The British critic William Empson liked describing the power of ambiguity in literature. If an author insists that only one view is true, there's little we can do but accept or reject that view. It easily gets tedious, like a prose article we can read only once. But when the author holds two contrasting views and weaves a narrative where both are somehow true, then we're pulled to it more. (Good music is similar, being both powerful yet also evasive, so that we can listen to it over and over, our mind approaching it afresh each time.)

There was a great consolation in *Zadig,* for although the events seem random, Voltaire, scribbling away up in his isolated Sceaux room, was able to guarantee that there was meaning to it all. In these fables, he was not just the randomly twisting hero down below; he was also the God up above, controlling all that happened.

Once again, his writing was picking up on and furthering some-thing very topical in the wider world. He and Emilie had long been in-terested in contemporary architecture, where a switch was taking place from rococo exuberance to cleaner neoclassical lines. She'd helped cre-ate a mix of those two styles at Cirey. In these stories the random twists of the main character were like rococo details, while the calm narrator's voice carrying all those twists forward so calmly was like the neoclassi-cal columns holding a modern edifice up.

THE duchesse generally left Voltaire alone till midnight or 1 A.M. before sending for "Museo" to see her. Voltaire would then clamber down the secret stairwell—or use the creaking lift—to reach her rooms on the ground floor. There the director of the Honey Bee Society would be ("her aged face like transparent parchment") sitting up in bed, gestur-ing to a tiny table beside her, where she'd had candles lit and an ex-tra dinner laid out. Voltaire would have his meal and chat with her, then take out the manuscripts he'd been working on and perform the homage she'd always expected would one day come to pass in her château.

He would read to her, page after manuscript page of these new stories he was pouring out. Back in the 1710s, she'd devised a series of competitions for the young, energetic guests at Sceaux: there had been riddles, songs, and ballet steps to try on nighttime walks by the private lakes. The forfeit for losing was to tell her a story. The young Voltaire had once improvised such a tale for everyone's delight in that parkland at night, about a beautiful princess and her shy writerly admirer. She has the divine ability to achieve multiple orgasms at will; he, the humble scribe, can but observe in wonder.

Its whimsy had pleased the assembled audience then, and now, these many decades later—he in his fifties, she in her seventies—he sat again beside her, legs tucked under the small dining table. They both were too old to be embarrassed by what age had brought them: both were wrinkled and increasingly frail; he needed to wear his thick nightcap, since the felt pad he normally wore under his wig wasn't warm enough on these winter nights; she probably had her own wig off; they both seem to have been clad in dressing gowns. None of that mattered. In the stories he was reciting, he was young again, and she, listening to these words, was young as well.

Because he was speaking it to her—and because he always was highly attuned to what his audience wanted—Voltaire began to change the way he wrote. He was a famous writer, but to our ears most of what he'd written for the theater is hard to enjoy. This is because he'd accepted, as did everyone else in France, that there was a hierarchy in writing styles, and near the top was the form known as the alexandrine, where each line has twelve syllables and a pause is mandatory after the sixth syllable. Sometimes the repetitive singsong that results works well, as anyone who's taken trains in France will remember. The standard boarding announcement—*"Messieurs, dames les voyageurs, en voiture s'il vous plaît"*—is close to an alexandrine. But used for hours on end it gets hard to take.

> *One sentence must rise and, from that peak it must fall*
> *This may happen quickly, or it may then be slow*
> *But it must keep on thus, however dull the rush*

Voltaire's prose histories had been fairly free of this, but even there he'd felt pulled toward epigrams and balanced sentences that work well enough on the page but are too mannered to be compelling when read aloud at length. In these secret nights with the frail duchesse, though, he didn't have to fall back into that. In his rush of creativity, he even began playing with those formal alexandrine forms he'd once held so sacred.

To do this, Voltaire had Zadig write a four-line verse about the king. When his friends ask to read it, Zadig tells them that a true noble writes only for his beloved; he breaks the clay tablet it is written on into two halves, and throws them into a thick rosebush. An unscrupulous character pulls one of those halves out, and it looks as if Zadig is done for, for the broken fragment reads:

> *By all the greatest crimes*
> *Established on the throne*
> *In these our peaceful times*
> *He is the foe alone*

The king, of course, is going to consign poor Zadig to death, but at the last minute a bird flies into the rosebush and brings out the second fragment, which reads:

> *the earth is racked and sore*
> *the king controls our sphere*
> *'tis only Love makes war*
> *whom now men have to fear*

It seems useless, until Zadig's beloved and the king see the perfect alexandrines that were intended when the lines are joined:

> *By all the greatest crimes, the earth is racked and sore*
> *Established on the throne, the king controls our sphere*
> *In these our peaceful times, 'tis only Love makes war*
> *He is the foe alone, whom now men have to fear.*

The revised tale was called *Zadig*. The director of the Honey Bee Society was content—her plans for her château had come true, just as she'd expected—and Voltaire was more than content. He'd written a great deal since his failure with the fire experiments, which had been almost exactly a decade earlier, in the summer of 1737. But aside from his *Discourse in Verse on Man,* in 1738, he had been in a creative trough, made worse by the ridiculous years spent at court after his failure with Frederick. Now, though—jump-started by the isolated room, the gloomy Longchamp, and the chirpily confident duchesse—he had come up with the greatest new literary form of his life. These philosophical fables were—as he guessed, with accuracy—the writings that would ensure his immortality.

Voltaire could be lazy and dawdle beyond mortal sufferance when his writing was stuck—his whole Versailles interlude had been such a delay, in his desolation at losing Emilie's respect. But here he was fired up, amidst the candles in that shutter-dark room.

Longchamp was more worried than ever, for "now my M. de Voltaire engaged in less sleep than he ever had experienced before. Despite my remonstrations he took no exercise, and instead consumed the totality of his waking hours in this nearly continuous writing." One fable after another was coming out—*Zadig,* and portions of text that led to "Micromégas." They and Voltaire's later writings in this genre— most notably *Candide*—have remained in print for almost two centuries and given sweet, saddened consolation to generations of readers. Longchamp recounts:

Approximately two months passed, of this somewhat repetitive existence at Sceaux, until one wonderful day Madame du Châtelet arrived. I gather she was so excited that instead of addressing our distinguished hostess, the duchesse du Maine, she wished to inform M. de Voltaire in person of certain news that she carried.

She took the stairwell we knew so well, up to our solitary apartment, and there informed Monsieur—and my humble personage as well—that the gambling debt from Fontainebleau had been sufficiently paid. I swiftly recognized that this meant those personages who had been disposed to harm my master and mistress had seen the error of their ways. In other words, M. de Voltaire was now at liberty to exit our château.

I was most pleased at this information, and indeed—if I might say—I briefly experienced a sensation of great rejoicing. But all was not to be as I then expected.

Emilie thought she'd come to rescue him, but Voltaire didn't want to leave. His writing was going better than it had in many, many years; no setting he could imagine at Versailles, or in Paris, or even back at Cirey would inspire him in the same way. He wasn't about to tell Emilie to leave, however, and he knew how much she loved to act and sing (her voice was still excellent). Wouldn't it be kind to their hostess—and a further reminder of the good days at Cirey—to create an impromptu play at Sceaux? There were plenty of his manuscripts Emilie could get from Paris that would be ideal.

And that is what they did. Fresh servants were hired, and the château spruced up as it hadn't been in years. There were actors to hire, and dancers from Paris; letters to be sent to the duchesse's elderly friends who might want to act; pages of text and music to have copied for the more professional actors who would have to be involved as well; musical instruments to dust off; the great hall to rearrange; and dozens of other tasks.

Voltaire tried to stay out of it and keep on with his writing, but after a few weeks he gave up. All the noise and bustle was too much fun. He left the manuscripts where they were and joined in, directing and rewriting and giving advice to anyone who would listen. Emilie was happy. It was delightful to be with Voltaire when he was in this mood, and she enjoyed the quick teasing that she could give him when his directorial instructions—as often happened—were irrelevant, contradictory, or both.

After a few preliminary efforts they were ready for the big performance. It would be on December 15, and since it meant so much—and now that he finally was free of his upstairs room—Voltaire decided that they shouldn't stint on the invitations. He had Emilie arrange for a print run of several hundred, which they had their servants distribute to everyone they knew in Paris, and then Voltaire had more invitations printed, which might as well be offered to all those interesting people they *didn't* know. One guest jotted down what was written on the invitation:

> *A new company of actors will present an original comedy on Friday 15 December, at the theater of Sceaux. Everyone is welcome. Come at 6 o'clock promptly. Order your [returning] carriage to be in the courtyard between 7.30 and 8. After 6 o'clock, the doors will be closed to the public.*

It turned dark early that winter afternoon, but the carriages started coming anyway. There were dozens, then more dozens, and soon there were hundreds. By the time of the strict 6 P.M. cutoff—with Longchamp no doubt happily fussing to enforce the rules—as many as five hundred people had crowded into the director of the Honey Bee Society's no-longer-forgotten château. It was the greatest gathering Sceaux had seen—and the finest of thank-yous from one now-recovered writer to his trusting elderly friend.

VII

LUNEVILLE

22

The Court of Stanislas and Catherine

Neither of them wanted to go back to the coldness of the past few years after that. But Paris and the nearby court at Versailles had too many overtones of what had gone wrong. It was time to leave.

Without quite saying why—and carefully explaining to Paris friends that they were just trying this for a while—Emilie and Voltaire hired a carriage, loaded up crates of books and clothes, squeezed in Emilie's maid, and sent Longchamp a half-day ahead so that he could make sure hot meals were ready at all the inns they would use along way. They would return, once more, to Cirey.

It was cold when they arrived, and there hadn't even been time to warn Madame Champbonin, so there was no greeting committee as there had been most other times. But the few staff that always remained at the château had been alerted by Longchamp, and so several of the fireplaces were blazing; extra food would be brought in soon as well.

After they had been there only a few days, a carriage with striking insignia pulled into the graveled courtyard. It was the crest of Stanislas, the deposed king of Poland. His daughter had married Louis XV, and

Stanislas had been granted control of the wealthy duchy of Lorraine, to the east of Cirey. (French success at Philippsburg years before had given Versailles the power to install him there.) But stepping out was neither the great king himself nor one of his official ministers, but a medium-sized, middle-aged man, wearing the long black robes and distinctive collar crucifix of the Society of Jesus: Father Joseph de Menou.

He'd met Emilie and Voltaire before, and on this cold January day he accepted their hearty invitation into the warmth of the château. There was easy conversation about what was happening at Lunéville, where Stanislas's Lorraine court was located, and interested queries about the gossip from Versailles. Only as the day went on did Menou broach his purpose. Would, by any chance, these two individuals care to visit the great King Stanislas at Lunéville? They would be hosted in style, and because of Voltaire's stature as a poet and Emilie's renown as a scientific thinker, it would be an honor: exactly what Stanislas had long dreamed of for his loyal Lorraine subjects.

This was tempting: it could be yet another bonding adventure, and would also be less pressured than uninterrupted weeks facing each other at Cirey. After a brief private discussion, Emilie and Voltaire told Father Menou that they accepted.

Almost as soon as they got to Lunéville—and even though they were put up in grand apartments in the main palace—they realized that Menou hadn't actually been as altruistic as he'd pretended. Stanislas had a mistress, the casually sensual Catherine de Boufflers, and Menou couldn't bear her and her influence on the good king.

For over a year Menou had been trying to get rid of her, telling the sixty-six-year-old married Stanislas that fornication with the gorgeous Catherine would condemn his soul to hell for all eternity. Just to be sure the warning took—for Menou, although celibate, understood that fallible humankind, and male humankind in particular, is prone to lapses—Menou had the king fund a vast retreat building, where he would bring Stanislas for days of somber, chilling reflection.

Each time Stanislas emerged he was shaken, and his soul was hardened: nothing, he realized—and this knowledge was now in his body, not just in his mind—nothing was worth chancing the damnation that lurked just a few years ahead. That's why Catherine, the mistress, knew never to approach him in the first hours after Father Menou let go. She would wait, often till the next morning—even older, morally chastened men are liable to find a resurgence of corporeal interest upon waking—before sitting on the end of the royal bed, casually holding the royal arm, and perhaps letting a firm young forefinger trace circles on the royal shoulder.

The medieval logician Jean Buridan described the plight of what came to be called Buridan's ass, which was placed exactly equidistant between two equally tempting piles of tasty hay and consequently died of starvation, unable to decide which way to turn. Stanislas was more sensible in his decision making. He couldn't risk his immortal soul by not going to regular confession, let alone missing the more occasional deep spiritual retreats with Father Menou. But since his physical body was, as Menou pointed out, such a fragile, insignificant, ramshackle thing, it would be most inconsiderate to keep the thoughtful Catherine de Boufflers from offering her regular ministrations as well. In his dilemma, both body and soul had to undergo these regular salves.

This was the impasse that the frustrated Menou had resolved to break. A more discreet mistress might just have been acceptable, but a mistress who had lived in Lunéville for many years and built up an entire faction of courtiers and officials willing to mock Jesuit authority was too much. Menou couldn't force Stanislas to drop Catherine, tempting though that might be, for she had family connections at Versailles (and Stanislas, although easygoing in most things, was protective of certain pleasures). But if Menou could distract the king by offering him someone more worthy, then perhaps the king himself would drop de Boufflers. A famed thinker such as Madame du Châtelet would be ideal—hence the invitation at Cirey. Menou had heard how separate she and Voltaire had been in Paris, and thought she'd be attracted to the wealthy, distinguished old king.

It was a total misreading by the celibate Jesuit. It's true that Emilie and Voltaire were no longer the tightly bonded couple they'd been in the first years at Cirey. But this didn't mean that Emilie would have any interest in Stanislas.

Instead, to Menou's mortification, it was Catherine and Emilie who became fast friends. Although Emilie was renowned in scientific circles and received awards from foreign academies, she'd always had a healthy appetite for earthly pleasures, and in Catherine she recognized a kindred spirit. There was a popular doggerel that Catherine modified and proposed for the epitaph on her own tomb:

> *Here within this peace profound*
> *a most genteel woman rests*
> *Who took her pleasure while on earth*
> *as all her lovers can attest.*

The two women began gossiping about mutual acquaintances, and dressed as matching sultan and Turk for a masked ball, and in general showed no sign whatsoever of competing for the same lover.

The king was happy, for at his age he experienced only fear at the thought he might have to satisfy a second mistress (for no one who'd known the wondrous Catherine was going to drop her as the first one). What he wanted from his new guests was something very different. He'd heard about the massively popular new play that had been performed at Sceaux—like everyone in the small provincial courts that France was dotted with, he followed Parisian gossip with desperation—and now he had the chance of getting its creators to direct the same roles here.

Voltaire loved that. Could Zadig himself have had a greater transformation than to escape from the desolation of the Honey Bee's tower to the glory of Stanislas's luxurious court? They performed the Sceaux plays, which were so well received here that they performed them again; Voltaire even let himself be persuaded to bring out his other old manuscripts and let the Lunéville court perform them as well.

Through it all, Emilie was flourishing. She starred in one show after another, carrying the singing lead in Destouches and La Motte's opera *Issé* more beautifully than she'd ever done before. She and Voltaire both realized that their physical relationship was not going to start again—the way they'd hurt each other in the Versailles years was too much to overcome—but Emilie's exuberance here reminded Voltaire of what he'd always loved about her. From their friendship, he began to write little odes to her again.

Everyone admired the two of them. There was plenty of opportunity, for Stanislas always went to bed by 10 P.M., and once he was asleep, Catherine opened up her rooms for a livelier group to meet. The impossible Madame de Graffigny had long since moved to Paris, but several of her friends, who'd hung on every word of her letters during her breathless visit to Cirey in 1738, were still at the Lunéville court. Now they had the chance to lionize Voltaire and Emilie in person, and so they crowded around.

One young poet in those gatherings, Jean-François, the marquis de Saint-Lambert, was especially attractive for Voltaire. His family's seat had been in an isolated hamlet, and from his teenage years he had planned to be a poet, even admitting in a note to an older admirer when he was eighteen that, "yes, despite my youth, and I'm sure my weak talents, I'm going to let out my Muse. I know it's insolent, but that's the beauty of my plan!"

Voltaire had met him briefly then, and had been struck by the youngster's poetry. Now, seeing how his writing had matured, as well as seeing the confidence and dry wit this healthy young man had developed, he liked him even more. The fact that there were rumors that Saint-Lambert had managed to bed Catherine herself—with nothing more to offer than his charm and quick wit—was another mark in his favor. Saint-Lambert in turn worshiped Voltaire, as the hero he'd always wished to be.

Despite the attention and admirers, though, after barely a month Voltaire was feeling ready to go back. He'd made his point to anyone watching from Versailles that the queen's own father was happy to have him as an honored visitor, but even Voltaire had a level, albeit an elevated one, beyond which endless attention began to pale. But when he suggested to Emilie that they leave Lunéville and return to Cirey or Paris, she barely seemed to register it. Surely, she suggested, they could stay a bit longer.

Voltaire was bemused, and wrote in absolute secrecy as always to

Marie-Louise in Paris, with whom he was continuing his on-again off-again affair: "My dear child, I don't know when I'll return. I'm here without my cozy slippers, or—what's worse—without my books. Perhaps we'll leave in three or four days, perhaps in two weeks . . . Life in Lunéville is still charming—but ah, nothing is as charming as life with you, V."

The delay meant more plays, and then, when even that got tiring, more tours that Stanislas led around his miniature kingdom, proudly pointing out his new grottoes and water jets and canals. This usually excited visitors from rural Lorraine tremendously, for they were near-perfect replicas of what could be found at Louis XV's Versailles. Yet since Voltaire had just suffered several years stuck in the grubby reality of that court, he found this small-scale copy less than compelling. He made polite noises, but truly was ready to go. When he insisted to Emilie, she seemed to agree. Yet then, to Marie-Louise:

> *At Lunéville, 3 April [1748]*
>
> *My dear child, I've already forwarded my baggage; I suspect it's in Paris by now. But we've had a further delay, for Madame de Boufflers [Catherine] seems to be experiencing a female indisposition. With her raised temperature we can't abandon her. I've absolutely no idea when we'll be able to leave....*
>
> *V*

The only consolation was that Emilie was even more glowing than before. She'd often been tense about getting enough time for her work, yet now, when Voltaire would stroll through her rooms, he could see that her Newton papers were stacked to one side and not messily strewn about, as when she was working at full tilt. Something about the easy life at Lunéville was relaxing her. It was puzzling, actually. Why wouldn't she be working at this physics she loved, Voltaire wondered, now that she had so much time?

23

Saint-Lambert

She was in love: deliriously, wonderfully, inescapably. It was Saint-Lambert, of course—she'd eyed him from the very beginning, and found something about his confident eagerness irresistible. It helped that he'd grown into a strapping man, and, having just returned to Lunéville from several years in the cavalry—much as with Maupertuis a decade earlier—he had the gentleness that often comes from being physically confident.

Their affair had begun at a party that one of Catherine's friends had given ("If I hadn't gone up to you and spoken first, we'd never have started," Emilie wrote), and then had continued with walks, rides, and soon the first snatched nights together. It had been hard to make the arrangements at first—everything had to be kept private, for Lunéville was crowded with gossip-ready courtiers—but Emilie had noted a large harp that was kept in one of the king's public rooms, which anyone might walk past. It was only used for occasional concerts, but it was so well carved that it would be natural for interested visitors to pause in front of it, as if examining the woodwork or strings.

That's where she and Saint-Lambert left their first notes. Emilie would ink one on a small lace-edged card, fold it with a blue or pink ribbon around it, and then ever so casually, while strolling through the palace—but checking that no one was too close—leave it in the harp. Saint-Lambert, strolling a little later, would pass by the harp and collect it, leaving one of his own in return.

All of his are lost, but several of Emilie's survive, half crumbled and yellowed from the two centuries that have passed:

> *It's a beautiful day out, but I can't do anything without you! Let's go and feed bread to the swans. We can ride out on horseback.*

> *You whispered such wonderful things to me last night. You've conquered my heart, you know.*

> *I'm such a lazy girl. When I wake up, all I do is think of you. Come over as soon as you can, will you? I . . . think we can stay in today.*

A few years earlier, in the "Happiness" manuscript that she'd worked on when everything was falling apart with Voltaire, she'd written, with calm logic, that it was ridiculous to think that an intelligent woman needed a man to be happy; that even if there were pleasures such a relation could bring, no one who'd grown old—she gave the age of thirty as the cutoff—could feel them with the full intensity of the young. But that had been written before Saint-Lambert—and he was the most devoted of lovers. He described waking in the morning:

> *How wonderful to sense you beside me*
> *Bare, uncovered*
> *   naked in the fresh dawn light.*

> *I open the shutters*
> *   and you stretch your arms to me*
> *I seek your beautiful eyes*
> *   I press my lips to yours.*

You breathe faster.

And when you cry out
you barely hear me
when I whisper what I feel

When I whisper how I adore you

They helped each other, as all lovers must. She was given the confidence that she was worthy of love; he found that this famous, internationally respected woman thought him worth loving as well. They exchanged lockets; they found they'd read many of the same books—Montaigne and Virgil, Dryden and Hutcheson. At night, when it was safe, they would sometimes hold hands while strolling in the darkened grounds; once this led to her tumbling into a ditch and scraping her leg, which required a quick cover story when she got back—and as a result strengthened their bond.

She couldn't share the technicalities of her physics, but he'd always loved the night sky, and she no doubt told him what she understood of how the stars worked. Cautiously—for he'd been keeping it private for many years—he confided that he dreamed of writing a great poem on nature, with a series of verses on each season. It was a popular theme, as with Vivaldi's *Four Seasons* just twenty years before (and would burst into popular attention even more, with Jean-Jacques Rousseau's writings just a few years later). She'd already run into Rousseau in Paris, where he was still just an irritable minor music composer, and she probably sensed that a new, more personally emotive tone was developing. It helped draw her to her young poet here, with his confident reading of the latest cultural moods.

Saint-Lambert might have felt their time was infinite, but she was older and knew it would be different. Even though Saint-Lambert would have assured her that his affair with Catherine was over, Emilie understood that Catherine was the sort of woman who depended entirely on beauty and sexual attraction to survive. She would always view attractive males in the court as her potential catch, not to be taken without permission.

> *My sweet, it's not enough to love each other, and to say it a hundred*
> *times a day. We have to be as discreet as possible. Voltaire's only going*
> *to be a bit jealous when he finds out about us, but Catherine will be*
> *furious. And she will of course: it's just a matter of time.*

Emilie tried to avoid the worst of the future upsets by deciding to break the news to Stanislas before he heard it from anyone else. Once she even got so far as telling him before dinner that there was something very important she wanted to speak to him about, and when he said (as she recounted in a letter that night), "Go ahead, my dear," she whispered that it was too personal, and she needed to be alone with him after. But when the meal was over she couldn't bring herself to raise it, and just put off the appointment.

Soon Catherine did work out what was happening, but instead of being angry, as Emilie feared, she seemed only too glad to help. (Voltaire was so busy directing their plays that he still didn't suspect anything.) For Stanislas knew that Catherine had been involved with Saint-Lambert the year before. When Catherine let Emilie go ahead, it was a clear signal to Stanislas that he no longer had to worry about the good-looking young Saint-Lambert threatening to take the affection of his chief mistress.

As a result, Catherine gave Emilie and Saint-Lambert the keys to a hidden bedroom, reachable from near the main palace, and there the two lovers had an even safer place to meet. Emilie still suspected that Catherine's encouraging mood wouldn't last, but she did have to admit everything so far had been easier than she'd anticipated so far.

By mid-May the excuses to Voltaire were getting so implausible, however, that Emilie had to give in, and told him it was about time they went to Paris after all. (Everyone expected her to be there to supervise the court case lingering up in Brussels.) Even then the loyal Catherine seemed more than willing to help her new friend, making sure that Voltaire was kept behind in Lunéville on important "theatrical matters" for a while, so that Emilie could spend several days alone with Saint-Lambert in the nearby city of Nancy.

It was their best time. Saint-Lambert's mother and sister were in the city, and he offended them greatly by not bothering to see them, but he didn't care: he had eyes, heart, only for Emilie. She couldn't resist. "I used to make resolutions that I wouldn't fall in love," she wrote to him immediately afterward. "But that's finally over now . . . I had no idea I could love anyone so much."

From Nancy she joined Voltaire in Paris, but how could she stay away from Saint-Lambert now? Just eight days after arriving in Paris, the ever-equable Longchamp wrote:

> Madame du Châtelet has convinced M. de Voltaire to return to Lunéville immediately (where I must say she seemed exceptionally happy, during our somewhat extended excursion there previously). I have been engaged to arrange for driving the horses with such rapidity that we shall not have to stop at any point along the way. In consequence of this decision, it will fall to my services to provision the carriage with all the sustenance we shall require for this unexpected journey.

Voltaire didn't mind leaving again at such short notice, for he was going through certain difficult times with Marie-Louise. "I will," he'd been forced to write her after one rather embarrassing evening, "bring you my member, even if it is somewhat flaccid. . . . I know you won't mind." He wanted time out to avoid further embarrassment.

There were adventures along the way, and at one point when they did stop after all, for a simple bowl of soup at a roadside inn, the hostess brought out an elegant tray and a porcelain serving dish, all under a silver cover. It seemed a sign of great politeness, until Longchamp went to pay and was told, abruptly, that it would cost one pure gold louis—the equivalent of several hundred dollars today. Voltaire stepped down from the carriage and began to reason with the landlady, explaining that truly it was shortsighted to try this, for of course he would tell everyone else who took this road, and she would end up losing so much business that her paltry profit from this one encounter would not be worth it. In good innkeeper fashion, she replied to this forensic rebuttal by gesturing for all the other tradesmen in this town, Châlons-sur-Marne, to leave their shops and surround the visitors. Longchamp remembered:

> In but five or six minutes a substantial and most uncivilized group was around us, raising a striking clamor, and in lieu of reasoned discourse, was engaged—if I might summarize the gist—in declaring that the landlady was right. M. de Voltaire saw that he was unlikely to prevail in continued discourse, and expressed to me his opinion that we might find it wise to "fall back," and indeed, without excessive delay, abandon our position. It fell to me to pay the insufferable innkeeper, before we were again on our way.

When they arrived in Lunéville, Saint-Lambert had a bad cold. Emilie had spent over a decade dealing with Voltaire's absurd malingering, so this was nirvana: a healthy man who would soon be cured. She sent him tea and broth to sip ("take it very hot, but only small amounts to start"); she found chicken wings for him to eat, and assembled plenty of their favorite books to read. She sat in his room—with others around for propriety—and made sure his pillows were plumped, and the ventilation was right, and the doctors weren't bleeding him too often. Since he couldn't collect her letters from the harp, he brought his trusted valet Antoine in on their secret, to carry the sealed notes.

On one of Antoine's first missions she sent back: "You know, I could almost fall in love with Antoine, just for carrying me your words. I can't write back now—too many people around—but you've never been more tender, my love. Let's talk more tonight." While Saint-Lambert was still ill, she'd often stay and just watch him sleep; but when he got better, they went back to constant, regular lovemaking ("In our love," she wrote, "there's no such word as *enough*"). She'd already, quietly in a letter, told him of her plans—"I'd like to spend the rest of my life with you, either at Lunéville, or at Cirey"—and he'd responded with the affection they both craved.

By August Voltaire really did have to get back for rehearsals of his new play, *Sémiramis*. Emilie was at the resort town of Plombières, where she was accompanying an oddly moody Catherine for a few days. When a letter arrived addressed to Catherine—but clearly in Saint-Lambert's handwriting—Catherine opened it, read it, and then made a point of tearing it into little pieces. She said nothing about what was in it, and Emilie wasn't going to ask—clearly it was innocuous, and Catherine was trying to make her jealous. But a day later, a Thursday in late August, yet another letter for Catherine arrived from Saint-Lambert. This one, however, wasn't in its own envelope. It was inside a letter that Saint-Lambert had sent to Emilie.

By itself that wasn't too odd, for postal couriers were so expensive that friends would often share envelopes and use each other to pass on letters. But the note to Catherine wasn't sealed. Emilie couldn't resist, and opened it.

24

Collapse

It was a love letter. Saint-Lambert had written to Catherine that he missed her, that he loved her madly, that he'd "never cease to adore her."

Emilie was beside herself. "What do you mean by this?" she immediately wrote back to him.

> You took my trust, and yet you wrote Catherine so that I would see it. You've deceived me.
>
> I'm not going to let myself believe that you love her. If I believed that, I'd have to believe that you're a monster of deception and duplicity. You probably thought you needed to write like that to Catherine to flatter her and keep your friendship. Well, be brave enough to lose that friendship. Lovers don't go around telling other people that they "love them madly," that they "adore" them. Or at least, my lovers don't.
>
> Maybe I won't be able to say all this when we meet. But it's your choice if you want to threaten our life like this. I still

want you—but I'm not going to be the person you're trying to make me become.

It's up to you to change my views. My feelings are frozen, but at least there's one advantage in my feeling like this. I'd missed you desperately before.

I miss you less now.

While Emilie was deciding what to do, Voltaire was so preoccupied by rehearsals in Paris that he barely noticed that neither she nor Saint-Lambert showed signs of making it to his play. As part of his effort to get back in Marie-Louise's arms he'd asked her advice on an important bit of staging, but then, like a fool, he'd actually listened to what she said. It was a delicate matter, for his new play *Sémiramis* hinged on the discovery of the true murderer of a great king, and having seen *Hamlet* in London, Voltaire was tempted to bring a ghost onto the stage in Paris.

It was daring, for the rules for drama in France were much stricter than they were in England, and no one had succeeded in doing this before. The question Voltaire had asked Marie-Louise was whether the ghost should appear dressed in ordinary clothes or should be shrouded in big black robes. Marie-Louise had decided that voluminous black shrouds were best.

On the opening night, over a thousand people were in the audience, and the theater was so crowded that—as usual—many of them were crowded tight on the actual stage. Crébillon and others who had been insulted by Voltaire over the years—which meant a large percentage of all writers in Paris—had pooled together to hire a group of young aristocrats to hoot and yell insults during the play. Voltaire knew very well that Crébillon would try that, and so had paid substantially to get a larger group of applauders on his side.

The play was going well, with the two groups of interrupters evenly balanced, until the ghost appeared.

Possibly if it had been a more athletic ghost, Voltaire would have had a chance of victory. But it was an aged, stately actor who was now lost under Marie-Louise's chosen voluminous robes. There was no tra-

clague

dition of stage lights to guide such entrances, so there was a certain amount of ungainly staggering before he even managed to reach the stage. Crébillon's claque laughed. The ghost was angry and pushed harder to make his way forward. But the stage was crowded, and Voltaire's supporters made it worse, for they now pushed together, to try to see just who was coming their way whom they were trying to support. Dozens of young men were shoving back and forth; the other spectators onstage couldn't see what was happening, and so they had to push closer as well.

All royal institutions needed an official guard, and the Comédie Française was no exception. When this largely ceremonial officer saw how the poor lost ghost was struggling to get onstage, he realized he had an important job to do and called out in a drilling voice: "Come on! Come on! Make way for the ghost!" It was downhill from there. The next day Voltaire went dressed in a thick cloak, with a big hat tipped low, to listen incognito to gossip at the nearby Café Procope. What he heard was so distressing that he decided to leave Paris almost immediately.

He wanted Emilie's ministrations in this time of need, and told Longchamp to take him to Lunéville. His health had always been poor, he confided to Longchamp, and indeed, on the coach ride back he had a near-total physical collapse. He was unable to eat, losing ever more weight from his already thin frame.

Longchamp was so worried that at one stop, where Voltaire seemed barely able to walk, he called for a priest, and also for the official governmental supervisor for the region. Voltaire waved the priest away and dictated some final notes to Longchamp, which he managed to sign with a weak, quivering letter V. Sunk in the depths of self-pity, and desolate at the thought of his life ending in this lost town, he looked at his servant and said that his one consolation was that at least the loyal Longchamp would be there to toss a handful of dirt on his grave.

Emilie had little sympathy when she heard about this, and there's no evidence she even bothered to reply. She'd left the Plombières resort—suffering the embarrassment of realizing how much she'd confided about Saint-Lambert to Catherine—and had a far more serious matter to consider. Did she want Saint-Lambert back?

He'd shown he could be a liar. But was that fundamental to his nature or just something he was prompted to do by pressure from the admittedly highly skilled Catherine? For perhaps Saint-Lambert was just getting so smitten by Emilie that Catherine had to show she was still in control. Yet would Catherine leave them alone after that?

In the second week of September, everyone arrived back in Lorraine. (The court had moved to its autumn quarters in Commercy, a bit outside of Lunéville.) Voltaire had recovered, of course, as soon as Longchamp fed him some tasty, grease-soaked grilled birds, then gave him plenty of watered wine to drink, and made sure he had a long night's sleep. Catherine was smugly friendly again, though Emilie knew she couldn't trust her.

Emilie made her decision. She needed love, and Saint-Lambert could give it. All she had to do was persuade him to focus on her. That shouldn't be too difficult, for she'd managed to make even Richelieu a reliable lover, after all. And even though she was older now, she could offer a world in Paris that was beyond anything Catherine knew. She spoke at length with Saint-Lambert, and they imagined how he'd meet her literary friends, and soon he was more committed than ever, leading her on walks, late-night rowing on the lakes, and more shared horse rides. He asked her to send him her portrait so that he could wear it in a watch, and specifically asked for one with her dressed as she'd been when she'd sung in the opera *Issé,* those first days when he'd seen her at Stanislas's court.

Five years earlier, after Voltaire had been away for month after month at Frederick's court, Emilie had written that something goes out of a relationship when the partners are separated for too long. She didn't want that to happen with Saint-Lambert. They went back to regular lovemaking, sometimes in his room, and now increasingly often in hers. It wasn't the full love she wished, but she forced herself to believe that could come back.

By now Voltaire recognized that something was going on, and one evening that October he descended from his upstairs apartment a little before the usual dinner time to do some exploring. "Finding no servant outside Emilie's door," Longchamp later recounted,

> he felt free to enter without the usual procedure of being formally announced. My master then traversed her apartment, still without encountering any other person, until he came to a small room at the back, from which a dim light could be seen. He there came to believe that he saw Madame in close proximity with M. de Saint-Lambert, on a sofa in her chambers; engaged, if I might put it this way, in discourses which concerned neither poetry nor philosophy.
>
> Upon this striking turn of events, M. de Voltaire was struck with such surprise and indignation that he was unable to fully restrain his temper. He commented, with somewhat violent words, on what he had just seen. M. de Saint-Lambert, preserving an admirable sangfroid, remarked that he thought it inappropriate for M. Voltaire to censure *his* conduct, and that if the gentleman was unhappy, they merely had to leave the apartment, and step outside the château to conclude the argument.

Voltaire knew that the pen was mightier than the sword, but he also understood the difference between a stirring metaphor and stepping out to imminent death. He tactfully withdrew from this threat by the quite fit young soldier, and instructed Longchamp to ready a coach: he was leaving, and he was leaving now.

Emilie took Longchamp aside and told him to stall. Although she and Voltaire were no longer lovers, she realized that any male would be upset to so unambiguously see how she'd taken the obvious next step after the ending of their affair. She went to Voltaire's room, sat at the foot of his bed, and then said—while Longchamp prolonged the act of lighting the candles as long as possible—some words in English, which to Longchamp's ears sounded affectionate, but it was hard for him to tell. Only when he left them alone did they switch back to French, but since a humble servant was given a room across just a very thin partition from the master's room, he was able—or so he said—to hear most of what came next.

Emilie's first gambit was unimpressive. (She still didn't know the details of Voltaire's own affair, so she couldn't tax him with that.) Voltaire had weak eyes—he'd often said as much, hadn't he?—so had he considered that he might have been mistaken in what he thought he saw, given the low light in her rooms? This got Voltaire riled again— what he'd seen would have been impossible for a blind person to miss—so Emilie quickly changed tack and brought out her ultimate weapon: Voltaire's health.

He was ill, was he not? He suffered, in a way that hardly any other mortal did, from a body that was fragile, delicate. Voltaire agreed, almost sadly. It was a shame that it took an occasion such as this for her compassion to come out, but yes, he had to admit she was quite right.

With that major premise established, her syllogistic conclusion was swift. Did he not realize that she was doing all this—those endeavors he'd seen with Saint-Lambert—to *protect* Voltaire's health? Certainly he remembered how excitable her temperament in bed had been. A friend who was coldhearted would ignore all that and insist on making an invalid fullfil those requirements, with no care at all for his health. But Emilie cared. And given that she was going to be so considerate on his behalf, wasn't it best for the new partner to be a mutual friend, whom they could both admire?

Voltaire's resistance melted. He'd always loved Emilie's extraordinary quickness, her sparkling confidence; he also—though this is something he wouldn't tell her—had reason, from a successful visit to Marie-Louise's during the latest Paris stay, to believe that that other relation might continue as well. A delicate acceptance of Emilie's logic was in order.

The next day he met Saint-Lambert. But instead of demanding that the duel take place—which would have saddled poor Saint-Lambert with the dishonor of being the man who slaughtered Europe's greatest poet—Voltaire took the young writer's hands in a double grip and, almost in tears, refused even to accept his earnest apologies. "My child," Longchamp recounts Voltaire saying, "I've forgiven everything." He explained that it was he, Voltaire, who was in the wrong, while "you, however, are at the happy age where one can still be a lover." He told Saint-Lambert to enjoy those pleasures, so brief in our life, and explained that an old man, an invalid like himself, was no longer made for such joys.

It was such an attractive pose that Emilie didn't mind, even though they both understood it wasn't quite the truth. She knew he was having some sort of affair in Paris (though she guessed it was with a noted actress); he'd had his suspicions about her even before Saint-Lambert, when she'd taken to spending undue amounts of time with one of their most attentive lawyers in Brussels. But it didn't matter. If anything, their shared pretense that he was too old for romance brought their true friendship somehow closer. In their worst days, when he'd been racing back and forth to Frederick in Prussia, he'd written her a poem that captured how they could both imagine their relation to be. Liberally translated:

> *Were I to still be a lover,*
> *You'd need to bring me back*
> *   to the age of my first loving;*
> *to the start of my days.*
>
> *For I'm dying you see*
> *   I can't be your lover*
> *I'm old.*
>
> *(It's the worst death*
> *It's a death worse than death)*
>
> *I can give you friendship, though*
> *   from my heart I can;*
> *I swear I can . . .*

He wasn't too old to have sex, of course, as his times with Marie-Louise showed. What he was really saying was that he wasn't fully in love with Emilie—but that their years together had opened them up so much to each other that he still needed her warmth. Emilie understood that now, and she and Voltaire were ever more at ease with each other that autumn.

Voltaire's year was finishing well. He could write to Marie-Louise with confidence after his successful performances in Paris ("How is my beloved? . . . thinking of you gives me really quite frequent erections . . . I'm afire to see you every hour"). He was rewriting the mangled *Sémiramis* and was confident that by keeping spectators off the stage and working on the crucial last act, he would carry off another great success.

Even the insistently independent Madame de Pompadour at Versailles was acting in a way he approved of. The Church still paid virtually no tax, even though it supported many thousands of officials of no discernible religious inclination: the government paid for almost all their needs, despite their enormous landed estates. A new finance minister, Jean-Baptiste de Machault, was proposing a minimum 5 percent tax, to at least begin to rectify that injustice.

If the king supported Machault, then the Church would be his enemy—and that was something Pompadour was desperate to ensure. (For if, by contrast, the king *did* get emotionally close to the Church, he might drop her as a mark of his receiving divine grace, as he had dropped her predecessor Châteauroux in those fervid moments of sunstroke at Metz years before.) As a result, because of Pompadour's influence the king really did seem to be on the verge of establishing the country's finances in a rational, equitable way.

Voltaire also found an ingenious way to publish *Zadig*. Printers had regularly pirated copies of his previous books by preparing several thousand extra copies when he gave them the manuscript and then selling those copies under the counter. One of the worst offenders had been the Prault family in Paris. Voltaire now contacted them, explained that bygones should be bygones, and—ostensibly under extreme secrecy—let them prepare several hundred copies of the first half of *Zadig*.

He asked them to send him those initial copies for safekeeping until he could convey to them the second half of the text. (They, of course, had printed up thousands of additional copies of this first half, and were only waiting for his remaining text so that they could go ahead with their pirated editions and cheat him out of his payments as before.) What he neglected to tell them was that under similar secrecy he'd had a like-minded printer in Lorraine prepare a few hundred copies of the second half. He now collected the two sets of unbound pages, hired a few nimble-fingered local women, and had them do all the binding and sewing. The swindlers in Paris and Lorraine had been outswindled: he now distributed, through trusted business associates in Paris, small numbers of exactly the edition he wished.

The *Zadig* story was hailed as a masterpiece, and Voltaire took that in his stride. He knew how good it was. Repeatedly in his life he'd appeared to be a fool—the bragging that got him sent to the Bastille, the failure of his fire experiments, the seemingly inane goading of Versailles authorities over the years. Yet repeatedly he'd also managed to turn defeat into victory. His stay in the Bastille had led to the triumph of his *Oedipus,* the de Rohan assault to his Letters from England, the fire experiment to his *Discourse in Verse on Man.* He needed the energy he acquired from those apparent defeats. The weeks spent locked up at Sceaux with Longchamp hadn't been an embarrassment either, but had led to this conquering success with *Zadig.* Once again he was able to show that he'd ended up on top.

For Emilie, the rest of the autumn was far worse. For a while Saint-Lambert continued trying hard to romance her, with his mixture of elegance and occasional puppyish eagerness. But he was getting out of his depth. He laboriously wrote her a play now, about two Iroquois Indians who shared a wife. Emilie almost certainly kept from pointing out the obvious—how much worse it was than the texts Voltaire could dash off in a moment—but others at Lunéville undoubtedly made those comments for her.

It's the problem all younger lovers face. Saint-Lambert was barely thirty, while Emilie was already forty-two. When a couple first meets, their relation can just be of two bodies, entranced in a timeless space, and there the younger one naturally has the advantage. As time goes on, though, wider life enters in.

It would have been different if Saint-Lambert had been courting the usual possible companion for a man of his age, which would be a girl in her teens or early twenties. She would be impressed that he had occasional garrison command of an actual infantry group, albeit in the scarcely substantial army of Lorraine. Emilie's husband, Florent-Claude, however, had surpassed that level thirty years before and was now one of his country's most distinguished cavalry officers, having commanded large battle groups in Europe's most powerful army. Saint-Lambert might also have bragged to a youngster about the position he held at the Lunéville court, but that was as nothing to the Versailles that Voltaire and Emilie knew so well.

It wasn't much of a help that Emilie didn't care about these differences and even tried to encourage his career. To an old friend she wrote that she was sending "some verses written by a young man who . . . I know here. I feel sure that you'll like them. He's dying with envy to meet you—and he's quite worthy of it. I'd like to bring him to Cirey. Let's arrange for you to meet him there."

Saint-Lambert was humiliated. He knew he was failing—in skill, in charm, and in the ability to keep up with Emilie's social level, let alone ever support her. Even the romantic poem he'd presented to Emilie about waking up in the morning with her wasn't quite as effortlessly written as he'd implied. He'd labored over it for a long time, for he'd started it during his affair with Catherine a year before. But what young man is going to be happy admitting that he's incapable of matching a woman? It was made worse by the fact that he'd always been effortlessly attractive: handsome, yet shy enough in demeanor that women wanted to take care of him. He'd never had to face a truly hard problem before—and so he panicked. Instead of having the decency to say he couldn't continue their relationship, he began to shun her.

Emilie had to pretend to outsiders that everything was all right. To another old friend in Paris she wrote in her usual buoyant tone: "I send you a thousand greetings, fine sir, as does M. de Voltaire, who's here with me. I hope we'll see you this winter—you'll find me in Paris at the start of the New Year."

But with Saint-Lambert it was different. She tried friendly cajoling at first:

> *I wanted to wake up with you, and it was only 11 P.M. when the first party finished—but then you rushed off. Do write and tell me why. I've never loved you more, my sweet. Now I'll have to brush my teeth alone.*
>
> *My sweet, can't you even try to come see me tonight?*

His coldness got worse:

> *You stopped by at 4 P.M.—but we'd agreed to meet at 1 P.M.! You know I'm leaving for Paris soon. Please, please don't treat me like this.*
>
> *You barely looked my way today. Why? Why are you suddenly treating me so coldly?*
>
> *Are you trying to make us be apart for ever?*

Their relationship was ending, but they still spent a few more times together in bed. There was no love now. Saint-Lambert was just using her—and it's possible he tried to insist on his prowess, in this one realm where he'd been so pleasing to her before. Suddenly the one thing happened that she couldn't control. She'd always been careful in contraception with her partners before. Yet now she was pregnant, and in an era when just getting through one's forties was impressive, there was no way of telling if she would survive the labor to come.

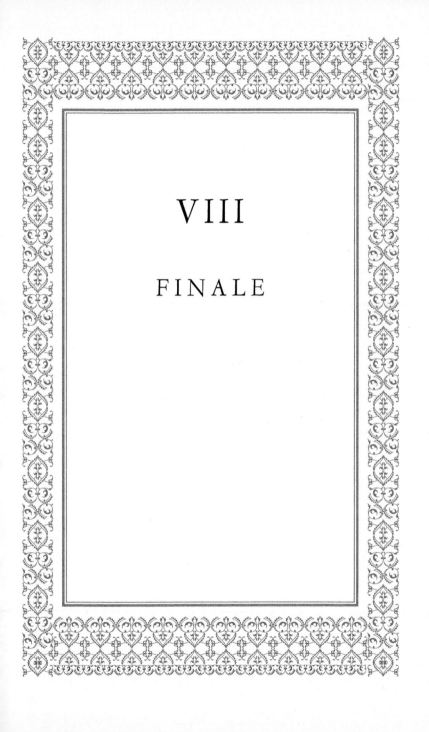

VIII

FINALE

25

Pregnancy

She didn't mention it to Voltaire at first, and just said that they should stop at Cirey for a brief while. Saint-Lambert stayed behind; he was barely speaking to Emilie now.

She was restless in the carriage with Voltaire, and at a stop they made halfway to Cirey for the horses to be watered and fed, she climbed down to investigate the town. When she found several locals and a priest amenable to some gambling, she sat down to take them on at cards. She didn't let it finish when the horses were ready, but instead insisted on playing more, almost as if she needed the intensity of that concentration, that diversion from what was going to come next.

They left late, when night had already fallen and a cold rain had begun. It was almost impossible to see ahead. Longchamp was out in front when his horse lost its footing in the dark, flipping him over into a waterlogged ditch. Then the horse landed partially on top of him— and made no effort to get up.

"This new position," Longchamp recounted, "seemed to strike my steed as being commodious for sleeping, and my struggles to extricate myself could not avail against his substantial weight. It was only when the carriage with Madame and Monsieur approached that my exhausted beast awoke, upon which he scrambled upward—a maneuver that, in its hastiness, placed me in greater anguish, I might say."

They arrived late on December 24. As a little girl, Emilie had gone to midnight Mass with her parents on that day; when she was twenty-six, she'd arranged to meet Maupertuis before an illicit night together in Paris; a little older, she and Voltaire had had years of blazing fires at Cirey on that day. Now, on this Christmas Eve of 1748, the stone and brick walls of Cirey were still icy cold; the fires being lit took hours to warm the main rooms. Longchamp directed the servants where to put the bags as Emilie and Voltaire went in.

She still didn't tell Voltaire she was pregnant, and for several days they went through the usual routine of unpacking and settling into their old rooms. Yet "instead of Madame being in her usual vivacious good humor," Longchamp noted, "she appeared, in my humble eye, to be unusually dreamy. I might even say sad."

When she finally did tell Voltaire, around January 1, he understood why she'd insisted they come to Cirey. Even if gossip was spreading that Saint-Lambert had been her lover, she and her husband had to at least make it seem plausible that Florent-Claude was the father of any living child she had. That was the only way to guarantee that the du Châtelet and de Breteuil inheritances stayed within the family. (Abortion would only have been considered as a desperate resort, for the ergot or other potions used for this purpose were highly dose-sensitive: too little and there was no effect, too much and fatal uterine bleeding would result.)

They sent word to Florent-Claude at his military base in Dijon, and when he arrived Voltaire left the two of them alone. Their son Louis was no longer at the house—he was serving in a regiment under Richelieu's command—and although Madame de Champbonin and the Comtesse de la Neuville were still in the area, and still eager to come over, they too respected what needed to happen.

Emilie and Florent-Claude spent days together: inspecting their estate on horseback and on foot. There were the forges outside, where the fire experiments from the 1737 Royal Academy competition had taken place, and the long stretching forests whose maintenance and harvesting they'd supervised for so long. They made a point of dining in clear view of the servants, Emilie in her finest gowns and with more jewels than ever, Florent-Claude also in his formal clothes, candles and silver and fine wines everywhere. After dinner there would be coffee, with Voltaire briefly joining their conversation, but then Florent-Claude and Emilie would go to a bedroom, to continue the crucial appearances for the servants.

"I believe," Longchamp remembered, "it was about three weeks into Monsieur le Marquis's most appreciated visitation that Madame announced she had reason to believe she was pregnant.... We certainly all congratulated her." Soon, from the staff's letters to their friends and relations serving at the great houses in Paris—as well as the "confidential" gossip that Champbonin and de la Neuville were soon to spread—it would be general knowledge in Paris and Versailles that Emilie du Châtelet was pregnant at the age of forty-two. Her husband, it was to be noted, was overjoyed. So too—and this would seem no odder than how she'd run the rest of her life—was she.

THE one thing that remained was to try to finish her scientific work. Since she'd been in Cirey too briefly after the Fontainebleau gambling to move the bulk of her library and papers there, she needed to return to Paris, where her best resources still were. She and Voltaire left in early February, when the weather had turned colder and snow was thick everywhere. They took their largest carriage, but it was so loaded on the outside with extra crates for their books and papers that the horses found it hard to gather speed. For warmth the carriage's wooden doors were sealed tight, and the occupants—Voltaire, Emilie, and Emilie's maid—were snuggled under furs and lap rugs. A bruised Longchamp was once again riding in front, on his not quite trusty steed. Dusk came early, so again it was dark when they left.

They'd been traveling many hours from Cirey when suddenly the rear axle on Voltaire's side broke, sending the wheel loose. The carriage skidded, then toppled over, with Voltaire at the bottom.

It was dead quiet outside, in the isolated cold, but from the carriage a weak call could be heard. It was Voltaire, informing everyone that he was alive, albeit steadily being compressed. The servants who'd been perched on the outside of the moving coach were thrown off, but unhurt in the deep snow. They climbed up onto the overturned coach, reached down through the now topside door, and "as one hauls a bucket up a well" started pulling the occupants free: first the bags, then the maid, then Emilie—and finally a startled and disoriented, but remarkably undamaged, Voltaire.

The accident was far enough from any town that it would be hours before servants could arrive back with help. But there were plenty of blankets, so although the temperature was below freezing, it wouldn't be too dangerous to wait. Emilie and Voltaire placed cushions in the thick snow beside the road, got under their favorite furs, and then lay back beneath the stars. Longchamp never would have lauded his own poetry, but even he briefly transcended himself in describing their wait that night:

> Despite the extreme froideur, [Madame and Monsieur] admired the beauty of the sky. It was serene, and stars were burning with a most vivid brightness. I detected no house or tree to disturb the least part of their view.
>
> We were aware that astronomy had always been one of their favorite studies. Ravished by this magnificent spectacle spread above and around them, they discoursed—while shivering, I should point out—on the nature and paths of the stars, and on the destiny of so many immense globes spread in space.
>
> I believe that only the fact that they lacked a telescope kept them from being perfectly happy. Their spirit being lost in the depths of the heavens, they no longer saw their situation on the earth—or, if I might be exact, their situation on the snow and in the middle of so much ice.

It was their last truly quiet moment together. The night was long; the nearest town was far. Emilie had spent a long time getting the skills to discover how this vast universe worked. If she'd been right in her Academy paper on the nature of light, there were even more stars than they could see now blazing away invisible to their sight.

They remained there for hours, pinned alone under the cold starlight. Finally the rescue party arrived: four local men lugging ropes, tools, and a new axle. Emilie and Voltaire slowly got up: there was work to do, a voyage to resume.

In Paris they moved into their old apartments on the Rue Traversière St. Honoré. Although Emilie tried to sequester herself from the crowds who wanted to invite her out, the bustle was too much for her to concentrate. Voltaire wanted to be helpful, but he was becoming brittle from the tension of her condition. Although he sometimes tried to joke about how easy it might turn out to be ("the new baby shall be categorized among [Emilie's] miscellaneous works"), he also remembered how Richelieu's even younger wife, Elisabeth, had died, as the complications from her pregnancy led to bleeding that no doctor could stop.

He snapped at Emilie when she was late for a meal, even though she was just trying to get extra time for her work. One morning, after he'd been especially short-tempered the night before, he knocked one of her favorite expensive cups from her hand when he abruptly jumped up from his sofa as she approached. He apologized, and immediately sent Longchamp to get a replacement—with instructions to pay whatever it took—but this wasn't the mood she needed.

Saint-Lambert was making it worse. "I've told you I'm pregnant," she wrote to him from Paris, "and that I need to make arrangements for my labor. Yet you haven't said a thing!" She was past anger. "This is a cruelty beyond all description—just as the sorrow I feel is beyond all expression."

The smoothly insincere Catherine came to Paris from the Lunéville court and invited Emilie out for meals, ostensibly as her friend. But then she pointedly dropped remarks about Saint-Lambert and how he was thinking of traveling to England in the autumn, saying

that apparently—and she really shouldn't be sharing this with Emilie—
he was telling everyone that nothing else important was coming up
that he needed to do.

Despite the ease of the pregnancy, Emilie was getting ever stronger
premonitions that her labor would be difficult. It wasn't only her good
friend Elisabeth who'd died from complications after childbirth. The
king's daughter-in-law had also died horribly in labor (after which there
had been the further indignity of her body being immediately sliced
apart in public dissection).

Emilie knew enough to be wary of most medical remedies but did
accept the consensus that moderate bleeding by surgeons was sometimes a sensible precaution to take. She went to Versailles, where the
surgeons went through the procedure. First they tied a tourniquet
around her arm till the veins in her forearm swelled up. Then they
brought out the mechanical marvel known as the scarificator: a small
brass box, with about a dozen spring loaded blades inside. The blades
were extremely sharp, and released in groups to cut into her.

While that was going on, an assistant was heating the cupping
glasses that would be applied over the open gashes. As the cups cooled,
the vacuum inside helped pull even more blood out. (If the surgeon
was especially advanced, the glasses would have valves on top, and he'd
use a vacuum pump to make his subject's blood spurt especially fast.)
The whole process left her with a sharp headache, but after a few
hours she recovered enough to explore Versailles a little.

She soon came across Stanislas, which was easy enough—since
his daughter was married to Louis XV, he regularly visited Versailles.
The mood was different with him now, though. Back in Lunéville,
Stanislas had always seemed slightly distracted, but that was only what
was appropriate for a king in his own court. Also, Emilie had made
him feel shy, for he'd never met anyone who spoke as fast as she did;
he'd certainly almost never seen a couple—her and Voltaire—where
the woman was respected for her views so much. But he'd been paying
attention to her conversations, perhaps more than he'd let on, and as a
result he'd finished his own book!

This was ideal for Emilie to hear. New authors need favorable editorial comment, and the fame of Emilie's book on Leibniz had spread even to Lunéville. She and Stanislas had one dinner, and then another, and then a third. He was trying to merge Catholic traditions with rational science and had many questions for her. He was sincere in his religion, a good Polish Catholic, yet he didn't quite believe the graphic stories of damnation that Father Menou tried to scare him with. He had picked up fragments from Emilie and Voltaire about a different view. That's what he wanted to know more about.

It was a significant precedent, for in the decades to come many other seemingly conventional individuals would be inspired by Voltaire and Emilie—by their writings, and by the example of their unconventional life together—to question traditions around them that had apparently been accepted since time immemorial. With this attitude, authority no longer had to come from what you were told by a priest or royal official, and the whole establishment of the established church or the state behind them. It could now come, dangerously, from small, portable books—and even from ideas you came to yourself.

Stanislas's daughter, the French queen, had been furious when she'd first heard of her father's new interests, blaming those visitors to Lunéville for having corrupted him. But Stanislas had long grown used to ignoring her. And since he was Louis XV's father-in-law, his lodgings now were not miserable rooms of the sort Voltaire had once been granted. Rather, he had chambers in the magnificent Trianon palace at Versailles, and there he graciously invited Emilie to stay if she wished.

She'd planned to try finishing her scientific work in her Paris apartment, but this would be better—the ideal refuge if she was to take her writing to the deepest level. Very quickly, she had her main books and manuscript brought over from the Rue Traversière apartment. Much like her father, Stanislas was not the bumbling older man he appeared. Catherine was but a plaything to him. In his youth he'd had more serious affairs of the heart, and understood how much Emilie was missing her dreams of love now. "I don't want anyone to know what I'm feeling," Emilie had written to a stone-cold Saint-Lambert, "so I'm quiet about it. But I cry for where my heart took me."

Stanislas also recognized—again, almost certainly without stating it—the medical position that Emilie was in. Her pregnancy still barely showed ("aside from my breasts swelling, and feeling tired, I'm still as thin as before"), but he assured her that when her time came she could be given the finest rooms in the main palace at Lunéville for her labor. It would be more tranquil than Paris or Versailles, and also safer; she could be assured that the manure piles she'd seen there of the sort that were omnipresent at Versailles as well—would be cleared from anywhere near her lying-in rooms.

He was an old man, and there was a further understanding they shared. At his age—close to seventy—death could be counted on to be close. He wanted to learn from Emilie what remained of God when science replaced the literal beliefs he'd been raised with. Voltaire had never been able to answer that. But anyone facing possible extinction, as he and Emilie both were, needed an answer. And here Emilie could console this kind old man. For she was convinced that in the writings of Newton, which she was now exploring more profoundly than ever, she could find the answer.

26

A Portal Unto the Stars

Isaac Newton had been a resentful, suspicious young man, angry that he'd never known his father (who'd died two months before Isaac's birth on Christmas Day 1642); that his mother had quickly remarried and sent him away to boarding school, where he'd been bullied; that even when he did get to Cambridge she gave him so little money (even though she was middling rich from her remarriage) that he was forced to work as a servant, waiting on tables, cleaning other students' boots, even, if they gestured him over, combing their hair or preparing their wigs. But he learned at a speed no one else had, almost as if he already understood what was in the books and lectures. Within six months, his first passive notes on the mathematics on offer began to turn into original queries; six months more, and he had all of what was then known in seventeenth-century mathematics behind him.

Then, in the hot moist summer of 1665, something sickening began to spread across England. It "pleased Almighty God in his just severity, to visit this town of Cambridge with the plague of pestilence." The university immediately shut down, and the students and faculty

and any townspeople who could afford it fled. The young man returned to his mother's isolated farm, at Woolsthorpe in Lincolnshire.
And there a storm burst in the young, angry, secretive Isaac Newton's
mind. Recounting it much later:

> In the beginning of the year 1665, I found the Method of
> approximating series. . . . The same year in May I found the
> method of Tangents . . . and in November had the direct
> method of [calculus] & the next year in January had the
> Theory of Colors. . . . And the same year I began to think
> of gravity extending to ye orb of the Moon & . . . I deduced
> [what] the forces wch keep the Planets in their Orbs must
> be . . . & thereby compared the force requisite to keep the
> Moon in her Orb with the force of gravity at the surface of
> the earth, & found them answer pretty nearly.
>
> All this was in the two plague years of 1665–1666.
> For in those days I was in the prime of my age for inven-
> tion & minded Mathematics & Philosophy more than at any
> time since.

It was the sort of genius that has arisen only a very few times in
human history—but Newton didn't publish what he'd found. He
knew that what he kept secret could never be criticized by anyone else.
When the plague ended and he returned to Cambridge, he seems to
have told almost no one of what he now knew. For decades he became
immersed in secret worlds: alchemy, biblical interpretation, and discovering the truth about Solomon's ancient temple, scribbling his results
in volume after volume of cryptic notes.

What inspired him to finally publish his early science results was
the realization, almost two decades later, that other researchers were
beginning to touch on a few of the results he'd uncovered on his
mother's farm. He loved secrecy, but he also loved acclaim: not petty
academic acclaim, but the awe that being known for coming closer
than any other mortal to uncovering God's plans could inspire. In a

quick, two-year burst, he began writing up what he knew, in the enormous, impressive folio volumes that he labeled his *Principia*.

To VOLTAIRE and most others, the *Principia* was a great storehouse from which to pluck useful results: that apples fell to the ground at particular speeds, that planets orbited following certain rules. But *why* did this happen? That was the question Emilie had become fascinated with from her several years' excursion into Leibniz, and she believed that Newton had intentionally hidden the answers away deep within his convoluted text. What was the true reason—what had he been puzzling over?— that he'd felt obliged to wait twenty years before writing up what he'd seen? And then, why had he presented it through elaborate, old-style geometry when he clearly had the skill to present it more directly, using the modern tools of calculus (which he himself had invented)?

Emilie knew, from her readings of biblical commentaries, that there was a great tradition of hidden writing, in which mystics, prophets, or others who felt they had access to powerful knowledge presented their findings to be read in two ways. There would be a surface interpretation, which ordinary readers or listeners would grasp, but there would also be a deeper level, hidden away.

Newton lusted for immortality—or at least for understanding how God's universe could be immortal. For seventy years people had read his *Principia* but missed these deeper findings. Emilie was convinced she could unearth them amidst the immense range of theorems in the thick *Principia* volumes. By revealing the right ones, it would be as if she could see through a portal.

She could, in what might be these last months of her life, glimpse what it would be like to survive forever.

That was what she had been doing in Paris once she'd collected the books she'd left, and made contact again with key researchers she knew from the Academy of Sciences. Her previous achievements weren't enough: the essays, books, and fame, the skills at languages and mathematics and everything else. She needed this deeper work—but there wasn't much time. "I lost a year in Lorraine," she wrote to her mathematician colleagues Father Jacquier and Johann Bernoulli, "where it was impossible to work. . . . I'm here to finish my Newton. I won't leave until it's done."

The bulk of the direct translation was already complete—she'd managed that even before the Sceaux escapade and the trips to Lunéville. But that wasn't what counted. Now, in her limited time, she made sure she didn't miss the two central groups of theorems in Newton's work.

Voltaire had simply accepted that apples and moons and everything else tumble *down,* falling at a predictable rate. Emilie, however, was hunting through Newton's vast text to find the seemingly casual theorems where he tried to work out how gravity stretched *up,* shooting from the very center of the Earth and going outward.

The answer was in the theorems that Newton had numbered 70 through 75. In the complicated geometrical form in which Newton had presented them, their significance was hard to see. Emilie translated the ideas behind them into more modern, transparent language: showing how the Earth, Sun, or any other body could be imagined as divided like an onion into one slender inner layer wrapped around another. She went through the analysis of how those layers would affect each other—all the rock or magma or whatever else might exist for the thousands of miles beneath our feet—and confirmed the wondrous conclusion that the entire bulk of a planet or star acted as if its huge mass wasn't spread out at all.

As a result, it was possible to treat the whole planet as a single mathematical point, suspended in an empty cage, right at the center of our globe. It was from that single point that the ruler of the universe had arranged matters for the streaming gravitational force to emerge.

The other group of theorems she made a point to bring out were—to use modern terminology—the ones on the conservation of energy. She'd struggled with that in her own work following on from her fire experiments; she'd also engaged in lengthy public debates with senior researchers at the Academy of Sciences about what it meant.

But the deepest answer was already in Newton—if one just knew how to look.

The seemingly minor corollary 40, attached to theorem 13, was where it was hidden. There had been hints of that in Leibniz's work too, but Emilie wanted to go further in showing exactly what the idea meant, and thus guide her successors for their research to come. Somewhere in there might also be the answer to all her questions about free will: about why she'd had to go to Lunéville and take up with Saint-Lambert; about what would happen to Cirey, centuries in the future, after she and everyone she knew was gone.

From the time she'd been a little girl at her father's table, she'd wondered what the future would make of us. With this task, she could get a glimpse. She was confident now. Her work was important, and her life could be a success.

All she needed was time.

Emilie was about four months pregnant when she accepted Stanislas's offer to stay at the Trianon palace. In the quiet rooms there, she started driving herself even harder than she had before. She stopped seeing other friends, and aside from a coffee break around 3 P.M. would work all day, only stopping for a single meal around 10 P.M. She'd chat with Stanislas over dinner, or Voltaire if he was visiting from Paris, but when Stanislas went to bed, or Voltaire withdrew for political machinations, she'd return, candles lit, to her writing for hours more.

George Bernard Shaw once said that for someone who didn't comprehend the music of Bach, it sounded as tedious as the empty clacking of an industrial sewing machine with no fabric going through it. But once you understood the music, you saw the beautiful multicolored tapestry being poured out. Voltaire couldn't follow Emilie's mathematical symbols and begged her to start going to sleep earlier. He told her it was bad for her to stay up so late—increasingly till 3 or 4 A.M.—but she shrugged him off. How important was her health, anyway, if her notion that she wasn't going to survive the labor were to come true? In her old manuscript "Happiness" she'd written: "It's rare to admit it, but we all secretly like the idea of being talked about after our death. In fact, it's a belief we need." This is what she was desperate to ensure now.

She kept up her work pace during that strange Paris summer. The weather was odd, sometimes unseasonably cold, with driving rain under gray skies, then abrupt, humid, thick air. Her son was angry at her, embarrassed by her being pregnant at her age. Voltaire was more and more tense. The reformist minister Machault, who was trying to get the king to push for even a minimum general tax on the wealthiest groups in society, was being blocked. At one point, when Voltaire was attending a play of his own at the Comédie Française, he started screaming at the crowd. There hadn't been a professional claque acting against him. It was just a few ordinary theatergoers, laughing more loudly than he wished. His rage was so extreme that they went quiet.

By June, Stanislas had to leave for Lunéville, and it would be hard for Emilie to remain at the Trianon without him. She moved back to Paris, but it was getting too uncomfortable to stay there. The police were on edge, for the recent peace treaty with Austria was leading to the appearance of large numbers of unemployed veterans on the Paris streets; there were religious mobs crowding in ominous numbers. Roundups of popular religious leaders and radical thinkers were under way. It was time to take up Stanislas's offer and follow him to Lorraine. Saint-Lambert was still mostly withdrawn, but just occasionally his letters were warm. Emilie kept on writing to him, desperate for companionship ("I feel an emptiness that I would love you to fill"), even though she knew he couldn't really be trusted.

Voltaire was coming with her. He knew that no one had ever understood him as she had; if the worst happened, no one would ever understand him in that way again. "These links have lasted a lifetime," he wrote. "How could I possibly break them?"

Late in June they all got in the carriage again, Voltaire and Emilie and her maid—and this time all the manuscripts she was working on packed tight with them. Longchamp again had to ride a certain distance ahead, and although he clearly wouldn't have minded traveling in safe daylight, "it was the wish of Madame that we travel in these nocturnal hours. Her reason, she informed me, was that since there is always time lost during a voyage, it was better that this be a portion of one's sleep, rather than to lose time in which one might work."

They stopped at Cirey for a few weeks, and there she worked even longer hours, settling in for work sessions after late dinners and coffee, and continuing them almost till dawn, just as she'd done during her fire experiments years before. Voltaire couldn't get her to slow down: "She believed that death was striking," he wrote, and ". . . all she thought about was how to use the little time she had left, to deprive death of taking what she felt was the best part of herself."

At Lunéville Stanislas had prepared a summer guest house for her, even painting it a gentle blue inside. (Charles Stuart was another guest in Lunéville that summer, for after his failure in Scotland he'd ended up expelled from France—and Stanislas had a great understanding of the plight of monarchs who lacked a country.)

Saint-Lambert was kind to Emilie at first, helping her walk around the grounds, but it didn't last long. After one dreadful dinner she quickly wrote him: "My God, you treated me cruelly, you didn't glance my way once. I was used to looking in your eyes and seeing how much you cared for me, how much you loved me. I looked tonight, and didn't find anything. . . . I bitterly repent for having been seduced by your love; for once having believed your feelings matched mine."

There were still calculations for the Newton project to finish off, but she also began speaking confidentially to Longchamp, asking him to help put her private papers in order. "Lunéville had the most excellent facilities for Madame's health . . . yet she approached me with various sealed envelopes, and made me promise that, if she were not to survive the dangers she was soon to face, I was to execute her instructions with complete accuracy."

Saint-Lambert, now in full cowardice, had found reason to leave Lunéville and serve at his garrison in Nancy. Late in August she wrote asking him to see her one more time. Voltaire never left her, and although not disparaging her fears, he assured her—for who would know as well as he how amazingly one's greatest health worries can be false?—that she really did have a good chance of surviving. She was fit; the pregnancy had advanced with no complications; Lunéville was clean and the air was fresh.

He might well be right. In the direct translation portion of her work, she'd written out Newton's words: "The admirable arrangement of the sun, the planets, and the comets can only be the work of an all-powerful and wise being." Not everyone her age failed to survive childbirth. If there was any justice, shouldn't she be one of the fortunate ones?

Sometimes the uncertainty was too much ("I'm terrified when I think my premonitions might be true"). But she continued her intense writing schedule and did manage to finish the manuscript, on August 30. She wrote to the director of the King's Library that her pages were on the way: "It would be most kind to . . . have them registered so that they can't get lost. Mr. de Voltaire, who is here beside me sends you his tenderest compliments." In her final letter, dated August 31, 1749, she was tired, but still had hope:

> *I walked to my little summer house today, and my stomach is so swollen, and my back so sore, that I wouldn't be surprised if I had the baby tonight.*

Emilie du Châtelet gave birth on the night of September 3. She died on September 10 of infection stemming from the labor; the child—a girl—died soon after. Her translation and commentary on Newton's *Principia* became fundamental to key eighteenth-century developments in theoretical physics, laying the groundwork for much of contemporary science.

Voltaire was bereft: "I've lost the half of myself—a soul for which mine was made." Months later, after Voltaire had abandoned Cirey and moved back to Paris, Longchamp would find him wandering at night in the apartments he'd shared with Emilie, plaintively calling her name in the dark.

I shall await you
quietly
In my meridian
in the fields of Cirey
Watching one star only
Watching my Emilie.

—Voltaire, "Ode"

What Followed

Emilie's great work, *Principes mathématiques de la philosophie naturelle de Newton, traduits du latin par Mme du Châtelet,* was published ten years after her death, when the return of Halley's comet in 1759 stimulated a burst of interest in Newtonian mechanics. The key notion she brought out and elaborated from Newton proved to be as important as she'd hoped. This was the new concept of "energy," which showed that there was a total amount of movement in the world, and although the way it was arranged could fluctuate wildly—there could be cities that rose up and took dominion over others; there could be civilizations that were broken apart, and their inhabitants dispersed—despite all those shifts, that total amount would never change. Just as she'd hoped, it was a proof that nothing ever fully disappears, that nothing ever dies.

More technical aspects of her work played a great role in energizing the French school of theoretical physics, associated with Lagrange and Laplace, whose formal achievements (the Lagrangian and Laplacian stability calculations) ended up as fundamental working tools in subsequent science, from Faraday and Maxwell's field theory of the nineteenth century to quantum theory and relativity in the twentieth. English researchers, lacking the advantage of seeing Newton's work clearly brought out with Emilie's more modernized notation, stuck to Newton's cumbersome original forms, which slowed their progress for over two generations.

Emilie's role in focusing and spreading the political ideals of the Enlightenment continued to the end. In 1748 she'd carefully helped an obscure Parisian investigator with questions he'd had about the equations for the air resistance faced by a moving pendulum. The following year, he hesitantly sent her a long essay he'd written on the origins of morality. Her thoughtful, encouraging reply was what the author—it was Denis Diderot—termed one of the "two sweet moments" of his life.

When Diderot was imprisoned in the fortress of Vincennes for this essay, in July 1749, Emilie interrupted her own writing to use family connections to ensure that he was treated well, even though she was almost eight months pregnant. After his release, Diderot went on to be the main developer of the grand, twenty-eight-volume *Encyclopédie,* which built on Cirey's approach of sharing and analyzing all knowledge, extending it for the next generation.

AT THE time of Emilie's death, Voltaire's greatest work—*Candide*— was still before him. Its themes of optimism versus pessimism and whether God intervenes in our life had been at the heart of his discussions with Emilie. Her abrupt death made its cynical conclusions impossible for Voltaire to resist; yet the model of their earlier years together—sharing a life with this vigorous, brilliant woman—was behind his constant calls for liberty and freedom of opinion, which were important not just in the ideas leading to the American Bill of Rights, but also in the intellectual case for feminism, as developed by Mary Wollstonecraft and then others in generations to come.

Voltaire left France a year after Emilie's death, moving to Berlin, where he was abortively involved with Frederick's planned Berlin Academy of Sciences. In 1758, at age sixty-four, he settled in the small town of Ferney, just across from Geneva, yet inside the French border. He lived there for twenty years, publishing *Candide* and other works, leading public intervention against cases of religious persecution, and encouraging Diderot and others associated with the vast progressive *Encyclopédie* project.

Visitors came by when Voltaire was very old:

> I sent in to enquire whether a stranger might be allowed to see Voltaire's house & was answered in the affirmative. The servant conducted me into the cabinet . . . where his master had just been writing. I should have said that close to the chapel . . . is the theater that [Voltaire] built some years ago, but which he uses only as a receptacle for wood and lumber, there having been no play acted in it these 4 years.
>
> . . . When the weather is favorable he takes an airing in his coach, with his niece, or with some of his guests. Sometimes he saunters in his garden; or if the weather does not permit he employs his leisure hours in playing at chess with Father Adam, or in dictating and reading letters, for he still retains correspondents in all the countries of Europe, who inform him of every remarkable occurrence, and send him every new literary production as soon as possible.
>
> . . . Seeing me . . . [Voltaire] approached the place where I stood. It is not easy to conceive it possible for life to subsist in a form so nearly composed of mere skin and bone, as that of M. de Voltaire. He complained of decrepitude, and said he supposed I was curious to form an idea of the figure of one walking after death.
>
> However, though emaciated, his eyes are still full of fire, and a more lively expression cannot be imagined. He enquired after English news, and what poets we had now. . . . Said he: you seem to have no one [anymore] who lords it over the rest like Dryden, Pope and Swift.

During this conversation we approached the farm buildings he was constructing near the road to his château. These, said he, pointing to them, are the most innocent, and, perhaps, the most useful of all my works. I observed that he had other works, which would be much more durable than those. . . .

After dinner, passing through a little parlour, where there was a head of Locke, another of the Countess of Coventry, and several more, he took me by the arm, and stopped me—Do you know this bust [Newton's]? It is the greatest genius that ever existed: if all the geniuses of the universe assembled, he should lead the band.

It was of Newton, and of his own works, that he spoke with the greatest warmth.

Voltaire died in Paris, age eighty-four, a decade before the French Revolution, feted by crowds of admirers. In his final eulogy of Emilie, he'd written:

Her memory is treasured by all who knew her intimately, and who were capable of perceiving the breadth of her mind.

She regretted leaving life, but . . . the image of a man sadly tearing himself away from his distressed family, and calmly making preparations for a long journey, would in a faint way depict her sorrow, and yet her firmness.

Emilie's family home overlooking the Tuileries in Paris still survives, although its interior has been divided into several smaller apartments. With the clay quarries in the Tuileries filled in and the area around the yew trees no longer used as open toilets, the gardens are now salubrious enough for the many tourists and locals who walk through them on their way to the Louvre.

Renée-Caroline, the snobbish teenage cousin who stayed with Emilie in 1715, became ever more reactionary as she grew old. Arrested and imprisoned during the Revolution, she was saved from execution by the fall of Robespierre.

The elderly astronomer who visited Emilie's family when she was a little girl, **Bernard Le Bovier Fontenelle,** used to say that he would be glad if he lived long enough to see "just one more strawberry season." His wishes were fulfilled, for he survived to the age of ninety-nine, dying only in 1757, nearly a decade after Emilie.

The **château at Semur,** where Emilie and Florent-Claude had their first married home, is now a hospital.

The unfortunate **Inspector Ysabeau,** whom Voltaire inveigled into the sewers of Paris in the hunt for nonexistent writings, became intrigued by Voltaire's work. When the public executioner burned Voltaire's Letters from England, he obtained an illegally printed extra copy to keep for himself.

The grimly turreted **Bastille** prison had fewer political prisoners as the years went on. In 1789, when it was stormed by the citizens of Paris, only seven inmates were left inside: four forgers, two lunatics, and one aristocrat (who had been consigned to the prison by his family). A café stands on the location today.

Suzanne de Livry, who had so entranced Voltaire when he was young, was living in Paris in later years after his English exile. When he knocked at her gate to visit her, she instructed her servants not to let him in: she had married an aristocrat and did not want any reminders of her less noble past. She did, however, keep the portrait he'd commissioned of himself for her, apparently giving it pride of place in her drawing room.

Adrienne Lecouvreur never married, though she had an illegitimate daughter who became the grandmother of Amandine Dupin, a young woman who was fascinated by stories of her ancestor's links with famous men. Dupin had relations with de Musset and Chopin and became a writer in her own right, publishing under the pseudonym of George Sand.

The **Duc de Sully's** town house remains as an imposing mansion in Paris's Marais quarter. The wastrel aristocrat **Auguste de Rohan-Chabot,** who had Voltaire beaten for impudence, lived a long life, protected first by his cardinal uncle and then by other family members.

The attempted taxation reforms of **Jean-Baptiste de Machault** failed.

Voltaire's nemesis **Jean-Frédéric Phélypeaux, comte de Maurepas,** remained at Versailles for many years, until he responded to Pompadour's charge that he should be more respectful by mockingly asserting that he was respectful to *all* the king's mistresses. Within the week he was expelled.

Brought back in old age by Louis XVI, he insisted on the construction of thin-hulled French naval vessels, which were easily destroyed by the more heavily timbered British ships they fought against. He also continued encouraging the king to resist calls for increased taxation of the old nobility or the Church, thus undermining the national finances and necessitating the eventual meeting of the Estates General—leading directly to the Revolution and the overthrow of the monarchy.

The amiable Englishman **Everard Fawkener** remained Voltaire's lifelong friend and correspondent. He became Britain's emissary to the Turks, and also served the English commander during the battle of Fontenoy. His daughter married into the family of the great military leader Marlborough, thus putting him in the same family tree as Winston Churchill.

Though now surrounded by London, the bucolic wonderland of **Wandsworth village** has scarcely changed since Voltaire stayed at Fawkener's home. The **Drury Lane** theater, where Voltaire further perfected his English—and where the enthusiastic amateur actor Mr. Bond died during a performance of Voltaire's play *Zaïre*—remains a center of London's West End.

The mathematician **La Condamine,** who worked with Voltaire on manipulating the Paris lottery to their mutual advantage, became head of the official French expedition to South America. The goal of the mission was to measure the Earth's curvature close to the Equator for comparison with measurements from Maupertuis's expedition to the far north. Lacking Maupertuis's calming nature, the French explorers became so irritated with each other that for months on end they pushed through the jungle refusing to say a word to each other. La Condamine returned to France a decade after he left, having performed the first scientific exploration of the Amazon along the way.

After the death of Elisabeth, duchesse de Richelieu, the ever-voluble **Madame de Graffigny** had no one to stay with in Paris. She lived in great poverty for many years, but then, in old age, wrote a novel— *Lettres d'une péruvienne*—that became a bestseller. Renowned as a dispenser of wisdom and head of an important salon, she wrote dozens more plays.

Although Emilie and Voltaire had given up on the slothful tutor **Michel Linant** ("perhaps in fourteen more years he'll finish the fifth act of his play"), he actually did submit an essay for the royal prize competition of 1740, on the topic "The Advancement of Eloquence in the Reign of Louis XIV." When the results were announced there was a greater surprise: he'd won.

Frederick the Great's unceasing militarism led to the catastrophe of the Seven Years' War, which saw his country of approximately 5 million people engaged in at times simultaneous battle against an array of enemies—Russia, France, Austria, Sweden, and others—with a combined population of about 100 million. Prussia's citizens were murdered and brutalized in a manner that hadn't been seen in Europe for centuries. The result was a terrified, blindly obedient Prussian citizenry and a mercilessly efficient officer corps.

The huge debt that Britain incurred in supporting Frederick led to Parliament calling for the distant American colonies to pay their fair share—a call that was received with a noted lack of enthusiasm by the thirteen colonies and was a proximate cause of the American Revolution.

The once curvaceously beautiful **Marie-Louise,** Voltaire's niece, had always liked to eat, and as she gradually took over her uncle's wealth ("I gave her my house in Paris, my silver, my horses, and I increased her fortune"), she was able to indulge that passion as much as she wished. She became very fat, and in time moved in with Voltaire, ostensibly as her uncle's housekeeper. Despite arguments and sulks, they lived together for the last twenty years of his life.

The handsome rosy-cheeked youngster **Charles Stuart**—whence the appellation "Bonny Prince Charlie"—never recovered from the destruction of his Scottish forces at Culloden and ended up disconsolate and drunk, traveling restlessly around Europe. He converted to Protestantism in yet another vain attempt to recapture his throne. He died in Rome.

Despite constant slurs from the higher-born women at the court, as well as ceasing sexual relations with the king fairly early on ("He finds me very cold"), **Madame de Pompadour** (the onetime **Jeanne Poisson**) became so much Louis XV's friend that she remained his official mistress for seventeen years, dominating the French government most of that time. The magnificent porcelain works now at Sèvres are due to her patronage.

At the start of **Louis XV's** reign, France was the dominant power in Europe, America, and India. By the end, sixty years later—and due in large part to his impressively incompetent decisions in diplomacy, military strategy, judicial appointments, and taxation—France's dominance was over, and Britain's had begun.

Emilie and Voltaire's efficient servant **Sébastien Longchamp** remained discreet about his services till many years after Emilie's death, when he finally published his memoirs, for which he'd made copious notes while in their service. He'd further prepared for his retirement by stealing spare copies of Voltaire's manuscripts, which he sold at great profit in later years.

The young **Jean-François, marquis de Saint-Lambert,** made a habit of borrowing the mistresses of famous writers. After leaving Stanislas's court and moving to Paris, he became romantically involved with Jean-Jacques Rousseau's Madame d'Houdetot as well. He tried staying in amiable correspondence with Voltaire for many years, and wrote an article on "genius" for the great *Encyclopédie.* Late in life, he became honored for writing a popular child's catechism of the Catholic faith.

Although the evidence is unclear, it seems that Emilie had entrusted him with eight leather-bound volumes in which she'd collected all the many hundreds of letters she and Voltaire had written to each other. Most likely Saint-Lambert burned them all, shortly after her death.

Louis-François Armand du Plessis, duc de Richelieu, continued with his numerous affairs so notably, and so impressively, that the young Pierre Choderlos de Laclos, a generation later, naturally modeled the Valmont character in his novel *Les Liaisons Dangereuses* on him.

Richelieu's successful assault on the British base at Port Mahon in Minorca in 1756 was commemorated in the creation of a convenient egg-and-oil mix that was first called "mahonnaise" and is now known as "mayonnaise." He married for the final time in 1780, when he was eighty-six.

With admirable timing—as always—Richelieu died in 1788, one year before the Revolution.

After the acclaim from his Arctic explorations died down, **Pierre-Louis de Maupertuis** got married and moved to Frederick's court in Prussia, where he elaborated on fundamental scientific work he'd begun when with Emilie, especially the principle of "least action," which is central to later physics, and especially to quantum mechanics. After Emilie's death, he was joined at Frederick's court by Voltaire, who soon began writing sarcastic pamphlets to mock his onetime rival for Emilie's affections.

In old age, Maupertuis returned to France, spending some of his last months in his old home town of St. Malo in Brittany.

Florent-Claude du Châtelet lived to age seventy. He did not marry again after Emilie's death.

Nothing more survives from the historical record of **Michelle,** Emilie's elderly half sister. Nor is it known how her mother, **Anne Bellinzani,** responded to the news of her discovery, for Bellinzani had been young when Michelle was born and was still alive a half century later, when news came that the daughter she'd had with Louis-Nicolas had been found. Bellinzani died in 1740, at the age of eighty-two.

Emilie's daughter, **Françoise Gabrielle Pauline,** inherited her mother's quick intelligence, once apparently memorizing all the lines for her part in a long play during a half-hour carriage ride. After marrying an Italian noble and moving to Naples, she never saw her parents again, though she remained a regular correspondent with her mother.

Emilie's son, **Louis-Marie Florent,** rose in the royal administration to become the ambassador of Louis XVI to the English court. During the Revolution he was guillotined in the Place de la Révolution, just yards from the river Seine. His own son died in prison, thus ending the du Châtelet line.

Partly ransacked during the Revolution, the **Château de Cirey** is now occupied by a private family, which has invested considerable funds in restoring it. Open to the public every afternoon from July to mid-September, it's conveniently reachable from Paris's Gare de l'Est.

Notes

4   **One terrified homosexual abbé:** This was the Abbé Desfontaines, who never forgave Voltaire for saving him, and ended up attacking him through sarcastic articles and malicious intrigues for years. His role in leaking the Adam and Eve poem is central to the events in chapter 10.

4   **In France, if the king had chosen:** The tax exemptions ostensibly began in medieval times, when nobles were supposed to give services in kind to help the king in war, and thus had already "paid" their taxes that way. Such exemptions became less justifiable when feudalism was over. This was to some extent recognized in legislation, for although in our period nobles were exempted from the basic tax of the *taille,* they were supposed to pay the later taxes known as the *capitation* and the *dixième.* But—and it's a big but—there were a huge number of exemptions that had built up over the years, be it from exempted sources of income, obscure "traditional" privileges, or simply through corrupt arrangements with local officials (who were often related to the individuals they were supposed to collect tax from).

4   **Working for pay was demeaning:** The problem was the dreaded *dérogeance*—the losing of nobility through practicing forbidden occupations.

The provisos were of Talmudic intricacy. Manual crafts such as carpentry or metalworking were disallowed, although glass-blowing was not. Commerce was forbidden if it was retail, but wholesale commerce was allowed, although maritime commerce was allowable both wholesale and retail (which exempted it from questions about what size of purchases distinguished wholesale from retail, which was much debated). Farming your own land was acceptable, but farming someone else's was severely unacceptable, even if you'd paid full rent. Owning a mine was acceptable, so long as your income came directly from its products, but not if you earned money through selling the value of the ownership. If there was any underlying logic, it was that (1) only God could create something from nothing (which is why retail commerce was out), and (2) aristocrats were warriors, not of the caste of laborers (which is why carpentry was out).

7   **By the end of the eighteenth century:** Kant, *Observations on the Feeling of the Beautiful and Sublime,* tr. John Goldthwart (Berkeley, 1960), p. 78. The attitude long continued. In the 1833 paper in which the English academic William Whewell coined the term *scientist* he went on to say that "notwithstanding all the dreams of theorists, there is a sex in minds." Even in 1911, Marie Curie, winner of two Nobel Prizes, wasn't allowed full membership of France's Académie des Sciences. The Royal Society in London only opened full membership to women in 1945, the French Académie in 1979.

9   **Since du Châtelet's life was focused on science:** In Mitford's world, women in France ended up as mistresses, whom one could treat humorously; English women became adulteresses, who had to be treated tragically. See Allan Hepburn, "The Fate of the Modern Mistress: Nancy Mitford and the Comedy of Marriage," *Modern Fiction Studies* 2 (1999), pp. 340–68.

11   **Translations presented more of a difficulty:** When Denis Connor used a catamaran to win an America's Cup heat against a New Zealand monohull, he defended it by telling the world's press: "We have a cat, not a dog." In languages where *dog* only means a four-legged furry beast, one can translate either the meaning or the brevity, but not both—for the multiple registers into which words fit rarely cohere across languages. See Douglas Hofstadter's *Le Ton Beau de Marot: In Praise of the Music of Language* for an eloquent discussion.

15   **"illusion is not something you can have":** Robert Mauzi, ed., *Discours sur le bonheur* (Paris, 1961), p. 79.

16   **The moonlight that streamed past:** The full moon was on June 29 (right when Emilie stopped over at Cirey), as Britain's Nautical Almanac Office has kindly computed, and that June was especially dry, as harvest records confirm. Whatever moonlight did enter the room would have had to strike the head of her bed, as visitors to the château can observe (there's only one natural place for the bed if it's not to block the doorway).

19   **Gabrielle-Emilie Le Tonnelier de Breteuil:** Her mother was very formal, and would have insisted on following the fashion for children of pinning in this manner.

19   **"Nothing is so beautiful":** Fontenelle's *Conversations on the Plurality of Inhabited Worlds,* "Fifth Evening" (Berkeley, 1990), p. 64. The interpolated "solar systems" replaces "vortices," i.e., I'm omitting the author's assumption of Cartesian rather than Newtonian physics. The preceding sentences, too, closely paraphrase Fontenelle.

19   **It was dark outside:** Up to twenty guests were regularly present, so this is a low estimate of candles.

20   **"I don't think that anyone ever saw her smile":** Modified from *Souvenirs de la Marquise de Créquy* (7 vols., Paris, 1834), p. 104.

20   **"Don't ever blow your nose on your napkin":** The source was the very old and much reprinted popular guidebook *La Civilité Puerile et honnête.* At the start of chapter 4 of Créquy's memoirs she describes Gabrielle-Anne's recourse to it. I've modified the paraphrase in Mitford's *Voltaire in Love* (London 1834) after comparison with the original text.

21   **For hours on end she would happily gossip:** The nobles of the sword, who'd been ennobled many centuries earlier and believed—whether justifiably or not—that it was for brave military service, lorded it over the nobles of the robe, who tended to have acquired their positions in more recent centuries and through administrative service. Emilie's mother was a Froulay, and in the former category; several relations of Emilie's father belonged to the latter.

There were many distinctions within each category, based on region, duration of ennoblement and the like. The key dynamics were to always look down on those below you, always act as if you're entirely comfortable wherever you are; and always try to rise higher. Thus Renée-Caroline's conversations with Gabrielle-Anne; thus too Louis-Nicolas's purchase of an estate at Preuilly-sur-Claise in Touraine as soon as he was rich enough, so transforming himself into a Baron (and explaining why Emilie was sometimes known, before her marriage, as Mademoiselle de Preuilly).

21 **Her mother and cousin:** Renée-Caroline—Gabrielle-Anne's friend!—describes the mother's sighs and glaring. *Créquy,* p. 96.

21 **Emilie was relegated:** In fairness to Renée-Caroline, she was desperately envious of Emilie. Her own childhood bore a resemblance to a nasty fairy tale: she'd largely been raised in the tower of an isolated château, not knowing if her parents were alive. Only shortly before the events in this chapter did she learn that her father was in fact living, and established at Versailles. She was sent to Paris, but there discovered that he didn't want her to live with him—upon which she was fobbed off on relatives and, most particularly, Gabrielle-Anne.

21 **"I don't believe":** Mauzi, ed., *Bonheur,* p. 13. She was writing after her break with Voltaire, but before meeting Saint-Lambert.

21 **Fontenelle told the ten-year-old Emilie:** Emilie's father held these dinners every Thursday, and Fontenelle was a regular. He liked talking to women, and especially about his *Conversations on the Plurality of Inhabited Worlds,* for it was the book that had made his reputation, and he nurtured it carefully through numerous editions over the years. Emilie would be the only attendee who could follow his technical points. M. Terrall's "Gendered Spaces, Gendered Audiences: Inside and Outside the Paris Academy of Sciences," *Configurations* 3, 2 (1995), pp. 207–32, shows why it was so important for Fontenelle to spread his ideas among the next generation of aristocratic women.

21 **"You will soon discover":** Fontenelle, *Conversations,* "Fifth Evening," p. 70.

22 **Most European thinkers:** It was a common view. Molière's satire *Les Femmes Savantes,* for example, which ridiculed women who tried to think for themselves, had been a great success among women as well as men. A few decades later a *female* anatomist in France, Thiroux d'Arconville, made a point of sketching female skeletons as if they had far smaller skulls than those of males. See Schiebinger, *The Mind Has No Sex?* (Cambridge, Mass., 1989), p. 197.

On the other hand, there was a significant handful of thinkers who did support women's rights. John Locke had written in his 1693 *Thoughts on Education:* "since I acknowledge no difference of sex . . . relating . . . to truth, virtue and obedience, I think well to have no thing altered in [an educational programme for daughters] from what is [writ for the son]."

22   **Even when Emilie had been younger:** Renée-Caroline: "My cousin Emilie . . . was immensely clumsy . . . and had big feet." *Créquy,* p. 96.

22   **"Men can choose lots of ways":** Mauzi, ed., *Bonheur,* merged from pp. 21, 22.

22   **Even the most distinguished girls' school:** This was Madame de Maintenon's Maison Royale de St. Louis. See Samia I. Spencer, ed., *French Women and the Age of Enlightenment* (Bloomington, 1984), pp. 84–85.

22   **One of Louis XV's daughters:** Ibid., p. 86.

23   **Luckily, though, when Emilie was fifteen:** Puberty came late then, since nutrition was so poor compared to later eras. Record books of Bach's students, for example, show that it was common for boys to still sing soprano till their mid- or late teens.

23   **"my cousin was three or four years younger":** *Créquy,* p. 96.

23   **Her face took on an attractive oval shape:** Even the most envious of women, such as Voltaire's niece Mme Denis, remarked on Emilie's physical beauty. Although Nancy Mitford was vague about Emilie's ideas, she was insightful about her looks: "Over and over again," Mitford writes, Emilie "is described, in letters and memoirs of her day, as beautiful; reading between the lines one can conclude that she was what is now called a handsome woman. . . . In spite of a great love of dress, [she was never] really elegant. Elegance, for women, demands undivided attention; Emilie was an intellectual; she had not endless hours to waste with hairdressers and dressmakers." Mitford, *Voltaire in Love,* p. 15.

23   **At age sixteen she was sent to:** Under the Regency, in a break from the extreme formality of Louis XIV's final years, and the somber influence of the severely pious Madame de Maintenon, the court had largely moved back to Paris. When Louis XV was old enough, it went back to Versailles.

24   **It didn't help:** Louis XIV had lived so long that his son and grandson had both died. His great-grandson was the direct heir, but was only five years old when he assumed the rights to the throne, hence the need for a regent.

24   **As one account has it:** Jonathan Edwards, *The Divine Mistress* (London, 1971). As discussed in the reading guide, Edwards's errors tend to be in transposing events, rather than wholesale invention.

24   **"She . . . wields a sword like a hussar":** Richelieu, quoted in ibid., p. 10.

24   **"My youngest . . . frightens away the suitors":** Ibid., p. 12.

24   **What she learned:** What she learned was more Whiggish than the

reality, for researchers were proud of emphasizing their break from past centuries. In fact—though unknown to her—medieval investigators had engaged in powerful examinations of the foundations of mechanics, as well as developed inductive aspects of Aristotle, building especially on his *Posterior Analytics.*

25   **Emilie was desperate to learn more:** He had a large library, but it wouldn't have had the maths and science books she then wanted.

26   **"My daughter is mad":** Edwards, *Divine Mistress,* p. 11.

26   **Finally, though, late in 1724:** Since she was born near the end of 1706 (on December 17), many biographers who use simple subtractions to arrive at her age are off by one year.

26   **With some help from her friends:** Often spelled "Chastellet," till Voltaire chose to simplify it. Spelling was more variable in that period than now; even many of the founding fathers of the American republic happily spelled words and names in different ways at different times.

27   **One aristocrat, for example:** It was the Comte d'Evreux, in his marriage to Crozat's daughter; from St. Simon's memoirs.

29   **The verses attacked . . . the liberal Regent:** Orléans was supposed to rule in conjunction with Louis XIV's beloved though illegitimate son, the duc du Maine (for although Orléans was the King's nephew, he was exceptionally dissolute). Orléans broke with that arrangement, however, even though the late king had written it into his will. The consequences—including du Maine's effort to overthrow the state—arise again in chapter 20.

30   **He smiled, and asked:** From Beauregard's letter, D45. Throughout these notes, a capital *D* followed by a number refers to letters in Besterman's comprehensive edition. (Generations of students have puzzled over why he began his numbering with that letter: it simply stands for *Definitive.*)

30   **The new court that had been built at Versailles:** Louis XIV's famous assertion *"L'état, c'est moi"* is generally taken as his bold, military-backed claim that the king outranked the potentially divisive nobles and Parlements. It suffers, however, from being almost certainly apocryphal. The first known reference is in Dulaur's 1834 *Histoire de Paris,* almost two hundred years after Louis was supposed to have declared it to Parlement in April 1655. But how could such a succinct summary of his overriding power have been ignored over all those years? It's also unlikely that the seventeen-year-old Louis would have dared be so insistent in 1655, when the Fronde wars were so recent.

Throughout his reign he was nervous, moving even between rooms in his palaces only when loyal guards protected the corridors and stairs. The fate of his relations emphasized what could go wrong: his English uncle, Charles I, had been beheaded; his French grandfather, Henri IV, had been assassinated; his English cousin James II was deposed.

31   **It didn't help . . . sexual relations with his own daughter:** Paraphrasing Besterman's elegant slur (*Voltaire,* p. 62).

31   **A little later . . . a commoner named Desforges:** René Vaillot, *Avec Madame du Châtelet 1734–1749,* p. 359. It was not the only such case: "One Dubourg, the editor of a satirical gazette, was put in a tiny cage at Mt. Saint-Michel in 1745 and died there in a fit of madness a year later . . . in 1757 the poet La Martellière was sentenced to nine years on the galleys." P. Gay, *Voltaire's Politics: The Poet As Realist* (New Haven, 1988), p. 78.

32   **There was no reliable sewage system:** The several miles of sewers that did exist in the city worked poorly, frequently getting blocked and flooding when it rained.

32   **There was a spurting:** From the far too vivid account Ysabeau wrote to his superior officer soon after.

33   **"M. Arouet, with his active imagination":** D54.

33   **The cell was deathly silent:** The phrases are modified from Voltaire's later *L'Ingénu,* which—written with the vividness of personal experience—describes the feelings of a young man unjustly flung into the Bastille after a *lettre de cachet.* Pomeau discusses this in his *D'Arouet à Voltaire: 1694–1734* (Oxford, 1985) p. 111.

34   **It didn't help that Arouet was probably illegitimate:** Theodore Besterman, *Voltaire* (London, 1969; rev. ed., 1976), pp. 20–23, gives indirect evidence that in a fury his father once told François that he wasn't even his real son: that a minor poet named Roquebrune had been his true parent. As François's mother had died when he was seven, this was a severe, unanswerable calumny. Years later, when the charge was hurled at him again, François apparently replied "that what was to his mother's honor was that she had preferred an intelligent man like Roquebrune, musketeer, officer, writer, to his [legal] father, who was by nature a very commonplace man." The attribution of the quotation is only second-hand, but seems plausible, especially after further evidence that Besterman presents. However, René Pomeau, *La Religion de Voltaire* (Paris, 1956; 2nd ed., 1969), p. 35, makes the point that Voltaire might

just have been engaging in Freudian projection, trying to create a father more gallant and romantic than the narrow-minded official who raised him.

34   **Arouet wouldn't be able . . . the books that were passed around:** One book circulating in the Bastille that Voltaire saw was a 1690 text on pseudonyms; another, earlier, inmate (around 1710) had penciled in much of a poem that bore some similarities to Voltaire's later epic on Henri IV. Wade, *Voltaire and Mme du Châtelet,* suggests Voltaire's partial plagiarism, though I'm more inclined to Pomeau's suggestion (*D'Arouet à Voltaire,* p. 112) that both authors were using standard sources, and had just converged on similar results.

35   **Another theory:** There have been many other explanations, as with Casanova's suggestion that it was to avoid the poor pun on Voltaire's original name of Arouet (*à rouer*—to be beaten). The key question, however, of *why* he chose to make the change then, is easier to answer. "I have been too unfortunate under my former name," he told Mlle du Noyer; "I mean to see whether this will suit me better."

35   **Voltaire was supposed to stay away from Paris:** Curiously, it was Emilie's father, Louis-Nicolas, who pulled the strings to enable him to return so quickly. Voltaire had dined at the Breteuil home when Emilie was a child, but seems to have paid no attention to her then. Louis-Nicolas, however, liked him, for in this young man's flamboyance and wit he recognized the grandeur of France in his youth, and probably hoped that Voltaire would be able to help bring that back. Knowing Voltaire's reputation, though, he was careful to keep him from meeting his daughter again once she was older.

35   **"who would not sin . . . those alabaster breasts":** Paraphrase and reordering of lines from his later epistle on the charming Suzanne; in the Moland edition of Voltaire's works, vol. 10, p. 270.

35   **There were some changes . . . young man named Génonville:** "Easygoing" is Voltaire's own description of Génonville; D91.

35   **What we are feeling, our Kings cannot know:** *Oedipus,* Act II, scene V. As with most of the poetry in this book, this is a very free translation. See Besterman, *Voltaire,* p. 76, for a flatter reading.

35   **Yes we can have faith:** Act I, scene V.

37   **"ye best poet maybe ever was":** Besterman, *Voltaire,* p. 80.

37   **A distinguished prince:** The prince de Conti, indirectly related to the great Condé of the Fronde. It was at a dinner in Conti's presence that Voltaire said, "Ah, are we all poets, or are we all princes?"—a presumptuousness that

could have been punished with prison, but which the young Voltaire got away with because of his charm and *Oedipus*'s great success.

38 **But there was also an up-and-coming actress:** Lecouvreur had been popular for several years, since her late teens, but still found it hard to be accepted by many of the elders who controlled patronage within the theater.

38 **"it was routine to offer a performance in bed":** Paraphrase of Baron von Grimm, *Correspondence Littéraire,* vol. 9, p. 209.

38 **"felt so well that he was astonished":** D125.

38 **If conversation turned to sibling rivalries:** This particular remark is from his later notebooks, jotted in English during his English exile. Like all good writers, he used and reused his material; this is typical of his repartee.

38 **If they were discussing . . . an ode to posterity:** His famous remark to the unpleasant Jean-Baptiste Rousseau, about the latter's "Ode to Posterity." Again, it is from a later period.

38 **Many distinguished women visited:** It's where Voltaire had first met Suzanne de Livry.

39 **There were evenings spent gossiping:** D92, Voltaire to Fontenelle, 1 June 1721, for the muddling and the opera glasses.

39 **"in this world . . . either hammer or anvil":** Voltaire, *Philosophical Dictionary;* entry on "tyranny."

40 **Now de Rohan called out:** The best evaluation of the sources for this incident is Lucien Foulet's, in Appendix 1 to his edited collection, *Correspondance de Voltaire (1726–29)* (Paris, 1923), pp. 211–32.

40 **The theater was plush . . . clusters of candles:** This was long before gas lighting, or even smoldering limelight; stage lighting was generally controlled by having hefty servants crank up or down a long plank packed with lit candles.

40 **It was cold outside on this winter midday:** The accounts have the attack happening at *souper,* which wasn't evening soup, but rather the midday meal.

41 **The sentence for murder was death:** The official penalty for killing anyone was death, but extenuating circumstances were easy to find if the culprit was distinguished, and the victim was not; much harder if the victim was a nobleman.

41 **But Phélypeaux:** Usually referred to by his title, the Comte de Maurepas; I'm using Phélypeaux simply to reduce confusion with Maupertuis. Voltaire usually referred to him by other, ingeniously crude labels.

41   **He had been granted high office as a boy:** His grandfather had been Chancellor Pontchartrain (as in the name of the lake in Louisiana); his father had been head of the navy, and at fourteen that job was passed on to him.

42   **Yet where were any of them:** Unknown to Voltaire, a handful actually were supportive, most notably the retired military commander, the duc de Villars. Another powerful individual who would have helped Voltaire was Mme de Prie—the official mistress of the Prime Minister, and with whom Voltaire had been close, possibly having an affair. But not only was de Rohan's uncle a cardinal, but that cardinal was also probably the illegitimate son of Louis XIV—which made de Rohan the late Sun King's grandnephew. (Richelieu would have tried to help, but he was too far away, in Vienna on a diplomatic mission.)

43   **Her father, whom she loved . . . out-of-date geometry texts:** The kindly neighbor was M. de Mézières, who lived near d'Avallon. The future great biologist Buffon was actually in Semur at the time, but still just a teenager, and Emilie had no way to meet him, let alone realize his potential or interests.

44   **"women would be able to take part":** From the end of her later preface to her annotated translation of Bernard Mandeville's *Fable of the Bees.*

45   **"nothing is more neglected":** Fénelon, in his *L'Education des filles,* 1687. See Gwynne Lewis, *France 1715–1804: Power and the People* (London, 2005), p. 59; also Spencer, ed., *French Women,* p. 85.

45   **"I felt . . . as if I was swimming":** Mauzi, ed., *Bonheur,* p. 16.

45   **"I gave in too often to my big appetite":** Ibid., p. 10.

45   **At one point . . . an affair with . . . a pleasant young noble:** Phélypeaux later wrote an account of Emilie attempting suicide out of desolation at the breakup, with Guébriant instantly finding a perfect antidote in his rooms to save her. It makes no sense though, for a simpleton like Guébriant would never have been able to diagnose a particular poison, let alone "happen" to have all the right antidotes at hand. Also, Emilie was more than capable of showing her feeling for men she'd broken up with in letters, but she never showed any upset from breaking with Guébriant. The more likely explanation is that Phélypeaux, detesting Emilie as a traitor to her class, was making up a story about her—as he did about the many other individuals he tried to insult.

47   **He'd inherited a fortune and been thrown into the Bastille:** The second time, when he was sent in for dueling, was typically convoluted. The

young comtesse de Gacé had become drunk one evening, then undressed herself, and ended up being passed along among the guests at a dinner party. Richelieu found it difficult not to recount the story at another ball, on February 17, 1716, where de Gacé's husband unfortunately was in attendance. Since the story was true, the husband had to challenge him to a duel.

No one was hurt much—Richelieu had a slight stab wound in his thigh—but both were sent to the Bastille. The two men became great friends there, especially when Richelieu commiserated with the comte about the flighty wife he'd been induced to marry. As the weather turned hot they were seen spending hours walking together on the top of the Bastille's ramparts: investigating the vegetable garden there; waving to passersby far below. When a surgeon did come to identify the marks of the duel, he found two friendly young aristocrats insisting that it was merely an ordinary birthmark, which meant that the two friends were soon released.

47 **He was a renowned soldier:** Though, in fairness, Richelieu's success here was due more to British incompetence than to his own skills. When the king later did give him a marshal's baton, it was largely to stop his complaining about not being appointed as a minister of state.

47 **"He was woman's idolized lord":** Observations of Voltaire's friend d'Argenson, and of de Goncourt; modified from Frank Hamel, pp. 30–31, and Hubert Cole, *First Gentleman of the Bedchamber: The Life of Louis-François-Armand, Maréchal Duc de Richelieu* (London, 1965), p. 153.

48 **"I can't believe that someone as sought-after":** Emilie's *Lettres,* vol. 1, pp. 64–65, n. 36. (All references are to the Besterman edition.) The quotation comes from a slightly later stage of the relationship.

49 **Marriage was a matter of . . . alliance:** Florent-Claude and his contemporaries recognized that it was different in other, more coldly rational countries, where this easy French pragmatism didn't arise. When the Frenchman La Rochefoucault visited London a generation later, he was struck that wealthy English couples actually went out with each other, and postulated this was why the women there delayed marriage to the advanced age of twenty-five or even twenty-eight: it might take that long to find a partner they could stand spending so much time with.

49 **Two vastly wealthy young women:** Mme de Polignac and the Marquise de Nesle.

49 **Louis-François Armand du Plessis . . . was in love:** Cynics have suggested that if Richelieu was ever in love, it was with the face he saw in his

shaving mirror. Certainly, like many womanizers he generally didn't like
women, and spoke of them with scorn (though he spoke of most men with
scorn as well). However, with Emilie he always made an exception; keeping
an extraordinary, moving correspondence going for over a decade. The reason, I suspect, is that she was no longer sleeping with him; also, that early in
their relationship she'd seen through much of his nonsense—and had
enough trust in their friendship to let him know it.

49   **Indeed, one aristocratic young woman had reported:** To Brantôme,
in his *Les Dames Galantes,* a work straddling the genres of biography and personal memoir. First published in 1655, its reputation grew in the eighteenth
century.

50   **"putting it in and frolicking":** Ibid., pp. 38–39.

54   **"Most educated Frenchmen had snubbed":** "In France . . . a merchant hears his profession so disdainfully spoken of that he is foolish enough
to blush for it." Voltaire, quoted in Ballantyne, *Voltaire's Visit to England,*
p. 178.

55   **"He cured his wife of the spleen":** From *Voltaire's Notebooks: Edited,
in Large Part for the First Time,* by Theodore Besterman (Institut et Musée Voltaire, 1952), pp. 52, 53. For his notebook Voltaire used twenty-one big sheets
of paper, folding them to make eighty-four pages.

55   **When he needed help . . . the prompter loaned him a copy:** The
prompter at Drury Lane remembered a foreign gentleman—"this noted
author"—who began to come to the theater, where "I furnished him every
evening with the play of the night, which he took with him into the orchestra
[so he could look at the words while hearing the actors speak them]: in four
or five months he not only conversed in elegant English but wrote it with
exact propriety."

56   **"Sir, I wish you good health":** D338.

56   **He also learned . . . servants didn't have to carry water:** The idea
wasn't too complex, even in the pre-steam-engine era, but the execution was.
Colbert had proposed a comprehensive system for piped water in Paris
decades before, but it had never been implemented.

56   **He found his way . . . "the Jew, the Mahometan, and the Christian
transact together":** Compare Thomas Jefferson, a great fan of Voltaire, in
his *Notes on Virginia,* sixty years later: "It does me no injury for my neighbor
to say there are twenty gods, or no god. It neither picks my pocket not breaks

my leg." That attitude is central to the separation of Church and State in the U.S. Constitution. "It is error alone," Jefferson continued, "which needs the support of government. Truth can stand by itself."

56   **In France . . . Protestants had been . . . tortured:** A handful of Catholic priests or administrators would furtively violate that prejudice, giving families known to be Protestant the false label *nouveaux convertis* so that births, deaths, or marriages could be registered. But that was rare, and as late as 1752 Protestant vicars were still being hanged.

57   **"The reason of our not using the outward sword":** I've slightly reordered the quotation, which comes from early in Voltaire's Letters from England.

57   **"stick to the first [volume]":** D310 and D318. Voltaire has a good explanation of why the latter parts of *Gulliver's Travels* are so much less compelling. In the same letter (which is in English): "The reader's imagination is pleased and charmingly entertained by the new prospects of the lands which Gulliver discovers to him, but that continued series of newfangled follies, of fairy tales, of wild inventions, palls at last upon our taste. Nothing unnatural may please long. 'Tis for this reason that commonly the second parts of romances are so insipid." He could have been writing of Hollywood sequels.

58   **"I do not know . . . orders for [Bombay] . . . of the world":** His actual usage was "Surat," north of Bombay, where the English East India Company had its headquarters. Here I'm using Archibald Ballantyne's old translation, in his *Voltaire's Visit to England* (London, 1898), p. 178.

58   **There was a lot more to learn . . . although Newton had had the bad grace:** Newton died in 1727, about eleven months after Voltaire's arrival, but Voltaire hadn't been well enough connected in the UK to get to see the (ailing) Newton before he died. He did attend the funeral in Westminster Abbey, though, and conducted a famous interview with Mrs. Conduitt—where the apple story (see p. 70) first saw the light of day.

60   **In other words, they bought:** The details were slightly more complex, for the exact flaw was that the probability of winning was *not* proportional to the cost of the tickets needed for entry. This meant that the chances of winning would, in fact, be hugely multiplied if one merely purchased an overwhelming number of the least expensive tickets—which Voltaire, with the help of a corrupt notary, was quick to do. See Jacques Donvez, *De quoi vivait Voltaire?* (Paris, 1949), esp. pp. 39–55.

60   **Voltaire amassed a fortune:** Most nobles were not well off, and many of those that were had the bulk of their cash tied up in land. Voltaire's funds were highly liquid.

60   **And they had all been complacent . . . after the beating outside Sully's:** In retaliation, Voltaire had removed all references to his friend Sully's direct ancestor from his epic on Henri IV (which took some doing, for the original Sully had been Henri's right-hand man).

61   **since she was an actress . . . excommunicated by the Catholic Church in France:** An important qualification. Italian Catholicism was generally more liberal, and when Italian actors came to Paris they were careful to ensure that they remained under Italian rather than French Church law.

62   **But although he wanted . . . his Letters from England:** There were various titles and editions. The main distinction is between the English-language *Letters concerning the English Nation,* printed in London, and the slightly later French edition *Lettres philosophiques,* printed in Rouen. For simplicity I use the shorthand "Letters from England," which is how they were often referred to.

62   **the mathematics was too hard for him to advance:** This is when he seems to have first made contact with Pierre-Louis de Maupertuis (see p. 71), asking him for help in the calculations of Newton's inverse square law for gravitation: Voltaire, always a superb popularizer, was working out how much the moon "fell" toward the Earth in one second. He wanted to compare it with the distance an apple closer to the Earth's surface fell in that time, to show that both followed Newton's laws, and that the exact amounts were in accord with the true orbit of the moon that we see.

62   **"If you neglect to enroll yourself":** *Select Letters of Voltaire,* tr. and ed. T. Besterman (London, 1963), p. 72. Voltaire here addresses Le Fèvre, several years later, giving this prospective writer counsel on what awaits him if he does choose that career: "If your talents are unfortunately mediocre (which I do not believe) your regrets will last all your life; if you succeed you will have enemies." Voltaire goes on to describe book reviewers who will enjoy being witty at the author's expense, scholars who will "despise you, or pretend to do so"; cabals, an easily bored public, and much else that has changed little over the centuries.

62   **To save the effort . . . he moved in with:** This was the baronne de Fontaine-Martel. Old and suffering from severe eczema, she made it clear that not only was there to be no sex with her, but that Voltaire was not to

have any mistresses visiting either. He was, however, getting a large rent-free suite of rooms, with dinners and servants all laid on.

65 **The friends and Emilie turned up:** By other accounts their first meeting was at the Opera, but the dating is inconclusive. Besterman suggests the first week of May, but the letter D607 that he assigns to that period has no date on it. By June, however, their letters are unambiguous.

65 **But he and Emilie had become lovers . . . he wrote a poem:** This is his "Epistle to Uranus"; again, not so much a translation as a retelling.

66 **"She was born with a fairly good mind":** Besterman, *Voltaire,* p. 181. He compared this much repeated diatribe against the original letter in which Du Deffand wrote it.

68 **"I swear to you, she's a tyrant":** René Vaillot, *Madame du Châtelet* (Paris, 1978), p. 78.

68 **There was a slight amount of mixing:** Voltaire's ranking was only of the medium-high bourgeoisie, for his father had been merely a prosperous notary, and Voltaire was only a writer. This made a marriage between Voltaire and an aristocrat entirely impossible.

68 **But that was only for . . . the evening gatherings:** Moderated slightly by the fact that salons were rarely run by women from the highest nobility: more commonly, they were organized by women from newly wealthy merchant families, who had married into more established aristocratic families.

68 **Emilie was breaking all that:** If a woman from her background did, inconceivably, marry down, she would lose her claims to nobility. (If a male noble married a commoner, however, he kept his position.)

69 **"Why be so horrified by our existence?":** From Voltaire's 25th Letter.

69 **We take this for granted today:** Many of these ideas were around before, but held by thinkers who were not at all as well known as they became once Emilie and Voltaire had helped focus and boost them (especially via all the correspondence from Cirey). Without amplification, the earlier thinkers held to "start" an intellectual trend are readily forgotten.

69 **Ordinary people were . . . placed on Earth to work:** Our common word *weekend,* for example, was scarcely known at this time. The concept made no sense. Rich people never worked, so for them there was no working week in need of an ending. Ordinary people, by contrast, worked all the time—except when they were at church, or on Church-given holidays—and so their secular working had no end.

70   **He'd been a hypochondriac:** "From time to time during his long life [Voltaire] complained of apoplexy, blindness, catarrh, chronic colic, deafness, dropsy, dysentery, erysipelas, fever, gout, grippe, herpes, indigestion, inflammation of the lungs, insecure teeth, itch, loss of voice, neuritis, paralysis, rheumatism, scurvy, smallpox and strangury." Modified from Derek Parker, *Voltaire: The Universal Man* (Stroud, 2005), p. 79.

70   **Emilie was in her late twenties . . . a servant who later saw her nude:** This was Sébastian Longchamp, valet and secretary. He was slightly ill at ease about her throughout his *Mémoires,* constantly on the edge of undercutting her, and had no reason to give unwarranted compliments.

71   **"my machine is totally exhausted":** D691.

71   **Paris's population was several hundred thousand:** Since the sewers worked so poorly, homes further from the Seine usually couldn't use them at all. Sewage was either poured into the streets or taken away in carts—and although some of that was intended for fertilizer, much ended up in the Seine.

72   **He'd grown up on the coast of Brittany:** The corsairs were encouraged by the royal administration, for the French Navy was barely functional in the 1690s and there were no funds to pay for ships and sailors. Offering the prize of British ships was a way of encouraging private entrepreneurs from the French coastal ports to attack Albion, with no upfront costs to Paris. See Mary Terrall, *The Man Who Flattened the Earth* (Chicago, 2002), pp. 16, 17.

72   **When they weren't in bed:** It even seems that they brought a microscope into the bedroom, to continue their scientific discoveries there. For although the nature of sperm cells was roughly known, no one was quite sure how or where women provided the matching cells. Maupertuis examined the fluid that could be collected from a woman during, as he put it, "the tender moments shortly after intercourse." But although he and any partner looked carefully ("I have searched several times with an excellent microscope"), the magnifications they could achieve weren't enough for them to find the source of female reproductive cells (Quotations from Maupertuis's *Vénus physique.*)

72   **There seemed to be numerous cases of "slippage":** Late in the eighteenth century Joseph Lagrange and especially Pierre Laplace were thought to have shown that there were no such instabilities, though in the early twentieth century Poincaré and then much later the developers of chaos theory made clear how precarious the solar system really is. To Newton the issue was even simpler. Because of universal gravitation, everything pulled on

everything else, and so the universe should collapse inward—whence his finding it natural that there would be detailed imbalances that God needed to fix.

Note that long after Laplace's simple stability assumptions faded out of physics, they continued on in economics, especially as codified by Walras and his followers—an attractive notion to anyone seeking the comforting assurance of divine harmony guiding our lives.

74 **"The sublime Maupertuis":** Vaillot, *Madame du Châtelet,* p. 85.

75 **But the de Guise ancestors who had cheated:** French rulers who were low on funds were liable to send out blank letters of royal grant, which local administrators would auction off: the winner would get to be a noble, and the king—after the percentage skimmed off by his administrators—would be richer. The practice occurred at least as early as the late thirteenth century, while an especially great surge of direct purchases took place at the start of the sixteenth century, under Louis XII, when the government was again desperate for funds. The second-tier category of "nobles of the robe" was created at that time, offering further opportunities for royal enrichment.

75 **The Richelieu fortunes, however:** Although nobles of the sword, the Richelieus had been quite minor within that grouping. Worse, the present duc was only related to the cardinal through his aunt, and was a direct descendant only of the less-distinguished du Plessis family.

75 **Such variations within the aristocracy . . . biologically superior:** Think of the bitchiness and squabbling that develops among rich families after just one or two generations today. Now carry that over centuries, extend it to several thousand families, and then have the prerogatives that the different individuals are fighting about become enshrined in law. To make it more complicated, although all titled individuals were noble, not all nobles were titled. (The title was not the personal quality, for that was the status of nobility; rather, the title was linked to particular lands, as with Emilie later being a "princess" because of holdings in the Low Countries.)

What was at issue here was not quite our modern biological racism, but more a strong snobbery toward different groups. Thus families that were nobles of the sword would mock and despise others that were nobles of the robe—even if they were related.

77 **"From Jean Frédéric Phélypeaux, to the Crown's agent:"** The message was to the local *intendant,* Pierre Arnaud de la Briffe. The *intendants* were a relatively new category of officialdom, appointed directly by the king, in the

hope that they would be more likely to do his bidding than the traditional—and often unresponsive—local nobles. (It was similar to the creation of the National Security Council in the United States, overlain on a not-quite-trusted State Department.)

77   **"The King has deemed it appropriate":** D731.

78   **"My friend Voltaire":** Emilie's *Lettres,* vol. 1, p. 40, n. 14.

79   **The printer was thrown into the Bastille:** They also found other intriguing and not quite approved titles that the printer had high hopes of: *The Reluctant Nun* was one, *The Fifteen Joys of Marriage* another. The warning that Voltaire received was from his friend Argental, another schoolmate of his and Richelieu's from Louis le Grand, and also, conveniently, quite close to Phélypeaux.

79   **What Voltaire ended up deciding:** Voltaire stayed briefly at other locations, including Cirey; but the details are unclear, for he made sure that any letters in his hand were sent by courier from a range of places, the better to mislead the Paris authorities. Some historians suggest he went to Philippsburg only by chance, but that seems unlikely, for Cirey was still scarcely inhabitable, and Voltaire liked his luxury. Also, he'd just spent weeks under Richelieu's hospitality at Montjeu, and visiting the military camp would just be a continuation of that in a safer place. Perhaps most compelling of all—to the authority-mocking Voltaire—was that he knew it would irritate Phélypeaux beyond measure when the truth finally came out.

81   **Also, more and more nobles . . . needed to defend their status:** For those who weren't nobles at all it was worse, as they were blocked at the level of noncommissioned officer, however skilled or dedicated they might be. Come the Revolution, their resentment meant that this important core of the army readily took the anti-royalty side.

82   **The officer was the son of the prince:** The prince de Conti: no great genius, but a loyal fan of Voltaire.

83   **Voltaire wrote to an acquaintance:** D766. To the comtesse de la Neuville, who would become one of his two most important neighbors at Cirey.

84   **The printer had been interrogated:** D760. He quickly implicated Voltaire.

84   **Now, on June 10, the city's Parlement:** The Parlement was strongly Jansenist, as was Voltaire's hated older brother. Versailles officialdom might

personally be at ease with critiques of the official religion, but fervent Jansenists took more of a Savonarola-style line and hated Voltaire's mockery.

87   **The siege had ended . . . misfortune of having his head separated:** Phrasing from the eloquent Cole, *First Gentleman of the Bedchamber,* p. 79.

89   **"To be able to keep an audience interested for five acts":** D841. Frank McLynn has proposed that this difficulty with sustaining a long play might explain why Voltaire was so insanely jealous of Shakespeare and tried, absurdly, to disparage him. He is one of a trio of famous Shakespeare-haters—the others being Tolstoy and George Bernard Shaw.

89   **At one important moment . . . Phélypeaux chose as admiral:** Not only had the relative—the young duc d'Enville—never been on the Atlantic, but he had never been on a sailing ship, either. He led his fleet of sixty-four ships in the vague direction of the French fortress on Cape Breton Island, but he'd brought so few war materials that the attack had no chance of success. Since he also had little idea how much food to bring for the expedition, on the long voyage home cannibalism broke out aboard the defeated French fleet.

89   **Though in fairness to Phélypeaux:** Admittedly he could never get Fleury or—after Fleury's death—the king himself to spend sufficient money on the French navy to allow it to match its archrival, Britain's Royal Navy. But he still didn't do much to improve that:

"In the British navy, the test to become a junior officer depended on having spent at least six years at sea and the candidate had to prove that he could: 'Splice, Knot, Reef a sail, work a Ship Sailing, Shift his Tides, keep a Reckoning of a Ships way by Plain Sailing and Mercator, Observe by the Sun or Star, find the variation of the Compass and be qualified to do his Duty as an Able Seaman and a Midshipman.' For the young French aristocrat officers there was no equivalent. They studied . . . nothing about fighting or sailing tactics. There were [however] daily sessions set aside for both dancing and fencing." Condensed from Adam Nicolson, *Men of Honor* (London, 2005), pp. 24–26.

90   **"This custom causes epidemic maladies":** Modified from Margaret Sherwood Libby, *The Attitude of Voltaire to Magic and the Sciences* (New York, 1966), p. 254.

90   **"It is time for . . ." one supporter wrote:** This was Voltaire's friend d'Argenson, yet another schoolmate from Louis le Grand and, for a while,

minister for foreign affairs; taken from his *Considérations sur le gouvernement de la France.*

91   **"I will be there":** D803. To Thieriot; the original is in English.

91   **He watched her countermand his orders:** This is usually described by biographers as delighted exuberance on her part. But almost immediately after she arrived at Cirey, she wrote to Maupertuis (D797), saying that it was awful in Cirey without him, and that she hoped to arrange her life "in the sweet hope of spending many years philosophizing with you." Voltaire had a habit of presenting a cheerful persona when things went wrong—as with his encomium to London at the start of chapter 4—and here too it seems he's trying to give a positive spin on Emilie's doings to friends who already have doubts about her commitment.

92   **"I've been reading Locke again":** Edited version of D764.

92   **"There's a woman in Paris, named Emilie":** Ibid.

92   **"Let's go to Midnight Mass together":** Emilie's *Lettres,* vol. 1, p. 55, n. 26.

93   **A police official:** D884. The official was one Dubuisson.

93   **Back home in the light of day:** Ibid. As Dubuisson pieced together the story from servants and night constables, she'd spent hours with Maupertuis and the other explorers going over charts and maps for their polar expedition; then "at midnight she suddenly remembered that she'd left her coachman waiting. It was too late to expect him to still be there, so she rode into Paris alone, but dislocated her thumb while galloping so far. When she was home she sent a messenger to Mr. de Maupertuis, and he set out right away to console her. Apparently his rhetoric was quite elaborated, for he stayed closeted with her from four in the morning till just before noon, when a courier told the household that Mr. du Châtelet was approaching.... If it weren't for that, I suspect de Maupertuis would still be there."

94   **"Perhaps there's folly in my shutting myself up at Cirey":** Emilie's *Lettres,* vol. 1, p. 74, n. 38. To Richelieu.

97   **What happened . . . dozens of letters and memoirs:** The format of this chapter was suggested by Besterman's ingeniously arranged chapter 18, in his biography *Voltaire.*

97   **Mme du Châtele has arrived:** Hamel, *Eighteenth-Century Marquise,* pp. 65–66.

97   **Voltaire says I'm busy:** D930.

97   **Madame wishes to order:** D1336.

98   **Now she is putting windows where I've put doors:** Hamel, *Eighteenth-Century Marquise*, p. 66. The note is from October 1734, but work would have stopped for the winter, and so would continue the following year.

98   **Please remember to buy two small . . . tweezers:** D1313, D1362.

98   **I spend my time with masons:** D943 except for the first sentence about masons, which is from a different letter. Emilie pointedly used the word *amant* of Voltaire, and *ami* of Richelieu, to clearly lay out the new arrangement.

99   **Would you please send the thermometers:** Collated from various letters to Moussinot, especially D1351 and D1306. In these Moussinot extracts I generally use Besterman's translations.

99   **I stopped at Cirey:** D2789.

99   **Would you very kindly send me a hundred . . . quills:** D1414.

99   **Please have two good copies made:** D1058. It's not a portrait of her, but one of him. See the image of Voltaire on page 2 of the photo insert.

100   **I only got there at two in the morning:** Unless specified otherwise, the de Graffigny quotations here are from her long compilation of letters near the end of vol. 5 and start of vol. 6 in the correspondence section of the *Complete Works of Voltaire*. She was writing to her equally gossip-desperate friend François-Antoine Devoux, nicknamed Panpan. This is from vol. 5, p. 394.

100   **"Could you please send . . . wig powder":** André Maurel, *La Marquise du Châtelet, amie de Voltaire* (Paris, 1930), p. 54.

101   **Yes, Hébert [the goldsmith] is expensive:** D1338.

101   **The next morning, when Madame woke up:** Sébastien Longchamp and Wagnière, *Mémoires sur Voltaire* (2 vols.; Paris, 1826), pp. 119–20. This dates from later on, but I'm aware of no evidence pointing to her having changed her habits. Linant describes, from the early Cirey period, her general obliviousness to those in a serving capacity.

102   **"Reflect on the advantages we enjoy":** Voltaire, *Philosophical Dictionary*, entry on "Love."

103   **By the way, is Maupertuis really going:** Emilie's *Lettres*, vol. 1, p. 75, n. 38. Aside from Emilie and Voltaire's letters, the main sources for the quotations in this expedition section are Terrall's *The Man Who Flattened the Earth*; the 1756 edition of Maupertuis's collected works (*Oeuvres de Mr. de Maupertuis*,

A Lyon, Avec Approbation, & Privilège du Roi), and the letter that he sent from his expedition to Mme de Vertillac (in *Mélanges publiés par la société des Bibliophiles Français* (Paris, 1829)).

103   **This voyage would hardly suit me if I was happy:** Terrall, *Man Who Flattened the Earth,* p. 101. The letter dates from late December 1735, the year that Emilie had definitely left Maupertuis for Voltaire.

104   **After [many adventures] . . . how to avoid the insects:** "On the river we'd been attacked by huge mosquitoes with green heads, which drew blood wherever they bit; we found ourselves on Niwa, persecuted by several other species even more cruel." Maupertuis, *Oeuvres,* p. 103.

104   **I will say nothing more of the rigors of traveling:** "If you try to stop a reindeer by pulling on the sleigh's bridle, it just makes them turn around and kick you. The Lapps know how to turn over the sleigh and use that as a shield. But we were so little used to it that we were nearly killed before working it out. Our only defence was a little baton we carried by hand, and had used to steer the sleigh and avoid tree trunks in the deep snow." Maupertuis, *Oeuvres,* p. 148.

106   **And my good Moussinot:** Libby, *Attitude of Voltaire to Magic,* p. 52.

106   **The text was written in Latin:** E. Asse, ed., *Lettres de Mme de Graffigny* (Paris, 1879) p. 50. See also Jonathan Mollinson's *Françoise de Graffigny, femme de lettres. Ecriture et réception.* In SVEC, December 2004.

107   **The punishment for adultery could include whipping:** The spectacular punishment of the comtesse de La Motte in a later generation—as depicted in the 2001 film *The Affair of the Necklace,* with Hilary Swank as the countess—was not so much for her adultery as for her embarrassment of the royal family through theft.

107   **"adultery is punished in the person of the wife":** Alain Lottin, *La Désunion du couple sous l'ancien régime* (Lille, 1975), p. 75.

108   **"The yogis of India":** Ira O. Wade, *Voltaire and Mme du Châtelet: An Essay on the Intellectual Activity at Cirey* (Princeton, 1941), p. 131.

108   **"I hardly spent two hours apart from him":** Emilie, *Lettres,* vol. 1, p. 151, n. 85.

109   **"each presided over . . . by a woman":** Besterman, *Select Letters,* p. 72.

110   **Undercut the Church . . . and the whole chain might come undone:** A similar concern is perhaps at the root of fundamentalist literalism in America, especially as it spread in the early twentieth century. In fast-industrializing America, as well as ancien régime France, turning back to the sources that

had once seemingly upheld old relations, and guarding them tighter than ever before, seemed to be the sole way to keep everything from dissolving. For a fresh take on the psychological assumptions behind this, see Arthur L. Stinchcombe, *When Formality Works: Authority and Abstraction in Law and Organizations* (Chicago, 2001). A more recent example is the Chinese government's great effort to block investigation of Mao's career. If the foundations of China's Communist Party were undercut, millions of careers could have to change.

110 **"I'm not a Christian, but that's only to love Thee:"** Vaillot, *Avec Madame du Châtelet,* p. 32. Voltaire was writing in 1722.

110 **It was . . . "like the rules of a game":** Modified from Esther Ehrman, *Mme Du Châtelet: Scientist, Philosopher and Feminist of the Enlightenment* (Leamington Spa, 1986), p. 64. It was a commonplace of writers such as Montesquieu in his *Persian Letters,* but here, at the start of her intellectual creativity, Emilie was making it fresh for herself.

111 **"Women usually don't recognize their own talents":** Modified from Ehrman, *Mme du Châtelet,* p. 61.

112 **This too was a fundamental step:** Greek writers had developed explicit typologies of polities, but that approach collapsed in the Christian era when mankind's doings were taken to be the unfolding of a divine plan. Only as that busy divinity was pushed aside could Montesquieu and Vico and others closer to Emilie's time reassert a meaningful pattern to purely secular activities.

112 **Hardly anyone had collected autographs before:** See Beatrice Fraenkel's *La Signature: genèse d'un signe* (Paris, 1992).

113 **"I couldn't whisper . . . the hoops of our dresses made us stand too far apart":** *Créquy,* p. 123. Her stranded friend was Mme d'Egmont.

113 **"There were supposed to be . . . strict arrangements of tiny patches":** "It required a special knack to place these patches where they would best set off the face—upon the temples, near the eyes, at the corners of the mouth, upon the forehead. A great lady always had seven or eight, and never went out without her patch-box, so that she might put on more if she felt so inclined, or replace those that might happen to come off. Each of these patches had a particular name. The one at the corner of the eye was the *passionate;* that on the middle of the cheek, the *gallant;* that on the nose, the *impudent;* that near the lips, the *coquette;* and one placed over a pimple, the *concealer (receleuse),* etc." From ch. 19 of Paul Lacroix, *The Eighteenth Century, with 21 Chromolithographs and 351 Wood Engravings* (New York and London, 1876).

114   **Now, though, a new form of publication:** See Dena Goodman, *Republic of Letters: A Cultural History at the French Enlightenment* (Ithaca, 1994), pp. 137, 142.

114   **It was much like a primitive Internet:** The phrasing is lifted from Tom Standage's wonderfully titled *Victorian Internet;* the concept is an old one, promoted by Tocqueville (in his *Ancien Régime*) and many others. What earlier studies missed, though, was the extraordinary power that a handful of "superlinkers" at the nodes can provide in spreading ideas. Albert-Laszlo Barabasi's *Linked: The New Science of Networks* (Cambridge, Mass., 2002) demonstrates that power with a number of clear diagrams.

115   **Even if someone did reach their thirties . . . much else steadily going wrong:** The less polluted air counterbalanced these ailments to some extent, as did greater physical exercise, especially for men. But poor nutrition and hygiene more than made up for that, as studies of skeletons even from wealthy areas show.

117   **"I am . . . like those brooks that are transparent":** Libby, *Attitude of Voltaire to Magic,* p. 47.

117   **"There are . . . a few great geniuses, such as M. de Voltaire":** From Emilie's preface to her translation of Mandeville's *Fable of the Bees.*

118   **that "brilliant light, so perfect for lovers":** Modified from Maurel, *Marquise du Châtelet,* p. 55.

118   **"Pascal taught men to hate themselves":** From a slightly earlier (1732) poem; in the Moland edition of Voltaire's works, vol. 22, pp. 33–34.

118   **"we guilty beings deserving to inhabit the crumbling ruins":** *Elements of Newton,* section 3, ch. 10.

120   **"My companion in solitude has . . . dedicated it to me!":** Emilie's *Lettres,* vol. 1, pp. 125–26, n. 73. She'd been disappointed at not receiving a dedication from the visiting Francesca Algarotti in his popular *Newtonism for Women,* which was based in large part on what she'd explained to him. This more than made up for it.

120   **"I spend my life, dear Abbé . . . with a lady":** Besterman, *Select Letters,* p. 49. The letter is dated December 9, so if that's accurate it would have been written immediately before the forced escape.

120   **"We have just left Cirey":** Ibid., p. 49.

123   **He'd sent copies . . . one draft had ended up purloined:** The thief was our angry ex-Jesuit, Desfontaines, the homosexual abbé who had been condemned in 1725 to be burned alive in a public square for his deeds, and

whom Voltaire had lobbied the authorities to save. On the principle that no good deed goes unpunished, Desfontaines spent much of his life trying to torment his savior. Voltaire had managed to brush off most of those attacks—once, after having had to endure the labor of reading and rebutting a scurrilous paper, he remarked that, really, it might have been better to have burned a monk, rather than now be bored by one. But the distortions Desfontaines added to the Adam and Eve poem could mean exile for life.

123 **Emilie knew that . . . the higher nobility lived in contentment:** Only a small percentage of the country's 100,000 or so nobles could live at Versailles. Most were far too poor; a few had fallen so far that they could only be told apart from the peasants they lived amidst by their right to carry a sword, and their reserved pews in church. See G. Chaussinand-Nogaret's *La Noblesse au dix-huitième siècle* (Paris, 1976) for sensible demographic estimates.

124 **It was . . . what the safety of the state depended on:** This wasn't the first time a king had decided to safeguard his position by concentrating or bankrupting his nobles, but it reached its pinnacle here.

124 **"I need to know":** Emilie's *Lettres,* vol. 1, p. 144, n. 82.

124 **It was Richelieu . . . sending a fast rider:** It was possible there would be only a stern warning from the court, but it was also sensible to prepare for an actual arrest, which would probably be carried out with forces directed by the local *intendant.*

125 **There were ambassadors, writers, businessmen:** Gustave Desnoiresterres, *Voltaire et la société au XVIIIe siècle* (8 vols., Paris, 1867–76), vol. 2, p. 119.

126 **It was the play he'd written:** Voltaire made a significant innovation in his text, for French had undergone a pronunciation shift in previous years. For example, what had been spelled and pronounced *les bordelois* in the seventeenth century was now pronounced *les bordelais* . . . but still spelled the old way. (It would be as if we pronounced the word *the* as we're used to, but the government insisted we still spell it *thee.*) In his play *Zaïre* Voltaire used the new spelling—*ais*—for all the many words that had that same *ois/ais* imbalance between sound and sight. He was the first writer to make that shift, and what was important was not just that, with his authority, it came to be accepted (whence today's Paris headlines about *Les Anglais* ("The English"); rather, that effect demonstrates how justified the authorities in tightly hierarchical France were to worry that more political aspects of his writings could catch on as well.

126   **"The Role That Kills!":** Jean Orieux, *Voltaire ou la royauté de l'esprit* (Paris, 1966), p. 225.

127   **For not only was ... Willem Jakob 's Gravesande:** The odd *'s* in front of his name is the Dutch way to write "of the," similar to the French *des* or the German *von*.

127   **The way ... 's Gravesande was determining this:** Voltaire also saw many other experiments, for (as I've written elsewhere) 's Gravesande also used hollow and solid brass balls, pendulums, scraped clay (of a deeply elaborate consistency), supporting frames, and a Laputan-like variety of other contraptions to carry out his contention that "The Properties of Body cannot be known à priori; we must therefore examine Body itself, and nicely consider all its Properties."

128   **He'd spent time with other scientists ... been made a member of the Royal Society:** Though that wasn't as much of an honor then as now, for membership was often granted to wealthy supporters or visiting dignitaries. (It was still somewhat more legitimate than the University of St. Andrews, notorious for selling rights to its doctorates, whence the remark that it was "getting richer by degrees.")

129   **[Newton's understanding] of gravity is not the final result:** *Elements of Newton,* p. 536.

130   **"I'm 150 leagues from him":** Emilie's *Lettres,* vol. 1, p. 151.

130   **For you see ... "my father had another daughter":** Ibid., pp. 145, 147.

133   **She'd teasingly called out:** From Anne Bellinzani's scarcely disguised *Histoire des amours de Cléante et de Bélise* (Paris, 1689), p. 168, in Présidente Ferrand, ed., *Lettres,* Notice par Eugène Asse (Paris, 1880).

133   **"I'm the tenderest lover":** Modified from Vaillot, *Madame du Châtelet,* p. 26.

135   **But Emilie also had a most unpleasant first cousin:** François-Victor Le Tonnelier, Marquis de Breteuil; he'd been in office 1723–26, and would be again 1740–43. Although not the minister responsible during Voltaire's stunt at Philippsburg, he would have felt the insult.

136   **He had a word ... this intense shame from the past was coming back:** It didn't help that a very elderly Anne Bellinzani was still alive.

137   **"M. du Châtelet ... is leaving [for Paris]":** Emilie, *Lettres,* vol. 1, p. 187, n. 99.

142   **"he was quite carried away":** D 894.

142 **Then Linant's sister arrived . . . efficiency:** Even Voltaire was moved to observe: "An extreme laziness of body and mind does seem to be the distinguishing characteristic of this family."

142 **"I don't want him to dedicate his tragedy":** Emilie, *Lettres,* vol. 1, p. 196, n. 107.

143 **This was Crown Prince Frederick:** He himself used the French-style *Frédéric* then.

143 **He regularly punched his son:** As reported by Frederick to his sister, Margharete; recorded in her memoirs.

143 **Only at twenty-one . . . was he trusted:** He hadn't been in the fortress the whole time, but his travel had been limited to just a few miles.

144 **"and often at the same time":** Desnoiresterres, *Voltaire et la société,* vol. 2, p. 128.

144 **The Academy of Sciences . . . had recently declared its prize:** It was officially termed the prize "for" 1738, since that was when it would be awarded, but the deadline for submission was September 1737.

145 **It was an expenditure . . . several million dollars today:** Estimating inflation rates over the centuries is nearly impossible, but there is some sense in asking what percentage of a population could afford a particular item. The equivalent of the high-tech laboratory equipment that Voltaire purchased would be out of reach of all but the wealthiest Silicon Valley or Wall Street individuals today. The era of the gifted amateur in physics was brief, Henry Cavendish in the late eighteenth century being one of the last independent top-level experimentalists; Oliver Heaviside, in the late nineteenth century, just managed to hold on as an independent theoretician.

146 **"Draw him into a conversation":** Desnoiresterres, *Voltaire et la société,* vol. 2, p. 123.

149 **Metals do gain weight:** The iron gained weight because oxygen from the air was joining with it. Voltaire lacked not just adequate scales, but also the very idea of weighing the encompassing air, for in his focusing on the iron he was missing the more important combined *system* of metal + air + smoke. He was close though, and Guyton de Morveau mentioned Voltaire's work in his 1772 paper, which finally showed that metals can gain weight when heated. Soon after, Lavoisier built on that finding to show that it was indeed oxygen from the air that caused this.

149 **The effect is so slight:** Voltaire had no chance, for the weight change was many trillions of times less than his scales could measure. There were

over 10^{25} atoms in the iron blocks, and only the top few surface ones would combine with oxygen.

149 **"I didn't want to be ashamed":** D1528; Voltaire's *Collected Letters,* vol. 5, p. 165.

150 **Maupertuis had needed to hide . . . his true interests:** For example, he'd had to pretend that his trip to the polar regions was only to investigate the "hypothesis" that Newton might be right.

150 **"I couldn't perform any experiments":** D1528.

150 **She'd helped Voltaire with this very calculation:** The mathematician Alexis Claude Clairault was a friend of them both, and had spent time at Cirey. "I had two students there, of very unequal value. One was really quite remarkable, while I could never get the other one [Voltaire] to actually understand what was meant by mathematics." P. Brunet, *La Vie et l'oeuvre de Clairault* (Paris, 1952), p. 14.

152 **Other times she stood and paced up and down:** Voltaire, *Collected Letters,* vol. 5, p. 469.

153 **"fruitful experiments could be conducted":** Desnoiresterres, *Voltaire et la société,* vol. 2, p. 157.

154 **She even put in a suggestion . . . in the direction of Herschel:** Herschel constantly tried to look beyond what was known, be it a new planet further than any then known, or new volumes of space beyond what was believed to exist—efforts rewarded by the discovery of the planet Uranus and the vast spaces in which our solar system resides. It's possible this reflex came from his own psychological dynamic, for he'd been raised to be a musician in Germany, yet had ventured beyond the confines of his family's assumptions and turned himself into an astronomer in England. Emilie too had broken from what was assumed to be right for her: she was no longer a proper aristocrat, and had left superficial female activities behind as well. That sheer phenomenology of "going into a new realm" may have helped Emilie—as perhaps with Herschel—to make this extraordinary conceptual leap to imagining supra-visible hues of light.

154 **There was a new tutor . . . and the painter:** D1677.

155 **"There's so much to do when you have a family":** Emilie's *Lettres,* vol. 1, p. 267, n. 148.

155 **"the originality of my ideas . . . would keep me from winning":** Desnoiresterres, *Voltaire et la société,* vol. 2, p. 159.

155 **"The one and the other [of those two essays]":** Libby, *Attitude of Voltaire to Magic,* p. 153.

156 **"Oh my God, Panpan":** D1686 and D1708.

157 **"I am curious," he eventually wrote to . . . Marain:** This was in 1741, when Voltaire sent Marain his own essay on *forces vives,* which meandered around the division we now make between momentum and kinetic energy.

158 **Did that not show . . . light could create magnetism?:** This wasn't as foolish an idea as it was then taken to be. A century later Michael Faraday found that a magnetic field would change the polarization of a beam of light traveling through leaded glass—a crucial link between what had hitherto been believed to be two totally separate realms. Voltaire's guess, though, was just a rhetorical counterpunch, unlike Emilie's powerful analysis of the possibility of ultraviolet light.

159 **Even before the Academy's results . . . one of these friends:** The friend was Formont.

159 **My friend I'll do what you advise:** D1410, in a jaunty eighteenth-century translation.

159 **there were twists and turns . . . ancient Greek warlords:** Parisian actors refused to be debased by playing in a chorus. When Voltaire had tried putting choruses in previous work, the roles had been taken by servants—who were often drunk.

160 **It could be a great way:** D1697.

160 **Voltaire toned it down:** As it was based on Desfontaines, the initial fervor is understandable.

161 **the palace they live in is clearly built for them:** Voltaire's theme of a mysteriously waiting beneficence has been interpreted in many ways, from similar mocking found elsewhere—as in Kafka's story about dogs who can't see humans and develop a whole theology about this invisible force lifting and feeding them—to more serious pondering, as with Einstein's image of our existing within a large library whose texts have already been written.

161 **Voltaire was writing fast now:** As evidenced by how quickly after the previous section he sent out Part 6, compared with the delays he'd experienced after each of the earlier parts.

161 **Voltaire's writing became beautiful . . . dreams of his Emilie:** Voltaire had a passion for such imagined visitors throughout his life—perhaps

from having lost his beloved mother when he was only seven. Consider W. H. Barber's "Voltaire's Astronauts," *French Studies* 30 (1976), pp. 28–42.

162 **"he's such a sweet-natured boy":** Emilie's *Lettres,* vol. 1, p. 203, n. 112.

162 **There was ever more construction . . . two young Lapp women:** The categories of geographical and ethnic identity were less distinct then than now. Although called Lapps throughout their stay, the women were more likely to have been ethnic Swedes.

162 **He knew that the main critic . . . was Jacques Cassini:** Known as Cassini II, in distinction to his father, who'd also been a somewhat deluded head of the Observatory. The sequence of hereditary incompetence continued on to a Cassini IV, whose run was ended by the French Revolution.

162 **"Maupertuis has flattened . . . Cassini":** Maupertuis's science was good, but he and Voltaire underestimated Cassini's pull over France's Academy-dependent scientists: the official word remained that Maupertuis's readings must have been inaccurate, and extra credence was given to a poorly designed expedition that Cassini himself supervised largely within France. Only when La Condamine staggered back from South America several years later were Maupertuis's findings independently confirmed, and Cassini, begrudgingly, had to give in. Bernoulli, observing the charade from distant Switzerland, wisely remarked that voyagers would always discover what they expected to discover.

163 **On the day of performances, Emilie's son:** De Graffigny reports only Champbonin's son, but it would have been surprising if he hadn't brought along the one other male youngster in the château, especially as Emilie's son had been underfoot during the earlier Newton experiments.

164 **Their rooms weren't quite as demarcated:** The trend toward more privacy is well discussed in Flandrin's *Families in Former Times: Kinship, Household and Sexuality.* A generation or two later and the transformation was near-complete, with Marie-Antoinette keeping a long gown on while she bathed and having a sheet stretched in front of her when she got out, so that no servants could see her.

164 **When it came time for more hot water:** Based on Longchamp's later description of her doing the same in Paris.

164 **But her bath was not . . . in a purely public space:** It was a significant cultural shift, but one can take matters too far. Daniel Roche described water closets being introduced in seventeenth-century Netherlands, and sug-

gested that "secretions of the body were being privatised along with the cogitations of the mind." Roche, *France in the Enlightenment,* tr. A. Goldhammer (Cambridge, Mass., 1980).

164   **She understood Maupertuis's calculations perfectly well:** If the Earth were flat, you would never see new stars lift up over the horizon as you walked north. If, however, the Earth were very small with a tight curve, then you would regularly see new stars appear, for your line of sight—the tangent to the Earth's surface—would constantly be shifting as you walked up the curved surface toward the pole. Our planet has a curve that falls somewhere between these two extremes, and by measuring how quickly fresh stars appeared at different latitudes one could deduce how curved the Earth was at those varying locations.

165   **"My uncle is lost to his friends":** D1488. She's confiding to Thieriot, just after the nine-day visit. Hamel, *Eighteenth-Century Marquise,* and a few others are vaguely polite about the niece, but Orieux, *Voltaire ou la Royauté,* p. 230, accurately demonstrates how much of a nitwit she was.

169   **But even though Marie-Louise:** The whispering words, and Voltaire's charm, are from Marie-Louise's letter to Thieriot; that they were standing close is a guess, but plausible for a couple newly in love—for despite what would come later, in choosing M. Denis she had followed her heart, turning down the far greater sums that she would have received for marrying others, such as Champbonin's son.

170   **Leibniz had certainly published it . . . Newton, however, had the habit:** If Newton had been a calm and sensible individual, he would have accepted the just claims of both sides—but if he had been calm and sensible he wouldn't have transformed the Western worldview. He was fierce about protecting his own glory, and for years used his position as head of the Royal Society to torment Leibniz and Leibniz's supporters as much as he could. You were either with him, or against him.

170   **Yet in exchange . . . betrayed!:** From de Graffigny's letters, composed either that night or the next day.

170   **It went on, louder and louder:** There have been attempts to exonerate her, but she loved passing on gossip, the more scurrilous the better; letters she received back from her sometime boyfriend Panpan make it pretty clear what she'd done.

173   **He needed Emilie's enthusiastic support, but she was . . . learning law:** She'd always liked languages, and when the young Italian Algarotti had

come to Cirey a few years before, she'd spent several weeks perfecting her spoken Italian so she could put him at ease.

175   **Emilie was far enough outside:** If one's too isolated it's nearly impossible to be creative, but if one has no isolated space for reflection it's difficult too. If Kant, for example, had been in Berlin, he probably wouldn't have been able to grapple directly with Hume, and create his unique new philosophy: there would have been too many establishment figures immediately at hand to offend. Similarly, T. S. Eliot needed to leave America (where he was held back by what everyone expected of him) and move to England before he could be creative; Jonathan Ive, the British co-designer of Apple's iPod, had to leave the world of UK design schools before he could create his unique style. There are striking analogies with speciation in population biology: selective pressure that's too strong makes it hard for new forms to build up, while a total lack of pressure often keeps the incumbent in position.

176   **Careers . . . seemed to be transforming:** The view that the current era was uniquely fast-changing was especially strong in early eighteenth-century France, not least because of Louis XIV's dramatic efforts to make the past seem relatively static.

176   **Emilie was one of the very first:** Leibniz had used the Latin *optimum* before, to mean "the greatest good"; the first mention of *optimiste,* though, is apparently in a 1737 issue of the Jesuit *Journal de Trévoux* (which regularly covered scientific matters).

177   **But at times he couldn't help . . . letting Emilie know how inane:** "Metaphysical writers are like minuet dancers; who being dressed to the greatest advantage, make a couple of bows, move through the room in the finest attitudes, display all their graces, are in continual motion without advancing a step, and finish at the identical point from which they set out." Voltaire's reply to a friend who'd asked his opinion of a particular overly abstruse thinker, cited in Archibald Ballantyne, *Voltaire's Visit to England,* p. 316.

181   **Then there was . . . a short ride to their house:** And it's still there today: 2 Quai d'Anjou. Mme Curie later lived nearby, at 36 Quai de Béthune.

182   **it "is without doubt the finest [house] of Paris":** Besterman, *Select Letters,* p. 64.

182   **His son, however . . . Johann Bernoulli:** The Bernoullis were to mathematics what the Bachs were to music, only here the talent was spread even more widely. Historians try to help by using numbers, e.g., Johann I and

Johann II. But there were also several Daniels over the years, and as they all often complained about each other, and on at least one occasion plagiarized within the family, it's a messy business.

183   **"Here you are back in Paris":** D2076.

183   **"I hope, sir," she wrote to him:** D2117.

184   **In Paris those five years before:** There had been a brief period of excitement about science before, but it was more of a fashion than evidence of any deep interest; also, it had not been specifically Newtonian.

184   **"All Paris resounds with Newton":** From the review of her and Voltaire's *Elements of Newton* in the *Journal de Trévoux;* cited in Mordechai Feingold, *The Newtonian Moment* (New York and Oxford, 2004).

184   **"Paris," he wrote, as if resignedly:** D2082. Which prompted one biographer to note, "To kill Voltaire under compliments, one must really make a lot of them."

185   **Those monarchs, for example . . . deserved our deference because:** As the sage Nealus O'Stephen once observed, of such systems that have accumulated over time: "Like Botany, they could be Memorized but not Understood."

187   **"Your Royal Highness, there is one thing":** Modified from D2110.

189   **"I am Don Quixote!":** D2363.

189   **he and the other young men "lost money at cards, danced till we fell":** Vaillot, *Avec Madame du Châtelet,* p. 204. What is translated here as "delicious moves" is literally "titillations."

190   **He wrote about Emilie . . . "like living in a chapel":** Modified from ibid., p. 205, and Hamel, *Eighteenth-Century Marquise,* p. 225.

191   **Nothing that Frederick had presented . . . was true:** Voltaire should have seen this coming, for even his very first visit to Frederick, not far from Liège, had been followed by an ultimatum against that town. (Prussian troops had been put in position before Voltaire arrived, and his presence was used as a cover for Frederick's arrival to supervise the possible attack.) But since Frederick did actually have a plausible legal claim to Liège—and because Voltaire wanted to believe in him—that aggressive ultimatum was taken as of no significance.

191   **This was Prussia's distinctive *Paradeschritt*:** Literally "parade march." Norman Davies, *Europe: A History* (Oxford, 1996), examines this and other European marching traditions, p. 612.

191   **Yet Frederick has created a true Newtonian machine:** As com-

pared to, e.g., Louis XIV's attacks on Spain in a previous generation, which he'd insisted were to reestablish the proper forms of inheritance and legal agreement.

191 **Keyserlingk was a trusted emissary:** Within, that is, Frederick's deeply distorted view of human nature. He mistreated Keyserlingk and called him a twit for being so incompetent. This meant he was nicer to him than he was to almost anyone else.

192 **"I've been cruelly repaid":** D2365. She said this to Richelieu, but it would be surprising if she didn't also say it directly to the culprit.

192 **And actually, did she have any idea:** His view of physics as a crushing tyrant is expressed in a letter to Argental, August 22, 1741.

192 **One wit said that there should be a clause:** Charles-Jean-François Hénault, court official, to Mme du Deffand; Hamel, *Eighteenth-Century Marquise,* p. 227.

197 **"[Monsieur de Voltaire] is in an appalling temper":** Archives de la Bastille (Paris, 1881), vol. 12, pp. 245–46.

198 **"The Court's ladies," as he'd noted:** From Voltaire's introduction to her (posthumously published) *Principes mathématiques de la philosophie naturelle de Newton* (Paris, 1759).

198 **But now, her concentration ruined . . . desperate for the sensation:** As she wrote in her *On Happiness,* this is when she really came alive.

198 **"Dear Lover, I'm so sorry for choosing to write you":** D2904.

199 **"I don't know," she wrote Richelieu quickly:** This particular letter is earlier, but is consistent with her turning to Richelieu in times of stress, be it confiding her feelings when wondering whether to leave Paris for Voltaire, or propositioning him during one of his stays at Cirey. (Other letters of hers suggest she did go ahead with an affair at this time with her loyal lawyer from the Low Countries, M. Charlier.)

199 **When one of the old guard . . . had criticized her:** This was the Marain incident of 1741. Vaillot *Avec Madame du Châtelet,* pp. 146–47, is good on the key timing, but I don't think he gives enough credit to her arguments and their importance in clarifying the concept of kinetic energy.

200 **Even by the undemanding standards . . . Louis was known:** "His education having been neglected, his mind remained under-furnished. He had a gentle and timid character and an invincible distaste for [public] affairs, which he could not bear even to have mentioned in his presence. . . . [He was] capable of friendship . . . [but] indolent, hating and fearing work." And this

was from Antoine Pecquet, one of Louis's own senior officials; in Robert Darnton, *Mademoiselle Bonafon and the Private Life of Louis XV* (London, 2003).

201   **She'd always been hated by ordinary people:** Louis was caught within a subtle transformation. In the seventeenth century, mistresses had been seen as revealing the king's power. Now, though, they were increasingly seen as revealing his weakness. For women were imagined as stronger than before. This was good for Emilie—it helped open at least some doors for her—but it was catastrophic for poor Châteauroux. The murder of a royal mistress would inspire no popular calls for revenge.

202   **"screaming with pain and at unknown horrors":** Hubert Cole, *First Gentleman of the Bedchamber: The Life of Louis-François-Armand, Maréchal Duc de Richelieu* (London, 1965), p. 134.

202   **Voltaire also recognized her as another outsider:** The majority at court actually were the comparatively new nobles of the robe. Such an infusion of energetic, relatively lower orders into higher ones was taking place across Europe at the time.

202   **Through a mix of bedroom skills and conversational ability:** Her official name at the time was Mme d'Etioles, for her mother had arranged for her to be married to a rich official of that name. At class-obsessed Versailles, however, this fooled nobody, and she was constantly harangued for her lowly origins. The fact that the mother tried to promote the story that the grandfather had been a weaver (which was a somewhat more acceptable profession but contradicted the family name, Poisson) just made them seem more ridiculous.

203   **On the morning of April 11, 1745 . . . the battle began:** There's a famous story about how the shooting started, based substantially on Voltaire's interviews with the survivors. It has too much the air of Voltaire's typical staging to ring entirely true, but at least in that version (and using some phrasing from Hubert Cole) the battle began with the British troops marching forward, in strict square formations, till they were scarcely a hundred yards from the French lines. The thousands of trained soldiers, with muskets aimed at each other, stood perfectly still, for everyone knew what had to happen before the firing began.

The overall British commander was George II's son, the Duke of Cumberland, but what was called for at this point was action too intense for him to participate in directly. It was a subordinate officer, Lord Charles Hay, who left the lines and moved forward. He took off his hat. The French troops' muskets didn't move. He lowered his hat. The British troops' muskets didn't move. He raised his hat again, and waited.

To his great dismay, the French officer, the comte d'Auteroche, now did something very ingenious: he refused to lower his hat! So Lord Hay had to return, dejected, to the British lines, no doubt to whispers of commiseration from his fellow officers. What had happened was that the British had offered the French the opportunity to shoot first. Auteroche had refused, because if he did fire first and his troops' musket balls missed—which was likely, since muskets didn't impart a smooth gyroscopic spin to the balls they shot out— then the British could charge while they were reloading.

The hat-lowering stratagem having failed, both armies now silently marched closer. When, at about thirty yards, the British officers lifted their canes slightly, the front two rows of French troops quickly knelt. The canes had been raised because the British troops were preparing to kneel as well. Scared soldiers aim high, and the British officers now began strolling along their lines, gently tapping down the pointed muskets. Nothing could be heard but the squelch of feet in mud and the brush of musket stocks against uniforms. Only then, with everyone in position, did the deadly shooting begin.

203 **The king was scared, and his generals were dithering:** The usually efficient de Saxe was the official overall commander but, being in poor health, he didn't directly control this part of the campaign.

203 **"as tightly wedged . . . as a square peg in a square hole":** Cole, *First Gentleman of the Bedchamber,* p. 147.

203 **Richelieu got back to the king and:** Victory has many fathers, and everyone wanted to take credit for the undoubted success at Fontenoy. De Saxe had seen that all the men and equipment were in position; Richelieu's role here—perhaps the most level-headed of his often self-promoting military career—was as described in the text; but the greatest credit might well go to Lord Clare, Irish and a Jacobite, who commanded the Irish regiments that, in the end, swung the battle.

203 **The king's generals, however . . . a very nice bridge:** They were also planning to leave their own (largely peasant) army behind.

204 **There were at least four French cannon available:** De Saxe was a superb commander—possibly the best of that era, of any side—but on this day he was slipping. He'd left orders for the cannon not to be moved from where they'd been placed, and it was those orders that Richelieu had to get the king to override.

205   **In July, the Catholic claimant . . . with promises of French support to come:** The qualifier "promises" is important, for French support was grudging, and only came after Charles Edward had successfully landed, raised the clans and won his first important victory (at Prestonpans). Had the support come earlier, and publicly, the more cautious of his Scottish followers would probably have been emboldened to keep advancing.

205   **Pamphlets had to be prepared:** What Voltaire wrote began:

MANIFESTO

Of the King of France in favor of
Prince Charles Edward

꩜

. . . THE DUKE OF RICHELIEU, commander of the army of his MAJESTY THE KING OF FRANCS, addresses this declaration to the faithful people of the three kingdoms of Great Britain, and assures them of the constant protections of the King his master. He comes to join the heir of their ancient Kings. . . .

208   **"what worries me now is free will":** D1486; also D1496. The term *energy* in its modern sense was still a century in the future; she wrote of "this quantity of force."

208   **In many respects he . . . was the last of the medievals:** The point was understood in his time but forgotten later, for Newton's ideas were taken up by anti-religious reformers, who wouldn't accept that Newton had these beliefs. The modern concept is Keynes's, promoted after he examined a long-forgotten collection of alchemical writings that Newton had left at Kings College, Cambridge.

208   **Hardly anyone could use it directly:** Looking back, in 1731, Johann Bernoulli senior wrote: "I tried to understand it. I read and reread what [Newton] had to say concerning the subject, but . . . I could not understand a thing." Feingold, *Newtonian Moment,* p. 67.

209   **That itself would be an immense undertaking:** She'd made a desultory start before, but now could do it properly.

209   **Indeed, she was now increasingly known:** Though the dauphin—when not in his father's presence—avoided saying "Madame de Pompadour," preferring "Madame Whore."

210   **The invasion of England had also failed . . . not helped by his ongoing arguments:** They weren't the only two who had it in for each other.

The Council of State, which had responsibility for the invasion and uprising, had six ministers at this time. In Frank McLynn's deft summary, "[Richelieu's] immediate boss was the war minister Comte d'Argenson, who was at daggers drawn with his brother the marquis d'Argenson, who in turn was at logger-heads with the king's personal favorite the duc de Noailles, who in turn despised Cardinal Tencin, the Jacobite promoter." The wonder is that the invasion plan got as close as it did.

210   **"Monsieur de Voltaire . . . begs the director-general":** Besterman, *Select Letters,* p. 90.

210   **Soon more honors came in:** Including, after several attempts, membership in the Académie Française. "This . . . is the subject of all literary men's secret hopes, it is a mistress against which they launch songs and epigrams until they have obtained its favors, and which they neglect as soon as they have entered into possession. . . . After forty years of work you [get to] deliver in a broken voice, on the day of your reception, a discourse which on the next day will be forgotten for ever." Voltaire's further summary to the aspiring writer Le Fèvre; in ibid., p. 72.

211   **Voltaire had begun an affair . . . incest . . . was much less abhorrent:** It was not uncommon amongst royalty, as witness Philip II; similarly, Lamartine or Voltaire's lottery colleague La Condamine.

211   **"I can barely believe, dear heart":** Vaillot, *Avec Madame du Châtelet,* p. 290.

212   **Voltaire, by contrast . . . a potboiler of a play:** A harsh charge against the long-famous *Sémiramis,* but try reading it.

213   **"When I finished consuming my repast":** Longchamp and Wagnière, *Mémoires sur Voltaire,* pp. 136–37. I've translated liberally, to capture his extraordinarily subservient tone, which is layered with just a hint of unctuousness and resentment.

213   **To be ready . . . she'd brought a great deal of cash:** She might have brought that much merely out of a gambler's confidence, but it's hard to see Voltaire lending her the substantial extra funds without a great trust that it was well founded.

214   **Voltaire had known not to interrupt . . . breathing deep:** It wasn't only in her text *On Happiness* that she recounts her excitement while playing; in other accounts she is described as playing for hours on end while Voltaire—and at times the coachman—stood waiting.

218   **The Fontainebleau cheats knew they'd gone too far:** There was a

certain amount of "allowable" cheating in aristocratic life, for country house owners often used rigged card or roulette-style games as a polite way of getting their wealthy guests to pay them, thus avoiding the crudity of having to make the guests produce a stack of coins and actually slip them into the host's hands. What happened at Fontainebleau had surpassed that.

218 **When those earnings did start coming in:** In modern jargon, she was securitizing the tax collectors' future income streams, which she'd acquired at a discount. (And since she'd arranged the initial purchase via a loan, she was never out of pocket.)

219 **The duchesse—although a tiny blond pixie:** She was always the driving force. When she did go too far, and got herself and her husband locked in prison for their planned overthrow of the state, she was brave enough to perjure herself, in an attempt to get him freed first.

219 **For such a task it helps . . . a magnificent château:** The duc's mother had realized how important the great finance minister Colbert was, and had charmed him when her royal beau was away. As a thank-you, Colbert had left her son the Sceaux château.

219 **There were messages in invisible ink . . . with the Spanish court:** Which wasn't as unpatriotic as it sounds, for the royal families were closely interrelated. (Thus of Louis XIV's grandsons, one became Philip V of Spain; another became the father of Louis XV.) Instead of an invasion, there would just be a quick coup, and a shift in who held power at the French court.

220 **He was old enough . . . and had kept in occasional touch:** Most notably via a recent visit to her summer home of Anet. Mme de Staal kept a wicked account, showing her incomprehension that Emilie should have insisted on staying in her room during the day to work on her Newton, pulling the tables together to make a sufficiently large workspace.

221 **He could be assured . . . liked being called "director of the Honey Bee Society":** Her motto was *Piccola si, ma fa pur gravi le ferite*—both were small, but stung sharply. Her fame then was so widespread that Couperin wrote his harpsichord diversion *Les Abeilles* [The Bees] for her.

223 **He could use this period . . . to write her a story:** Partly this was her prerogative as an aristocrat, and his hostess; partly it had been a constant of their relationship in years past, when he'd enjoyed night-long parties there. Voltaire also knew that she suffered from insomnia, and was going to be awake anyway.

226 **He took out a fresh sheet of paper:** How much of the story he wrote

was fresh? Vaillot believes hardly any of it was; Longchamp and the immensely careful Besterman think all of it was. The explanation, I think, comes from the way Voltaire worked and reworked his best ideas. Thus the lengthy, eloquent draft about the mouse thinking it's a god, which he sent in a letter to Frederick, became an even lengthier part of his *Discourse in Verse on Man* (as we saw in chapter 14). Similarly here. The story "Memnon," which he'd written a good draft of before, naturally slid into the deeper story he was developing at Sceaux, even though it hadn't quite reached what would be its final published form as *Zadig* (which, for clarity, is what I've called its various versions throughout this text).

What Longchamp had to deal with, then, was a mixture of previous writing (which explains why Voltaire was so insistent that he get the old writing table from Paris, with the key manuscripts in it), but also a great deal of redrafting and fresh writing (which explains why even as tireless a copyist as Longchamp was exhausted by the hours of transcription). The total number of words in the tales that Besterman suggests were written at Sceaux could easily have been read aloud in the hours that Voltaire stayed with the duchesse (arriving back up in his room, as Longchamp reports, often scarcely before the dawn). Given the time of year—end of autumn or early winter— that would be late indeed. But do also see Van den Heuvel's views, in the introductions within Frédéric Deloffre and Jacques Van den Heuvel, eds., *Romans et contes* (Paris, 1979).

228   **The British critic William Empson:** In Empson's *Seven Types of Ambiguity;* a point much developed by Sartre, and then especially by the cognitive anthropologist Mary Douglas (in her writings on our fascination with all category-shifting objects, be they honey, or lava, or social minorities). Voltaire had long understood the principle: "It seems to me," he wrote in 1739, "that sculpture and painting are like music: they do not express ideas. An ingenious song cannot be performed . . . and a clever allegory, intended only for the intellect, cannot be expressed either by the sculptor or the painter." To the Comte de Caylus, in Besterman, *Select Letters,* p. 59.

229   **They both were too old . . . clad in dressing gowns:** On the penultimate page of *Zadig* the hero is dressed in nightcap and dressing gown as he bests the swordsman—the type of insertion of actual life into a story that Voltaire loved.

231   **"By all the greatest crimes":** These elegantly split alexandrines are

the translation of Donald Frame in his edition *Candide, Zadig, and Selected Stories* (London, 1962).

231   **Now though—jump-started . . . the greatest new literary form of his life:** There were numerous precedents, but it was fresh for Voltaire and, I'd say, fresh even when compared to the others in the genre: less ridiculous than Rabelais's Pantagruel, more sincere and intense than Swift's Gulliver.

231   **"now my M. de Voltaire engaged in less sleep":** Longchamp and Wagnière, *Mémoires,* p. 148.

233   **One guest jotted down what was written:** The ever-present duc de Luynes, in his journal; quoted in Vaillot, *Avec Madame du Châtelet,* p. 302.

233   **"Order your [returning] carriage . . . between 7:30 and 8":** Notice that the duchesse is ensuring no one will bother her by staying on afterward for even the briefest of drinks.

240   **He'd heard about . . . the small provincial courts:** Lorraine itself was an independent duchy, which would revert to the French crown once Stanislas died.

241   **"yes, despite my youth, and I'm sure my weak talents":** Gaston Maugras, *La Cour de Lunéville au XVIIIe siècle* (Paris, 1904), p. 82.

242   **"My dear child, I don't know when I'll return":** D3632.

243   **Their affair had begun . . . one of Catherine's friends:** The friend was Chancellor de la Galaizière. He was the true power in the duchy, for he controlled Stanislas's French stipend, which came from Versailles.

243   **"If I hadn't gone up to you":** Emilie, *Lettres,* vol. 2, p. 172, n. 374.

244   **"I'm such a lazy girl":** The quotations are from Maugras, *La Cour de Lunéville,* pp. 292, 293.

246   **"My sweet, it's not enough to love each other":** Ibid., p. 293.

246   **Saint-Lambert's mother and sister were . . . offended:** Georges Mangeot, *Autour d'un Foyer Lorraine: La Famille de Saint-Lambert, 1596–1795* (Paris, 1913), p. 66.

247   **"I used to make resolutions that I wouldn't fall in love":** From her long letter of May 9, 1748, D3648.

247   **"I will . . . bring you my member":** Modified from the somewhat archaic translation in Besterman's edited *Voltaire's Love Letters to His Niece* (London, 1958), p. 27. It slightly predates these events in Lunéville, but given Voltaire's health and distraction, the problems were liable to recur.

248   **"In but five or six minutes"**: Longchamp and Wagnière, *Mémoires,*
pp. 195–97.

248   **"take it very hot, but only small amounts"**: Maugras, *La Cour de
Lunéville,* p. 310.

248   **"In our love . . . there's no such word as *enough*"**: Ibid., p. 326.

248   **"I'd like to spend the rest of my life with you"**: D3652.

251   "**You took my trust, and yet . . . You've deceived me**": D3753.

252   **Voltaire knew very well:** Not least because Voltaire's play was designed to supersede Crébillon's own version of thirty years before. Also, the
younger Crébillon was far more radical than his father (who called him "my
worst production"), and often took Voltaire's side in public issues.

252   **a larger group of applauders:** Led by the chevalier de La Morlière, a
master in these matters. Paid enough money, he would arrange a group of
over a hundred guaranteed loud supporters; they generally met at the adjacent Café Procope (still in existence) to arrange strategy.

253   **"Come on! Come on! Make way for the ghost!":** Vaillot, *Avec
Madame du Châtelet,* pp. 233, 236, has the details.

253   **His health had always been poor, he confided:** Longchamp and
Wagnière, *Mémoires,* pp. 218–21.

253   **Sunk in the depths of self-pity . . . his one consolation:** Ibid.,
pp. 215–19.

253   **Emilie had little sympathy:** Though she did probably send a lackey,
just in case Voltaire wasn't pretending this time.

254   **By now, Voltaire recognized that something was going on:** He'd
noticed at least one occasion when Emilie's fireplace had not been used all
night, even though the weather had turned chilly—which made it pretty clear
that she'd slept somewhere else.

255   **"Finding no servant outside Emilie's door":** Longchamp and Wagnière, *Mémoires,* pp. 200–3.

255   **Only when he left them alone . . . or so he said:** I'd trust him here,
for the geometry was as he described; furthermore, it's very much how Emilie and Voltaire reasoned and argued. It also matches the poem Voltaire wrote
soon thereafter for Saint-Lambert.

257   **He told Saint-Lambert to enjoy those pleasures:** Longchamp and
Wagnière, *Mémoires,* p. 204.

258   **"How is my beloved? . . . thinking of you":** Besterman, *Voltaire's
Love Letters to His Niece,* pp. 87, 103.

258   **One of the worst offenders had been:** Vaillot, *Avec Madame du Châtelet,* p. 350, corrects Longchamp here.

259   **The swindlers . . . had been outswindled:** Such finesse is crucial in any activity illegal enough to preclude turning to police law courts in case of disagreement. As with the drug trade today, the response "What are you going to do, sue me?" needed nimble preplanning to avert.

260   **"some verses written by a young man":** Hamel, *Eighteenth-Century Marquise,* p. 334.

260   **He knew he was failing:** In his poems and stories Saint-Lambert liked describing himself as a confident, world-wise traveler—and that made his inability to be like that when he was finally given the opportunity in real life even more galling. Consider the tone in his tale of a proud sea voyager landed in rural Scotland, *Contes de Saint-Lambert* (Paris, Librairie des bibliophiles, 1883), pp. 5–12.

260   **"I send you a thousand greetings, fine sir":** Emilie's *Lettres,* vol. 2, p. 234.

261   **Saint-Lambert was just using her . . . he tried to insist:** It's likely that her previous contraception had depended on the man respecting her when she said it was an unsafe time of month, or exercising control when practicing withdrawal. This is what Saint-Lambert would have violated.

266   **Abortion would only have been considered as a desperate resort:** See Merry E. Wiesner, *Women and Gender in Early Modern Europe* (Cambridge, 2000), pp. 62ff.

267   **"I believe," Longchamp remembered:** Longchamp was mocking about this, and pretended that Florent-Claude had been fooled into believing the child was his. But not only was Florent-Claude a thoughtful man, attuned to Emilie's feelings; he also knew the ins and outs of Lunéville gossip, for he kept close contacts there in his efforts to influence Stanislas's military appointments. It would have been impossible for him not to know of this very public affair. Furthermore, neither Emilie nor Voltaire had mocked him in all the years they'd been together; it would have been out of character for her to have abruptly done so now. A final giveaway is that Longchamp shifts abruptly to a gleeful and even more than usually unctuous tone at this point.

268   **It was Voltaire, informing everyone that he was alive:** Back in Paris afterward, he complained to one and all about his sore legs and back.

269   **"the new baby shall be . . . [Emilie's] miscellaneous works":** The

phrase seems to have originally been Frederick's, though used back and forth by the two men.

270   **The blades were . . . released in groups:** Information kindly supplied by Michael Stephens, archive assistant at the Royal College of Physicians and Surgeons, Glasgow.

270   **But he'd been paying attention . . . finished his own book!:** Emilie was partly aware of this, for Stanislas had asked Voltaire for editorial help on portions of the manuscript the year before.

271   **Stanislas's daughter . . . had been furious . . . blaming those visitors:** A fact that Father Menou, who'd started it all, found uncomfortably accurate.

273   **Isaac Newton had been a resentful . . . his mother:** In a brief confessional he wrote at Cambridge, Newton lists the sin of having bad thoughts toward his mother.

273   **where he'd been bullied:** Newton had fought back when he was picked on as a child, selecting the worst offender, one Arthur Storer, and although being shorter, Newton "had so much more . . . resolution that he beat [Storer] till he declared he would fight no more." Instead of stopping, the furious Newton then began to treat Storer "like a Coward, & rub his nose against the wall." In a brutal fit, he kept on pulling Storer "along by the ears . . . thrust[ing] his face against the side of the Church." Richard Westfall, *Never at Rest: A Biography of Isaac Newton* (Cambridge, 1980), pp. 62–63.

273   **so little money . . . forced to work as a servant:** It's possible he managed to sidestep the worst of these duties, and especially the onerous emptying of chamber pots; see A. Rupert Hall's discussion in *Isaac Newton: Adventurer in Thought* (Cambridge, 1992), p. 12.

273   **Within six months:** My phrasing here is largely from Westfall, *Never at Rest*, p. 106.

273   **"pleased Almighty God in his just severity":** E. S. Shuckburgh, *Emmanuel College* (London, 1904), p. 114; cited in Westfall, *Never at Rest*, p. 141.

274   **"In the beginning of the year 1665":** Perhaps the most famous quotation from Newton (along with his remark about being like a young child collecting seashells). It's been much critiqued (see, e.g., D. T. Whiteside, "Newton's Marvellous Year: 1666 and All That," *Notes and Records of the Royal Society* 21 [1966], pp. 32–41). But one has to watch out for revisionism for

revision's sake. In true creativity there's lots of preparation and then—in a rush incomprehensible to outsiders—it all comes together.

276 **Now, in her limited time, she made sure she didn't miss:** They were central to her old controversy with Marain, and at the core of her interest in physics.

276 **As a result, it was possible to treat the whole planet:** She was right about the importance of these theorems. In a letter unknown to her, Newton had written to Halley in 1686 that a major reason he'd delayed publishing his *Principia* was, in fact, that he had never extended his work "lower than to the superficies of the earth, and [until] a certain demonstration I found last year [the key theorem number 75], had suspected it did not reach accurately enough down so low, and therefore . . . never used it nor considered the motions of heavens." See S. Chandrasekhar, *Newton's Principia for the Common Reader* (Oxford, 1995), p. 12.

277 **There had been hints . . . but Emilie wanted to go further:** The key concept is what's now termed "least action": the way that a system appears to "ensure" that certain overall quantities, such as the amount of time it takes an object to travel a certain path, are kept to a minimum. Maupertuis, Fermat, and others were important in applying and clarifying the early suggestions. The concept's significance, for the birth of energy conservation, is the way it shifts our focus away from "mere" forces, to concentrate instead on these wider, unitary quantities. (Again note the similarity with Emilie's work on the fire prize in 1737: while Voltaire had stuck to one small part of a system—the heated iron block—she had been stretched further, imagining the range of possible lights hitherto unseen.)

277 **How important was her health, anyway?:** "She believed that death was coming long before she was taken from us. From then on her one idea was to use the little time she thought remained to complete the work she had undertaken and so cheat death of stealing what she considered to be part of herself. Hard and unrelenting work, and continual lack of sleep when rest might have saved her life, led to the death she had foreseen." From Voltaire's later introduction to her (posthumously published) *Principes mathématiques de la philosophie naturelle de Newton* (Paris, 1759), p. 175.

277 **"It's rare to admit it":** Robert Mauzi, ed., *Discours sur le bonheur* (Paris, 1961), p. 22.

278 **"I feel an emptiness":** D3876.

278   **"it was the wish of Madame . . . in these nocturnal hours"**: Longchamp and Wagnière, *Mémoires,* pp. 240–41.

279   **"She believed that death was striking"**: Voltaire's introduction, *Principes mathématiques de la philosophie naturelle,* p. 175.

279   **"My God, you treated me cruelly"**: Mix from Emilie's *Lettres,* vol. 2, p. 300, n. 479, and a slightly earlier letter to Saint-Lambert, D3879.

279   **"Lunéville had the most excellent facilities"**: Longchamp and Wagnière, *Mémoires,* pp. 245, 248.

279   **Saint-Lambert, now in full cowardice:** He had even hinted that he would stay closer to her—if, that is, she paid him (ostensibly it was to make up for the paid military service he would be forgoing in Nancy).

280   **"The admirable arrangement of the sun"**: Voltaire's introduction, *Principes mathématiques de la philosophie naturelle,* p. 175.

280   **"I'm terrified . . ."; "It would be most kind"**: Emilie's *Lettres,* vol. 2, p. 306, n. 485; pp. 306–7, n. 486.

280   "I walked to my little summer house today": Ibid., p. 306, n. 485.

281   **"I've lost the half of myself"**: Hamel, *Eighteenth-Century Marquise,* p. 370.

281   **Months later . . . plaintively calling her name in the dark:** Longchamp and Wagnière, *Mémoires,* p. 262.

284   **The following year . . . a long essay:** His *Letter on the Blind: For the Use of Those Who Can See.*

285   **Visitors came by:** Most of what follows is merged from accounts by Charles Burney and John Moore; in Theodore Besterman, *Voltaire* (London, 1969; rev. ed., 1976) pp. 500, 506. The final two paragraphs about Newton are from Martin Sherlock's account in Ballantyne, *Voltaire's Visit to England.*

285   **"When the weather is favorable he takes an airing in his coach"**: Voltaire, in 1775: "The harshness of the climate in which I live, within forty leagues of the icy mountains . . . obliges me to take precautions that one would not take in Siberia. I deprive myself of communication with the outside air during six months of the year. I burn incense in my rooms. I make my own particular climate, and that is how I have achieved a fairly advanced age despite a delicate temperament." Libby, *The Attitude of Voltaire to Magic and the Sciences,* p. 253.

287   **When the public executioner burned . . . he obtained an illegally printed extra copy:** Indeed, Pomeau (*D'Arouet à Voltaire,* p. 329) presents indirect evidence that the Letters from England were never burned at all.

Rather, the suggestion—based on a marginal note found in an old text—is that since copies of Voltaire's work were so hard to obtain, Ysabeau kept the original that was supposed to be burned, and substituted an innocuous volume on Spanish history instead.

288 **Brought back in old age . . . thin-hulled French naval vessels:** The gamble was that fast ships that could shoot high and destroy sails would impair enemy mobility. It was a plausible strategic choice, but often failed against the more bulldog-solid British ships. (Though battles where sheer maneuverability and speed were of central importance, as with Yorktown, showed that not all the funds invested in the French navy had been misguided.)

288 **He became Britain's emissary . . . also served the English commander:** George II's son, the duke of Cumberland; best known in later life as the "Butcher of Culloden."

288 **His daughter married . . . same family tree as Winston Churchill:** The link is distant, but proudly recorded. Fawkener's daughter Henrietta married the third son of the third duke of Marlborough. That third son was named Robert, and his brother was the fourth duke. The title proceeded normally through the generations to the seventh duke, who had two sons: the older became the eighth duke; the younger was Randolph, Winston Churchill's father. Thanks are due to John Forster, archivist at Blenheim Palace.

289 **"perhaps in fourteen more years":** D1410. Voltaire, *Collected Letters*, vol. 4, pp. 430–31.

289 **When the results were announced:** D2015 and 2016.

290 **"I gave her my house in Paris, my silver":** An aged Voltaire lamenting to an equally aged Richelieu; Besterman, *Select Letters*, p. 112.

290 **He converted to Protestantism:** It was during his secret trip to London, a few years after the catastrophe at Culloden. Charles had never respected Catholicism—taking a view similar to Voltaire's about the excesses of the clergy—and thought that his conversion would remove obstacles for English supporters of the Stuart line. Frank McLynn's *Bonnie Prince Charlie* (London, 2003) is excellent on the background.

290 **Despite constant slurs . . . ; "He finds me very cold":** Pompadour to Mme du Hausset; in C. P. Algrant, *Madame de Pompadour* (New York, 2002), p. 97.

291 **Richelieu's successful assault on the British base . . . in Minorca:** It was after this encounter that the unfortunate British admiral Byng was arrested for cowardice, and shot to death on his own quarterdeck. It's what led

Voltaire to the scene in *Candide* where he described the British "shooting an admiral from time to time, to encourage the others"; unfortunately, he and Richelieu were partly to blame. For although the new Pitt administration was trying to get Byng freed, Voltaire had Richelieu write a letter attesting to Byng's bravery. When that letter was intercepted, it made the court martial suspect Byng appear to be engaged in treason as well.

As to the name *mayonnaise,* there's also a suggestion that it honors Charles of Lorraine, Duc de Mayenne, famous for insisting he would finish his chicken with cold sauce before taking the field at the battle of Arques (which he lost to Henri IV) in 1589.

292   **for Bellinzani had been young . . . and was still alive:** See the wondrous volume, Présidente Ferrand ed., *Lettres,* Notice par Eugène Asse (Paris, 1880), including *Histoire des amours de Cléante et de Bélise* (Paris, 1689), p. xxvi.

292   **During the Revolution he was guillotined in the Place de la Révolution:** Its name changes summarize a century of commotion: first it was the Place du Roi, then the Place de la Révolution; now, with the American Embassy on the north side, it's the Place de la Concorde.

Guide to Further Reading

Voltaire

Candide is the most famous of Voltaire's writings, but it has so much slapstick that modern readers often put it down after just a few pages. I'd recommend instead starting with his brief fable "Micromégas" (in many collections, e.g., *Micromégas and Other Short Stories,* tr. Theo Cuffe, ed. Haydn Mason (London, 2002)), which is about an innocently wise giant who has come to Earth.

Voltaire's creature notices a tiny wooden splinter flipping over in a shallow salty puddle—that's Maupertuis's mighty sailing ship, which in fact was nearly shipwrecked in the stormy Baltic in July 1737. The giant is amazed that the minuscule bipeds on that wooden vessel know geometry and mathematics, and he's even more amazed when, trodding further across their tiny globe, he learns of their species' beliefs. It's a theme with wide resonance, from Hollywood's *The Day the Earth Stood Still* to Ted Hughes's *The Iron Man.*

After that, I'd ramble through one of the many one-volume collections of Voltaire's work, looking out particularly for extracts from his *Philosophical Dictionary* or from *The Century of Louis XIV.* To go with that, do try to find a copy of *Select Letters of Voltaire,* tr. and ed. by Theodore Besterman (London,

1963)—the ideal way for the anglophone reader to glimpse the oft delighted, sometimes petulant individual behind the flashing pen.

One of Besterman's great discoveries was a collection of letters that the elderly Marie-Louise had carefully put aside when she sold the rest of her late uncle's papers to the Russian empress Catherine. Those letters remained unread for almost two centuries; the selection published in *Voltaire's Love Letters to His Niece,* tr. and ed. by T. Besterman (London, 1958), makes clear that Voltaire's literary skill did not always correspond with wise judgment. The pastel sketch reproduced therein, showing an attractive though unenamored Marie-Louise beside a harassed yet accepting Voltaire, is a masterpiece of psychological observation (and is reproduced on page 6 of the photo insert). The magisterial *The Complete Works of Voltaire* (Oxford, 1968) includes over fifty volumes of his letters, and is ideal for the reader who wants to further explore a particular episode.

Voltaire's life was so exciting that a lot of famous writers have produced quick potboilers about him, recycling one unsubstantiated story after another. The biography by Maurois is just about acceptable; the one by A. J. Ayer is most politely left unmentioned. The number of worthwhile biographies is really quite small. In French, aside from contemporary accounts such as that of Condorcet, the best for a century was Gustave Desnoiresterres's *Voltaire et la société au XVIIIe siècle* (8 vols.; Paris, 1867–76), which builds diligently from original sources, and most notably from the deliciously revealing accounts of two key assistants, the former of whom we've met: it's Longchamp and Wagnière's *Mémoires sur Voltaire* (2 vols.; Paris, 1826). Several biographers—most notably Mitford—used Longchamp too uncritically; important provisos are to be found in the footnotes of Vaillot's 1988 volume mentioned below, as well as in William H. Barber's "Penny Plain, Two-pence Colored: Longchamp's Memoirs of Voltaire," in *Studies in the French Eighteenth Century Presented to John Lough* (Durham, 1978).

After Desnoiresterres's eight-volume study there was a long gap till Voltaire studies were rejuvenated in France with the works of René Pomeau. These began with *La Religion de Voltaire* (Paris, 1956; 2nd ed., 1969), and then, as he got government funding, led to the series *Voltaire en son temps* (5 vols., Oxford, 1985–94; reissued and revised in 2 vols., 1995). Pomeau wrote the first volume, *D'Arouet à Voltaire: 1694–1734* (Oxford, 1985), while the second is by René Vaillot: *Avec Madame du Châtelet,* 1734–1749 (Oxford,

1988). (Vaillot's volume here builds on his earlier *Madame du Châtelet* [Paris, 1978].)

Pomeau and Vaillot are thoughtful researchers and had much of Bester-man's collected correspondence to work with. But my personal favorite of the French biographers is Jean Orieux's *Voltaire ou la royauté de l'esprit* (Paris, 1966). Orieux writes like Voltaire would, if he could channel a bit of Falstaff along the way. It's a robust, delightful work.

In English, the best twentieth-century biography is Theodore Bester-man's *Voltaire* (London, 1969; revised ed., 1976), which built on his immense decades-long effort of collecting and annotating not just all of Voltaire's let-ters but relevant accounts by guests, spies, friends, servants, and others. Ira O. Wade's *The Intellectual Development of Voltaire* (Princeton, 1969) is also an excel-lent resource, though written in his usual style—at one point Wade succeeds in making the de Rohan incident boring, which takes some doing.

For the period after this book—when much of Voltaire's greatest work was still to come—Ian Davidson's *Voltaire in Exile* (London, 2004) is an ex-cellent start. The Oxford academic Roger Pearson has been a wise commen-tator on Voltaire's writings, as in his thoughtful *The Fables of Reason: A Study of Voltaire's "Contes Philosophiques"* (Oxford, 1993), and although his biography *Voltaire Almighty* (London, 2005) appeared too late to be drawn on for the present book, it's a good, comprehensive account.

There's a mountain of publications about various aspects of Voltaire's life; standout volumes from that heap include *The Attitude of Voltaire to Magic and the Sciences* by Margaret Sherwood Libby (New York, 1966); almost any-thing by Peter Gay, such as his *Voltaire's Politics: The Poet as Realist* (New Haven and London, 1988) or his *The Party of Humanity: Studies in the French Enlighten-ment* (London, 1964); also the old volume *Voltaire's Visit to England* by Archi-bald Ballantyne (London, 1898), which goes well beyond its declared title, to include captivating firsthand reports by many foreign visitors to the elderly Voltaire. Jacques Van den Heuvel's *Voltaire dans ses contes: de Micromégas à l'Ingénu* (Paris, 1967) starts with what seem to be summaries of stories, then opens them up to reveal a gripping cognitive anthropology of Voltaire's thought. Madeleine Raaphorst's article "Voltaire et féminisme: Un examen du théâtre et des contes," in *Studies in Voltaire and the Eighteenth Century* (hereafter SVEC), vol. 39, gives a further angle on that topic, of special relevance to our book.

Emilie

The reader who has some French is in for a treat, for that saint of a scholar, Theodore Besterman, along with finding out everything about Voltaire, also spent years collecting *Les Lettres de la Marquise du Châtelet* (2 vols., Geneva, 1958). Browsing them is the best way I know into her life.

Du Châtelet's own little volume *On Happiness* is fearsomely honest: written when she was feeling isolated from Voltaire, was making little progress on her Newton opus—and had not yet met Saint-Lambert. The edition by Robert Mauzi (*Discours sur le bonheur,* Paris, 1961) has a long editor's introduction, concentrating on the emotional and physical texture of her thought, but the less elaborated Badinter edition (Paris, 1997) is more easily accessible. (Several paragraphs of extracts can be found in English, in the volume by Esther Ehrman mentioned on p. 347.)

The introduction to Emilie's *Institutions de physique* is especially touching, with its remarks to her then not-quite-teenage son—"You are, my dear son, at the happy age when your mind begins to think, yet your heart isn't powerful enough to overthrow it." She recommends he start serious studying now, for she goes on to note that soon he'll be distracted by women, then by the quest for glory, and if he waits till all that's over to begin work in earnest, he'll find—as she knows only too well from her own experience—that he'll be frustrated at how much less supple his mind has become than when he was young.

The main biographer in French is René Vaillot, in his *Madame du Châtelet* (Paris, 1978), and then in his contribution to Pomeau's multivolume Voltaire biography (p. 344). Yet although his books are impeccable in accuracy, and earnest in tone, they somehow remain on the outside of Emilie's life, looking in (though the 1978 work was written at a better point in Vaillot's life, and has a vigor the latter one lacks). In Elisabeth Badinter, however (*Emilie, Emilie: l'ambition féminine au XVIIIe siècle;* Paris, 1983), Emilie has found her ideal biographer. Badinter knows, from firsthand experience, what it's like to be born to great wealth and live with a brilliant man, yet still feel that life isn't always quite as satisfying as she had hoped.

The dear cousin Renée-Caroline took hundreds of pages in her *Souvenirs de la marquise de Créquy* (7 vols., Paris, 1834), to recount the slights and the ingratitude she experienced in her long, prosperous life—which might not have been relaxing for the wealthy man she married, but is a boon for the historian: the time she spent in Emilie's childhood home fits neatly into our story. Many of the anecdotes about Louis XVI and Napoleon in her memoirs are apocryphal and were inserted well after her death; the early sections, however, seem more closely based on her actual notes. The estimable servant Longchamp spent years preparing the materials for his own memoirs (see under Voltaire, p. 344), and if he slightly overplays the occasions when he gets to see his mistress unclothed, or in a bath, it is always in the most dignified fashion.

Among English-language biographies, the most powerful has to be Nancy Mitford's *Voltaire in Love* (London, 1957): often bitchy, generally clueless—and a great romp to read. The deeper flaw is that although Mitford admits that science is not her strength, she does hint to readers that she has an inside track to the attitudes of European aristocracy. But she's writing in the 1950s—when successful social democratic movements were undermining belief in that world—and so a prickly, defensive tone creeps in. The wiser biographer Frank Hamel, in his *An Eighteenth-Century Marquise: A Study of Emilie du Châtelet and Her Times* (London, 1910), captures the rhythms of a genuinely aristocratic world much better—aided by his completing his book just before the First World War.

Esther Ehrman's *Mme du Châtelet: Scientist, Philosopher and Feminist of the Enlightenment* (Leamington Spa, 1986) is very brief, but good on the passion for gambling, and also has useful extracts in English of Emilie's writings—as well as Voltaire's proud memoir of Emilie's life, from his introduction to her posthumously published Newton translation *Principes mathématiques de la philosophie naturelle* (Paris, 1759). The volume by the writer Jonathan Edwards (pseudonym of Noel Gerson), *The Divine Mistress* (London, 1971), is less than trustworthy, not least in the author's habit of transposing events (as with his having Emilie enter a café in disguise, while in fact it was Voltaire who did that). Used with caution, though, it does highlight a number of areas that more thorough research can pin down.

An excellent biography promises to be the one currently being prepared by Judith Zinsser, a leading scholar of Emilie's life. Of her many articles, the brief "Entrepreneur of the 'Republic of Letters': Emilie de Breteuil, Marquise du Châtelet, and Bernard Mandeville's *Fable of the Bees*," *French Historical Studies* 25, 4 (2002) pp. 595–624, is especially insightful on Emilie's first creative efforts at Cirey, while her "Emilie du Chatelet: Genius, Gender and Intellectual Authority," in Hilda Smith's edited *Women Writers and the Early Modern*

British Political Tradition (Cambridge, 1998), pp. 168–90, is an excellent wider
survey. The overview she and Julie Candler Hayes edited, *Emilie du Châtelet:
Rewriting Enlightenment Philosophy and Science* (SVEC, January 2006), assembles
experts from art history, philosophy, and the history of publishing to probe
even further in those and other disciplines.

For the attitudes Emilie had to face from the male scientific community
throughout her life, I especially like Mary Terrall's "Emilie du Châtelet and
the Gendering of Science," *History of Science* 33 (1995), pp. 283–310. The volume edited by Natalie Zemon Davis and Arlette Farge, *A History of Women in
the West,* vol. 3: *Renaissance and Enlightenment Paradoxes* (Cambridge, Mass.,
1993), widens the perspective even more.

There's useful information in *French Women and the Age of Enlightenment,*
ed. Samia I. Spencer (Bloomington, 1984), as well as—though more dryly—
in *Cartesian Women: Versions and Subversions of Rational Discourse in the Old Regime*
by Erica Harth (Ithaca and London, 1992). But my favorite book on women
in this period is *Republic of Letters: A Cultural History of the French Enlightenment*
(Ithaca, 1994) by Dena Goodman, who observes, for example, that in the
same way that as many male thinkers were taking strength from the "primi-
tives" who were being discovered abroad, others were "colonizing" the new
domain of women in the metropolis, using observations on women such as
Emilie for their own political ends. Londa Schiebinger's *The Mind Has No
Sex?: Women in the Origins of Modern Science* (Cambridge, Mass., 1989) goes further on the mix of supportive and negative attitudes through which Emilie
had to navigate.

Of the many books on specialized topics, don't miss Thomas Kavanagh's
Dice, Cards, Wheels: A Different History of French Culture (Philadelphia, 2005),
with its subtle insights into the views different groups brought to bear on this
most compelling of time-wasting activities.

Cirey

The key source for daily life at Cirey is the account left by the most unembar-
rassable houseguest in history: Madame de Graffigny. Her gushing—and surprisingly touching—letters sprawl over more than a hundred pages in the
fifth and sixth volumes of the correspondence within the Voltaire Founda-
tion's *Complete Works of Voltaire;* they are also available (with some extraneous
material) in de Graffigny's own *Vie Privée de Voltaire et de Mme du Châtelet* (Paris,

1820). She has only the vaguest connection with numerical reality, so her account of the number of fireplaces in the château or the proximity of mountains can't be trusted, but anything involving emotions or envy is strikingly accurate—her impassioned descriptions of her hostess's furnishings are a close match to what was recorded in the inventory of Emilie's belongings a decade later. I used a few extracts in chapter 9.

Ira O. Wade is the modern author who first reemphasized Emilie's scientific work, and his early volume *Voltaire and Mme du Châtelet: An Essay on the Intellectual Activity at Cirey* (Princeton, 1941) is a basic source—although the author's difficulties with regard to non-obfuscatory exposition had already reached their full flowering. A balanced overview of the early years is in the 2001 special issue of SVEC, titled *Cirey dans la vie intellectuelle: la réception de Newton en France,* while the earlier study "Chemistry at Cirey," by Robert Walters (SVEC, vol. 58, 1967), elaborates on that central episode of attempted creativity there. William H. Barber, "Mme du Châtelet and Leibnizianism: The Genesis of the *Institutions de physique,*" in *The Age of the Enlightenment: Studies Presented to Theodore Besterman,* ed. W. H. Barber et al. (Edinburgh and London, 1967), pp. 200–22, is crisp on that next stage in her work (though see the reevaluation of his work in the 2006 SVEC in the Emilie entry above). The château's present owners have a good Web site, www.visitvoltaire.com, with useful links as well as details on the reconstruction of the attic theater.

Other Characters

There are biographies or memoirs available for all of the other characters; especially good ones include Hubert Cole, *First Gentleman of the Bedchamber: The Life of Louis-François-Armand, Maréchal Duc de Richelieu* (London, 1965); Elisabeth Badinter, *Les Passions intellectuelles,* vol. 1: *Désirs de gloire (1735–1751)* (Paris, 1999), which is chattily discursive on Maupertuis and his crowd; Gordon Craig's *The Politics of the Prussian Army, 1640–1945* (New York, 1964), superb on Frederick's place in the Prussian military tradition; Frederick's own wildly self-serving but psychologically astute *Political Testament* and *Form of Government* (extracts conveniently available in Eugen Weber's *The Western Tradition,* vol. II [Lexington, Mass., 1995]; and Margaret Crosland's *Madame de Pompadour: Sex, Culture and Power* (Stroud, 2000), which is more understanding than many earlier accounts—though for good gossip, there's nothing like the

Goncourt brothers' *Madame de Pompadour, revue et augmentée de lettres et de documents inédits* (Paris, 1878).

Gaston Maugras's *La Cour de Lunéville au XVIIIe siècle* (Paris, 1904) is the ideal introduction to Saint-Lambert and the world that let him thrive. Everything Frank McLynn has written on 1745 and Bonnie Prince Charlie, from his *France and the Jacobite Rising of 1745* (Edinburgh, 1981) to his *Bonnie Prince Charlie* (London, 2003; orig. published as *Charles Edward Stuart,* 1988), comes highly recommended. McLynn's research is comprehensive, his writing crisp, and his psychological observation astute—be it on the way the heart went out of Stuart's forces once they turned back at Derby with an undefended London a scant 127 miles away, or on the flurry of confusion that caused conflicts between Phélypeaux and Richelieu to hold back the French invasion force that otherwise would undoubtedly have led His Britannic Majesty's citizens to become His Bourbonic Majesty's subjects.

Readers who have access to a good university library will be touched by the *Histoire des amours de Cléante et de Bélise* (Paris, 1689), the novel a young Anne Bellinzani wrote, based closely on her love affair with Emilie's father, Louis-Nicolas, when he was first becoming aware of how powerfully a young woman could dream of happiness in the stars.

Louis XV's France

The ideal place to start is Tocqueville's *The Old Regime and the Revolution,* ed. François Furet and Françoise Mélonio, tr. Alan S. Kahan (Chicago, 1998), which has been justly famous for nearly two centuries. Not only does Tocqueville have a more nuanced view than Marx, but he also ingeniously shifts perspective as needed, homing in on Canada at one point, for example, since—with no feudal tradition to block central authority—"all the deformities of the government of Louis XIV are seen there, as if through a microscope."

Gwynne Lewis's *France 1715–1804: Power and the People* (London, 2005), or Colin Jones's *The Great Nation: France from Louis XV to Napoleon* (London, 2002), are both good on the researches that Tocqueville's insights have led to; William Doyle's edited volume *Old Regime France* (Oxford, 2001) is at times a bit bloodless but does show the state of academic research. Robin Briggs's *Early Modern France 1560–1715* (Oxford, 2nd ed., 1998) outlines the world Louis XV had to work with, and is written in the no-nonsense tone that makes visitors to All Souls, Oxford, wonder why there should be more than one Fellow there, as each, clearly, is wise enough to be a world unto himself.

P. N. Furbank's *Diderot: A Critical Biography* (London, 1992) is another of the volumes that's much broader than the title suggests, and sketches the wider setting with aplomb. Alistair Horne has a gift for titles, and his *Seven Ages of Paris* (London, 2002) is a loving homage to the city he's written about from many aspects over many years.

The stunning incompetence of Phélypeaux and others in Louis XV's administration—which makes certain recent residents of the Oval Office seem paragons of nepotism-free efficiency—is a leitmotif of the highly recommended *The Command of the Ocean: A Naval History of Britain, 1649–1815,* by N. A. M. Rodger (London, 2004); see especially his middle chapters.

One of the first twentieth-century books to show that tacit groupings of nobles were a *subversive* force in the years before the French Revolution, fighting back to regain the exemptions they'd been losing, was Franklin Ford's confident *Robe and Sword: The Regrouping of the French Aristocracy After Louis XIV* (Cambridge, Mass., 1953). G. Chaussinand-Nogaret's *La Noblesse au dix-huitième siècle* (Paris, 1976) has more of a filigree construction: it shows how deeply the idea of "honor" could shape an entire class's life, and suggests that defending it against ideas of competence, and of compassion, was at the heart of France's later social explosion. For fun, Norbert Elias's *The Civilizing Process* (tr. Edmund Jephcott; Oxford, 1978; German original, 1939) takes seemingly bizarre curios of what to us are the uncouth table manners of those nobles and their antecedents, using them to reveal the social and political pressures that created our "natural" manners today.

Annik Pardailhé-Galabrun's *The Birth of Intimacy,* tr. Jocelyn Phelps (Oxford, 1991), and Jean-Louis Flandrin's *Families in Former Times: Kinship, Household and Sexuality,* tr. Richard Southern (Cambridge, 1976) are calm, fairly analytical approaches to their topics. Uta Ranke-Heinemann's *Eunuchs for the Kingdom of Heaven: Women, Sexuality, and the Catholic Church,* tr. Peter Heinegg (New York, 1990), by contrast, as well as G. S. Rousseau and Roy Porter's edited collection *Sexual Underworlds of the Enlightenment* (Chapel Hill, 1988), tell us far more about eighteenth-century ejaculata than any normal person would wish to know. *The Libertine Reader: Eroticism and Enlightenment in Eighteenth-Century France,* ed. Michel Feher (New York and Cambridge, Mass., 1997), gives yet more firsthand accounts.

The Enlightenment

Getting direct exposure to the main writers of the Enlightenment is a treat, for most of them were writers of the highest order. Essays by Hume, Diderot, and almost all of the others make an ideal start; Isaac Kramnick's edited *The Portable Enlightenment Reader* (New York, 1995) is a convenient collection of bite-sized extracts. The volume edited by David Williams in the Readings in the History of Political Thought series, *The Enlightenment* (Cambridge, 1999), samples fewer thinkers, but at greater length.

Ernst Cassirer's *The Philosophy of the Enlightenment,* tr. Fritz Koelln and James P. Pettegrove (Princeton, 1951; original ed., 1932) is a profound work of intellectual history, successfully rebutting the Romantic criticism of "the shallow Enlightenment"; Carl Becker's classic *The Heavenly City of the Eighteenth Century Philosophers* (New Haven, 1932) takes those critiques in a sharply original direction. Since his book is a fairly close transcription of spoken lectures, it's also written in an easy, whimsical tone, though the corrective Carl Becker's *Heavenly City Revisited,* ed. Raymond O. Rockwood (Cornell, 1968), is good to go with it. The collection *What's Left of Enlightenment? A Postmodern Question,* ed. Keith Baker and Peter Reill (Stanford, 2001), is useful on more recent views from the academy, though the smugness of some of the essays would no doubt have made Cirey's residents sigh.

Robert Darnton will always be known for his classic *The Great Cat Massacre, and Other Episodes in French Cultural History* (New York, 1984), with its deep reading of seemingly meaningless oddities in pre-Revolutionary France. He's a natural writer whose ideas have been enriched by proximity to Clifford Geertz at Princeton, as also seen in his more comprehensive *The Forbidden Best-sellers of Pre-Revolutionary France* (London, 1996), though the corrective *The Darnton Debate: Books and Revolution in the Eighteenth Century,* ed. Haydn T. Mason (Oxford, 1998; originally vol. 359 of "Studies on Voltaire and the Eighteenth Century") is good to keep at hand, not least for Daniel Gordon's delightfully unfair article "The Great Enlightenment Massacre," which shows Darnton giving perhaps more importance than deserved to the scribes of Grub Street.

For general interpretative books, Alfred Cobban's *In Search of Humanity: The Role of the Enlightenment in Modern History* (London, 1960) is wise and clear, while Dorinda Outram's *The Enlightenment* (Cambridge, 1995) is much more thoughtful than its short format would suggest. The best introduction to

French approaches is Daniel Roche's *France in the Enlightenment,* tr. Arthur Goldhammer (Cambridge, Mass., 1980), where chapter headings such as "Time," "Spaces," and "Powers" immediately make it clear you've left the Anglo-Saxon world behind.

The ebullient Roy Porter contests France's importance vis-à-vis England in his less than compromising *Enlightenment: Britain and the Making of the Modern World* (London, 2000), while Gertrude Himmelfarb accepts France's importance, yet bemoans the way it got everything so wrong, especially through not being as inductive and practical as the British: her *The Roads to Modernity: The British, French, and American Enlightenments* (New York, 2004) is fluent, and not quite as reactionary as her marriage to Irving Kristol would suggest. A calm intermediate view, as seen from more neutral cantons, is *The Enlightenment: An Historical Introduction,* tr. William E. Yuill (Oxford, 1994), by the Swiss specialist Ulrich Im Hof, who mixes the best of English and Continental approaches in his text.

American writers often treat the whole matter as a prelude to the events in Philadelphia of 1776: cautiously in the case of Ralph Lerner in his *Revolutions Revisited: Two Faces of the Politics of Enlightenment* (Chapel Hill and London, 1994), more chauvinistically—but with good evidence—by the sturdy historian of a previous generation, Henry Steele Commager, in *The Empire of Reason: How Europe Imagined and America Realized the Enlightenment* (New York, 1977).

Science

Fontenelle's dialogue *On the Plurality of Inhabited Worlds* (in many editions since its original publication in the seventeenth century, e.g., Berkeley, 1990) is gracefully written, and imagines the author strolling on moonlit evenings with a beautiful young marquise, who has never learned the new astronomy that Galileo has recently discovered but is eager to see her horizons lifted outward. David F. Noble's *A World Without Women: The Christian Clerical Culture of Western Science* (New York, 1992) offers a fresh take on the background of the intellectual world Emilie was trying to join; Thomas L. Hankins's *Science and the Enlightenment* (Cambridge, 1985) is a clear and workmanlike account of the topics and approaches taken in the period in which she was working.

The key ideas here are those of Newton, who—in a neat match with the secretive manner of his own life—is the hidden yet most powerful protagonist of this book. Richard Westfall's volume *Never at Rest: A Biography of Isaac Newton* (Cambridge, 1980) is comprehensive, but more for reference than for continuous reading. James Gleick's biography *Isaac Newton* (New York, 2003) is a better read, and laden with insight; the volume that Westfall co-edited with I. Bernard Cohen, *Newton: Texts, Backgrounds, Commentaries* (New York, 1995), enriches the science and crucial theology even more.

Best of all, to understand what Emilie lived for, is S. Chandrasekhar's *Newton's* Principia *for the Common Reader* (Oxford, 1995), the finest biography of an idea I've ever read.

Acknowledgments

This book wouldn't have been conceived if it weren't for the fact that Sam Bodanis and Florence Passell, although they loved girls—so much that they had five of them—were also keen on having a boy, and so continued their family until a son was born. This meant that I grew up in a house with lots of women, at one point having five teenage sisters—which is pretty impressive for anyone, let alone a chatty kid brother—getting glimpses of their hopes, arguments, dating, and dreams. Whatever insight I may have had into Emilie's life began from that.

What love meant to me came more surprisingly: blindsiding me first in high school, then a few times after, most notably in France for a decade, where living on the isolated, beautiful Rue de la Vanade also taught me a little about what life at Cirey may have been like. Later, years in Oxford and then London gave me some feel for the journeys between scholarly and practical life Voltaire and Emilie regularly took. None of that was planned as leading to this book, but looking back, I see that—just as with the family I grew up in— none of what I've written could have taken shape without it.

Planning the book was easy, once I'd made a first survey of the letters and other sources, but when I started the writing I was still unsure whether the mix of romance, science, and history I had in mind was actually working. That's why—and I recommend this to all writers, though I suspect she's too busy, so you'll have to find equivalents of your own—I sent the first few chapters to my friend Julia Bindman, who mixes a warm, analytical mind with the extraordinary trait of being unable not to tell the truth.

When she told me those first chapters succeeded I was happy, and thanked her and said I'd send the rest of the book when it was done; when she went on to declare, "Like hell I'm waiting that long," and that she'd like to read each new chapter as I finished them—and then, quite independently, when Sue Liburd, Larissa Thomas, Julia Stuart, Rebecca Abrams, and Digby Lidstone said pretty much the same—I knew I was on to something that worked. As the book went on and the readership for each finished chapter grew, I began e-mailing what I'd written at near-weekly intervals to friends, officemates of friends, roommates of the officemates of friends, and others even more tenuously connected. That combined interest was the greatest of inspirations.

Even so, the first complete version wasn't quite right, not least because it was nearly twice as long as the present book. There was too much to-ing and fro-ing, too much textual analysis and historical background, and too much elaboration of science and the biographer's evidence. I was slipping away from the central story. Suzanne Levy and Rhonda Goldstein did wonders in bringing me back on track; so too did Gabrielle Walker, the closest of friends, who knows a great deal about being an adventurous, bright woman. In long canal-side walks, and over many teas, she helped me keep sight of the core points; at one point, near the end of the project, she crucially helped me focus the first chapter more directly on Emilie.

Other friends who commented on all or part of the book include Sunny Bates, Robert Cassen, Michael Goldman, Tim Harford, Frank McLynn, Leanne Savill, and Simon Singh (taking time before a round-the-world trip). Colette Blair helped, one sunny morning, with a graceful translation of de Bouffler's proposed epitaph; Mary Park showed what style could mean to a power couple in any era; new friends MeiLi and Robert Hefner further demonstrated how an elegant, thoughtful life could be lived. Larry Bodanis was a breath of fresh air throughout. Research help came from Sarah Dickinson Morris and Iona Hamilton; Tim Whiting and Sarah Rustin in London, and Rachel Klayman in New York, did wonders with the editing. Subeditors have a reputation of being narrowly concerned with grammar, but this is far from accurate in describing Sue Phillpott and Steve Cox. Steve helped shape the entire main text; Sue made a vast number of phrasing changes and editorial selections that greatly improved the endnotes. Katinka Matson and John Brockman supported this project from the very beginning. For all, many thanks.

While I was doing my revised draft, Gary Johnstone was filming a previous book of mine, which included a section at the château de Cirey. It was through his kindness, as well as that of Cirey's present owners, that I was able to explore the building for hours on end, looking at old letters of Emilie's, thumping on load-bearing walls and chimney foundations, examining the ceiling beams and scraped layers of paint in the upstairs theater. After strolling through some of the adjacent forests in a freezing February and seeing the marks of old forges and paths, when I found myself at the end of the day sharing coffee in plastic cups with characters dressed as Emilie and Voltaire and Maupertuis, it seemed entirely fitting.

I don't know what my kids made, at first, of having all the individuals from the book take up home with us for so many months, but soon it was natural for stories of sieges and sword fights and how God slides beads down suspension bridges to join our usual repertoire of stories on the way strolling, scooting, and—when a quick glance at the watch showed we'd dawdled for too long, again—sprinting to school.

When the time came for the final chapter, I had the key information and story in my head, but knew I needed several uninterrupted hours to get it written out. Due to travel plans, it had to be written in one day; due to school being over for the winter holidays, it was also a day the kids expected to hang out, and indeed we spent the morning strolling here and there around the center of London. Normally we'd have hot chocolate and puzzles and drawing when we got back, but this afternoon I needed to write. I explained the situation, and put my fate in their hands.

When we got home and thawed out, Sam and Sophie, suitably bribed, were happy to provide a few hours of quiet, and turned to their books and Game Boys and drawing pads; I packed the pillows up against the headboard of my bed, got out my writing pad, and then—for the final time in full freshness—let myself enter back in to the world I'd come to love: feeling what Emilie lived for, and trusting what she had wished. Knowing the tragedy that the chapter led up to, I don't think I could have written it, let alone finished, without knowing that my two beloved children were around me in our home, enjoying their youth.

Awaiting their life.

Illustration Credits

La Marquise de Châtelet, Gabrielle Emilie Le Tonnelier de Breteuil (1706–1749), by Nicholas de Largillière (1656–1746). Undated image. *Bettmann/Corbis.*

Portrait of Voltaire (François Marie Arouet de Voltaire, 1694–1778), after Nicholas de Largillière (1656–1746). Oil on canvas, 1718. *Musée de la Ville de Paris; Musée Carnavalet, Paris, France; Lauros/Giraudon/Bridgeman Art Library.*

Louis XV, King of France (1715–1774), by Hyacinthe Rigaud (1659–1743). Portrait in coronation robes. Oil on canvas, 208 x 154 cm. *Versailles 15.2.1710; Versailles 10.5.1774; Château et Trianons/akg-images.*

The Taking of the Bastille, 14 July 1789. French School (eighteenth century), oil on canvas. *Château de Versailles, France; Giraudon/Bridgeman Art Library.*

View of the Comédie Française Theatre in 1790, after an original by Gaudet and Prudent. French School (nineteenth century), color engraving. *Bibliothèque de la Comédie Française, Paris, France. Archives Charmet/Bridgeman Art Library.*

Portrait of Frederick II, King of Prussia, after Vanloo Michael Nicholson. *Corbis.*

Louis-François Armand de Vignerot du Plessis, Duc de Richelieu (1696–1788,) by Swedish painter Alexander Roslin (1718–1798). *Topfoto.*

Jeanne Poisson, la Marquise de Pompadour (1721–64), by Maurice Quenton de la Tour (1704–1808). Pastel on paper mounted on canvas, 1755. *Louvre, Paris, France. Giraudon/Bridgeman Art Library.*

Portrait of Sir Isaac Newton, by Godfrey Kneller (1689). *Bettmann/Corbis.*

Eighteenth-century French lithograph of the King's Games, published by Firmin Didot/Gianni Dagli Orti. *Corbis.*

View of the Château de Sceaux. French School (nineteenth century), photograph. *Giraudon/Bridgeman Art Library.*

Voltaire with Madame Denis (Marie-Louise Mignot Denis, 1712–1790), by Charles Nicolas Cochin II (1715–1790), ca. 1758–1770. Crayon on paper. © *New York Historical Society, New York; USA/Bridgeman Art Library.*

Postcard depicting the Château of Cirey-sur-Blaise, formerly the residence of Madame du Châtelet and sojourn of Voltaire between 1733 and 1740, before 1914. French School (twentieth century), black-and-white photograph. *Bibliothèque des Arts Décoratifs, Paris, France; Archives Charmet/Bridgeman Art Library.*

Le métamorphose de la Place Stanislas de Nancy. Gamma/Camera Press.

Le Marquis de Saint-Lambert (1763–1803), by an unknown artist. *Courtesy of the Visconte Foy/British Library.*

La Marquise de Boufflers, née Beauvan (1711–1787), by J. M. Nattier. *Courtesy of M. Knoedler & Co./British Library.*

Title page of Emilie's final work. *Courtesy of the British Library.*

Index

Je meurs en adorant Dieu, en aimant mes amis
en ne haïssant pas mes ennemis, en
détestant la superstition (1778)

Also by David Bodanis

DISCOVER ELECTRICITY

fight 151

Patti
11:15
Sues.

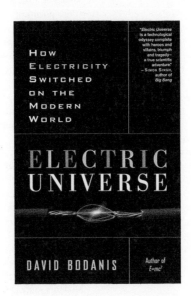

TAKING us from the frigid waters of the Atlantic to the streets
of Hamburg during a World War II firestorm to the interior of
the human body, *Electric Universe* is a mesmerizing account of
the invisible force that lies at the heart of nature and that drives
today's technological revolution.

ELECTRIC UNIVERSE
How Electricity Switched on the Modern World
$13.95 paper ($21.00 Canada)
ISBN-10: 0-307-33598-4 • ISBN-13: 978-0-307-33598-2

Available from Three Rivers Press wherever books are sold

THREE RIVERS PRESS • NEW YORK